The Hungry Years

The Hungry Years

CONFESSIONS OF A FOOD ADDICT

WILLIAM LEITH

GOTHAM BOOKS

GOTHAM BOOKS
Published by Penguin Group (USA) Inc.
375 Hudson Street, New York, New York 10014, U.S.A.
Penguin Group (Canada), 90 Eglinton Avenue East, Toronto, Ontario,
Canada M4P 2Y3 (a division of Pearson Penguin Canada Inc.); Penguin
Books Ltd, 80 Strand, London WC2R 0RL, England; Penguin Ireland, 25 St
Stephen's Green, Dublin 2, Ireland (a division of Penguin Books Ltd);
Penguin Group (Australia), 250 Camberwell Road, Camberwell, Victoria
3124, Australia (a division of Pearson Australia Group Pty Ltd); Penguin
Books India Pvt Ltd, 11 Community Centre, Panchsheel Park, New Delhi -
110 017, India; Penguin Group (NZ), cnr Airborne and Rosedale Roads,
Albany, Auckland 1310, New Zealand (a division of Pearson New Zealand
Ltd); Penguin Books (South Africa) (Pty) Ltd, 24 Sturdee Avenue, Rosebank,
Johannesburg 2196, South Africa

Penguin Books Ltd, Registered Offices: 80 Strand, London WC2R 0RL,
England

Published by Gotham Books, a division of Penguin Group (USA) Inc.
Originally published in the United Kingdom by Bloomsbury Publishing, Plc.
First American printing, September 2005
10 9 8 7 6 5 4 3 2 1

LIBRARY OF CONGRESS CATALOGING-IN-PUBLICATION DATA
Leith, William.
    The hungry years : confessions of a food addict / William Leith.
        p.   cm.
    ISBN 1-592-40155-4
    1. Leith, William. 2. Compulsive eaters—Biography. 3. Overweight persons—
Biography. 4. Obesity—Psychological aspects. 5. Food—Psychological
aspects. 6. Low-carbohydrate diet. 7. Atkins, Robert C.   I. Title.

RC552.C65L45 2005
362.196'85263'0092—dc22
[B]   2005046163

Printed in the United States of America
Set in Sabon with Block
Designed by Daniel Lagin

The Hungry Years

The Fattest Day of My Life

I wake up on the fattest day of my life, January 20, 2003. I am just over 6 feet tall, and weigh . . . how much? I step on the scale and off it very quickly, to limit the damage. 236 lbs. At best! My bathroom floor slopes slightly, and I have positioned the scale carefully to ensure the smallest possible reading.

236 lbs. Waist size: 36. This is how I feel: light-headed, shaky, with a raw sensation, almost a pain, just below my ribs. I can feel the acid wash of heartburn in my gullet and the gurgle of juices in my guts.

Hunger.

I splash water on my face.

Hunger is the loudest voice in my head. I'm hungry most of the time. I also feel bloated most of the time. I am always too empty, and yet too full. I am always too full, and yet too empty. Last night I ate three platefuls of mash and gravy. I also had chicken and vegetables. I can barely remember the chicken or the vegetables. The mash was fluffy, starchy. I could not relax until it had all gone. Then I licked my plate clean. I picked the plate up and licked the starch residue and congealing gravy. It tasted delicious, vile, shameful. People sometimes ask me why I have crusty stains on the lapels of my jacket or the bib area of my shirt.

My girlfriend said, "I hate it when you do that."

"I thought you thought it was funny."

"No, I hate it."

"It's a tribute to your cooking."

"No, I hate it."

Now it's early, and I want toast. God, I hope there's some bread in the kitchen. God, I hope there's some sliced bread in the kitchen. I really don't want to do any slicing. In the morning, with low blood sugar, it's like slicing a stone with a long, bendy razor blade. I could easily have an accident. I swing myself out of bed, my belly tight and sore under my T-shirt. When I was thin, I slept naked, but now I dress for bed, or rather don't fully undress; I wake up damper, hotter, hungrier. My hunger frightens me. The fatter I get, the more I want to eat. The fatter I get, the more comfort I need. Right now, I want thick slices of warm white bread, crispy on the outside, with butter soaking into the middle.

My girlfriend is sitting on the sofa, smoking her second cigarette of the day. This is seven-thirty in the morning. She has a serious addiction. She hates the fact that she smokes. She knows how hard it is to quit, but that's not the problem. She's quit before. But when she quits, she always goes back to smoking. In some deep psychological place, she needs to be a smoker. It's about her childhood, about protesting, about punishing herself. It's all mixed up with her identity. As a nonsmoker, she feels like someone else, and that scares her.

"First of the day?" I say, even though I can see there's already a butt in the ashtray.

"Unfortunately not."

In the kitchen, there is most of a loaf of sliced bread, and—yes!—the butter has been left out all night, so it will be soft enough to spread. When I was a kid, when I had my worst hunger, I hated cold butter. Later, it didn't bother me so much—I was patient enough to pare off thin slices, which I would arrange carefully on the toast. Then I would wait until the butter had melted, something I can't imagine now.

Now I'm in a hurry. The bread is brown. Damn. Still, I put two slices in the toaster, and, while I'm waiting, I take another slice from the loaf, butter it, fold it over, and eat it in three bites. I pop the toast, to see if it's nearly done, but it's not—nowhere near—so I butter another slice, and try, and fail, to eat it slowly. Now, when I pop the toast, it is slightly crisp, and slightly warm, so I take a slice, butter it, eat the disappointing, mushy result, and put another slice in the toaster. And then I realize I should have put the second slice in the toaster before I ate the first. As usual, I am falling behind.

I am in a toast frenzy. I have an urge, like in the Burger King ad, in which "urge" is an integral part of the word "Burger." Although, of course, "urge" isn't an integral part of the word "toast." But I am aching for toast. It's like a Mac Attack. (I have actually suffered from Mac Attacks.) It's like a nicotine fit. It's like the feeling you get in a coke-snorting frenzy, when you say, "Shall we, um, do another line?" and the reply is, "We've just done a line." Please believe me when I say that I am not a coke fiend, have not been one for years. I know about willpower. Looking at the toaster, glaring at it, listening to the buzz of its little engine or whatever, I stop for a moment to make a cup of instant coffee, and ask my girlfriend if she wants any toast.

"No thanks," she says. She never eats breakfast.

I open the fridge. Nothing for me in here. Tomatoes, bacon, eggs, salad vegetables. On the countertop next to the fridge, there is fruit in the fruit bowl. At the moment, I am not interested in any of these things. I am like a gay man looking at a girly magazine. I want bread, cereal, croissants, bagels. I could eat a baked potato, or some pasta, or some fried rice left over from a Chinese or Indian takeout.

This actually crosses my mind. Might there be fried rice in the house? Cold fried rice, the grains clumped together, sitting on a bed of congealed fat? In a silver takeout carton? Once I saw a show in which a man had got fat because he ate leftovers from Indian meals with his toast in the morning.

In any case, there is no fried rice in the house. In my heart, I already know this. (Some famous addict once said that a true coke addict knows when there is cocaine in the house, always, and cannot stop snorting until all the cocaine has gone. Well, I always know when there is fried rice in the house.)

And now, my breakfast is ready. Two slices of buttered toast. No plate. I eat standing up. These days, I do a lot of eating standing up. People seem to disapprove. Perhaps that's why I do it. I take a sip of my instant coffee—my girlfriend's brand, a brand which is supposed to give more money to the growers, although I'm not absolutely convinced. It is "ethically sourced." It scalds my mouth. I eat the first slice of toast, munching through it like a praying mantis eating a leaf. Then I eat the second slice. And, for a moment, I'm in a bad place—already bloated, but not yet sated. Too full. Too empty. Clouds of self-disgust are gathering on the horizon.

At least I haven't got a hangover. All I have is a slight memory of the hungover state—a phantom. My head still feels slightly fuzzy and sore when I wake up. This is the morning of my twentieth day without alcohol. I used to have a drinking problem. Now I might and might not have a drinking problem. We'll see. Apart from soft drugs, I am drug free. I am in a monogamous relationship, so I do not feel a constant urge to flirt with women. In any case, I'm too fat for this kind of behavior. That's all in my past, I think. When you get fat, these sorts of opportunities are no longer open to you. When you get fat, people find you a lot less attractive.

What happens to me is this: I get fat. Then I get fatter and fatter, over a period of years, until I'm fatter than I've ever been. Then I get thin again. But when I get thin, I'm never as thin as I was the time before. And when I get fat, I'm always fatter than I was the time before. Right now, at 236 lbs. I am close to obese. Another month, I'd say, and I'll be obese.

Perhaps there will come a point, perhaps quite soon, when it is just too late. Perhaps when I cross the border from fat to obese I will be stuck, never again able to claw my way back to thin. I'll be a lifer. Might this happen? It happened to Orson Welles, to Sidney Greenstreet, to Roscoe "Fatty" Arbuckle. Big sad men, communicating their pain slowly, silently, pound by pound. It happened to John Belushi, to John Candy, to Chris Farley. It looks like it happened to Marlon Brando, to Francis Ford Coppola, to John Goodman, and possibly to Tom Arnold and Drew Carey. It's almost certainly happening to Robbie Coltrane. Coltrane, a decent actor, who, by being fat, has ruled himself out of contention as a top-dollar leading man, who could never be James Bond, but who was, instead, a fat, smirking James Bond villain, and who ended up as Hagrid, the fat wizard in *Harry Potter,* gained an average of 14 lbs. a year for the best part of a decade. What was he trying to tell us? I once tried to interview Coltrane about his weight gain, and it was one of the most difficult interviews I've ever done. Did he talk about his weight? A little bit, maybe. Did he want to say how he felt? Much, much less. The feelings were locked up in an oubliette deep inside his brain. Fat people are not like coke fiends or alcoholics, who sometimes like nothing better than talking about their problems. With a fat person, there is an elephant in the middle of the room, and nobody's allowed to mention it.

Fat Shower

I am fat. Therefore everything I do is fat. This morning I take a fat shower, squirming around in the suds like an oversized cherub. Fatly, I towel myself dry. This is not like the toweling-dry of a thin person. Fat people absorb water like sponges. Fat people sweat more. Fat people don't want to walk, half-naked, out of the bathroom to a place that is less hot and steamy. Fat people don't like being exposed. Fat people take their clothes into the bathroom, so that they can emerge, magically, fully dressed, if a little damp and uncomfortable. Fat people wear fat clothes. Right now, I tend to wear tight jeans, and I tuck my shirt in, to advertise the extent of my fat belly. If I were balding, I'd be the kind of man who gets a haircut, rather than the kind who brushes hair over the bald patch. I know that the next stage, wearing loose, baggy clothes, will be the end. When you "Go Floaty," you have admitted defeat. Somewhere, there is still some fight left in me.

And when I pull my T-shirt over my hot, swollen torso, it feels like rolling on a condom. And when I stand on one leg to put on my sock, I feel a twinge. I am creaky.

And when I walk out of the bathroom, my girlfriend says, "Don't tuck your shirt in. I've told you before."

I smile, a rictus grin.

She says, "It just bulks you out."

The Cannon Conundrum

Today I am flying to New York, to interview a diet guru called Dr. Atkins, possibly the most famous diet guru in the history of the world, and yet it does not occur to me that I am doing this, that I have set this up, because I need help. This is one of the funny things, the queer things, about being fat. You don't want to admit to yourself that you are trying not to be fat, because you might fail—you will, in fact, almost inevitably fail—and every time you fail, you know you are more likely to fail in the future. And the other thing, of course, is that almost all diets actually make you fat. This is the Cannon Conundrum.

In 1983, diet guru Geoffrey Cannon wrote a book

called *Dieting Makes You Fat*. "Dieting," wrote Cannon "creates the conditions it is meant to cure." When you diet, your body just gets better at sucking calories out of the food that you do eat. What Cannon tells us is that dieting makes you hungry on the inside; it gives your body a secret hunger. This is because, when you diet, your mind wants to lose weight, but your body does not. When you diet, your body thinks you are unable to find food. You think: diet. Your body thinks: famine. And the more times you diet, the fatter you get. As Cannon puts it, "And what does the body need to keep it going between times of famine? Fat. The more often people diet, the more their bodies will protect the stores of fat."

Cannon began to study the effects of diets on the body because he had been an obsessive dieter himself. He had tried diet after diet, all with the same result: he lost weight, and then, when he stopped dieting, the weight came back. "Between 1964 and 1976," he wrote, "I lost about 200 lbs. If all my diets had worked, on New Year's Day 1976 I would have weighed minus 20 lbs."

What he discovered was that, when a diet stops, the dieter experiences "raging appetite." You can't help it. It's not you—it's your body. "The healthy body," wrote Cannon, "can adjust to a period of emergency, which in effect is what a diet is, but once the emergency is over the body's imperative demand is for the nourishment that succours it." Dieting, in other words, is like locking a sex maniac in a lap-dancing bar. He can look, but he can't touch. One day, inevitably, he escapes from the lap-dancing bar, and ventures into the real world.

Like Cannon, I have been on diet after diet. Like Cannon, I have been on diet after diet that didn't work.

Unlike Cannon, a little part of me, somewhere deep inside my brain, still has hope.

What if He Is Right?

Bumbling around my apartment, looking for things to throw into my travel bag, it occurs to me that, like all diet messiahs, Dr. Atkins seems to promise a miracle. In his new book, *Dr. Atkins New Diet Revolution,* which is more or less the same as his old book, *Dr. Atkins Diet Revolution,* which he wrote thirty years ago, he says, "If you believe that weight loss requires self-deprivation, I'm going to insist on teaching you otherwise." The Atkins regime is not about willpower. Atkins does not offer a twelve-step program. He does not advocate avoiding fat, or cutting down on calories. He does not tell us to look deep into our souls. He tells us to stop eating carbohydrates.

It's simple. Carbohydrates make you fat. If you radically cut your intake, you'll be thin. Meanwhile, you can eat all sorts of other stuff.

A miracle.

Does the Atkins regime work? Does it *work*? On a journalistic level, it would be a better story if he were a charlatan.

I could unmask him!

I pick up Atkins' book. The cover is orange and blue, like emergency warning lights at the scene of an accident. I have the "must-have" new edition. On the cover, Nigella Lawson calls the Atkins diet "the perfect diet for those who love food." I already have a problem with it: why is there no apostrophe after the word "Atkins"? It should be *Dr.*

Atkins' New Diet Revolution. Is it aimed at the sort of reader who is frightened off by the use of an apostrophe?

What Atkins says, to put it simply, is that carbs are addictive. Well, any fat person can tell you that. When you're in the grip of fat person's hunger, you don't want an apple, or an egg, or a slice of ham. You want carbs. So I think Atkins has a point. This, as I say, slightly disturbs me. I'm wondering how it might fit in with my story. "Here's a diet guru. He's right," sounds pretty lame to me. Not quite the same as, "Here's a diet guru. He'll take your money and you'll still be fat afterwards."

So . . . what if Atkins is right? What if carbs *are* the problem? Maybe it's that simple. But surely it can't be that simple. Etched in my mind, over a lifetime, is the notion, not that carbohydrates are bad, not that bread and potatoes are bad, but that fat is bad.

That it's fat that makes you fat.

That, gram for gram, fat has more calories than carb.

That you get trim by cutting down on calories.

That, therefore, you get trim by cutting down on fat.

I am anti-fat.

I hate fat.

I am fattist.

But what if Atkins is right? What then? What if carbs are the problem?

Unspeakable

A memory crosses my mind. I'm thirty years old. 205 lbs. Overweight but not quite fat. Waist size 34. I'm sitting on a train, and three of the fattest people I've ever seen get into my compartment. There's a mother, who must weigh 400 lbs., and her son and daughter, who are heavier—in the son's case, a lot heavier. I'm startled, riveted. The sight of these people is almost entertaining. They each carry a plastic bag full of snacks—bags of potato chips, cylindrical tubs of potato chips, chocolate bars, bags of sweets. As soon as they sit down, the show begins—they grab the snacks, they tear at them, they wolf them. Their hands—soft, oversized hands—begin to cram the snacks into their mouths. Constant eating has developed in them superhuman abilities to chew, to release enzymes in the mouth, to form the food into a bolus and swallow. They do not talk to each other. The guy inhales two large bags of chips in three or four minutes. The girl kills a Mars bar in a couple of gulps. Then she hits the Pringles. She eats the Pringles in 2-inch stacks. When she runs out of food, after about fifteen minutes of uninterrupted eating, she starts moaning. She tries to snatch her brother's food bag. There is panic, fighting. The girl is making sub-orgasmic noises. The guy is grunting. He's lashing out. The mother bops the girl on the head, and gives her a Mars bar to calm her down.

It is after breakfast and before lunch. These morbidly obese people are moving toward a meal, having recently finished a meal. I think: they are addicted—to starch, to sugar. They are like subsistence alcoholics, drinkers who have to drink all the time to stave off withdrawal. Perhaps, I think, the food is the problem. But then I think, no, it can't be that simple. There must be something else, something deep, ugly. Something unspeakable in these people's brains. When you see fat people, you want to blame them for their condition. Those fat bastards. You want to blame them.

I Decide Not to Drink It

Twelve years later, 25 lbs. heavier, I look for things to pack. Fat clothes. Fat bathroom products. Fat beard-trimmer. I need the beard-trimmer because, if I have a proper wet shave, my face looks too fat—I look moon-faced, with a smooth, shiny double chin that looks like a doughnut around my neck. So I make sure never to be clean-shaven. On the other hand, I don't want a full beard either. I can't go down the fat-and-bearded route. I'm not ready for fat and bearded, in the same way that I am not ready to be fat and jolly. Like I said, I still have some fight left in me. So I set the trimmer to the lowest notch, which gives me a stubbly look—enough to distract from the double chin, to mitigate the moon-face.

My doorbell intercom buzzes. The taxi has arrived. My girlfriend has gone to work. As always, I am running late. The panic of being late clears my mind—it enables me to pack. I bulk around the bedroom, bending over, crawling on all fours. My lower back is sore. My knees are sore. My ankle is sore. I pack tight, girdling T-shirts, short-sleeved shirts (long sleeves make me overheat), trousers, socks, books about being fat, and books not about being fat, so that I can sit on the plane, and eat, and read, and forget myself.

In the taxi I eat nothing, and at the station I buy a coffee in a cardboard cup with a cardboard sheath, a "java jacket," to stop my hand getting hot, and I consider buying a sandwich, maybe push the boat out and have toasted ciabatta bread with melted cheese and something, I suppose ham or olives, but I don't, partly because I'm in a hurry, and partly because I don't really want a sandwich.

Big Mac? No way. Not now, not ever.

It turns out I don't want the coffee either. Still, walking through the big, crowded concourse, past the snackpoints and mobile eateries, the bagel kiosks and baguette hatches, holding the java jacket gives me a kind of focus. I am doing something. I have agency. My train leaves in two minutes. On the way to the platform I stop to buy a bar of chocolate, to go with my coffee, which is fine because now I won't buy a sandwich. I promise myself I won't eat the chocolate until I get on the train, and then I promise myself I won't eat much of the chocolate until I get on the train, and then I promise myself I won't eat all of the chocolate until I get on the train. I screw the wrapper up and slip it into my pocket, into the springy rustling wrapper-nest that is already there.

On the train, I sip my coffee, which tastes bland and bloaty, and I decide not to drink it, but drink it anyway.

The Real Problem

I have a terrible problem.

I'm fat, obviously, because I eat too much. But I don't think that's the real problem. Like many, even most, fat people, I am fat because I have other, deeper problems. One of them is a desire to procrastinate. Being fat is like living on one side of a valley and looking across at El Dorado—the promised land of thinness, which can never disappoint you until you visit it. Deep down, every fat person is a little bit frightened of crossing the border into the thin world. What if it's not as good as it looks in the brochures? What then?

I get off the train at the airport and begin the process of being borne along, via escalator and moving sidewalk, toward the bars and food halls of the departure area. Airports are very fat places. Everywhere you go, you see fat people. Everywhere you go, you see things to help you get less exercise and eat more food. And airports are the future; every day, the world outside the airport gets a little bit more like the world inside the airport. One day, you'll park your car in the vast car-park of some supermall, and you'll step on a moving sidewalk that will bear you, salivating, toward a warm chunk of meat wrapped in a fluffy coating of starch, and you'll guzzle it, and lick your fingers, and step back on the moving sidewalk. Obese, snacking guys will sit and watch your progress on TV monitors.

A fat woman cruises toward me. She is walking splay-footed, with effort, taking careful steps as if walking up a steep path. As John Self, the fat anti-hero of Martin Amis' novel *Money* says, when you're fat, everything feels steep. Being fat is an uphill struggle. I look at her, at the eaves of flesh hanging from her sides, and for a moment, a split second, I feel the fat person's twinge of fear and self-pity: Will I get like that? Will I? The woman is in a much fatter place than me though—if I lost, say, 15 or 20 lbs., my fatness would be mentionable. This woman would need to lose 100. She might not have spoken about her weight for years. Every day, I guess, she lives with this dreadful, lonely secret, that something has gone terribly wrong with her life, and nobody will talk to her about it.

All I need to do is lose 45 lbs. Even 40. Hell, if I lost 30,

I'd almost be trim. If I lost 20, my friends would come up to me and say, "Hi, Fatboy." That in itself would feel like an achievement. Nobody calls me Fatboy anymore. I'm too fat.

I've been trying to keep a food diary. Yesterday I got up, walked to the newsstand, and bought a newspaper and a couple of magazines and a sandwich. I spent some time browsing through magazines, those travel brochures advertising the trim world; I took in thirty or forty images of girlish women's bodies—low-fat, low-carb, high-maintenance. Catherine Zeta-Jones, losing weight; Sophie Dahl, losing weight. Kirstie Alley, the woman from *Cheers*—the dark one Sam Malone always wanted to sleep with—gaining weight. Jennifer Aniston, steady. The magazines were explaining to women that it is, indeed, possible to book a trip to the thin world, if you work hard enough, if you spend enough money, if you diet, if you exercise, if you check yourself into a clinic for a bout of liposuction. The sandwich I bought was a BLT, two slices of thick, soft white bread with crisp, pale lettuce, bland slices of water-bomb tomatoes, somebody's own-brand mayonnaise from a tub the size of a bucket, and hard, oily bacon with fat the color of aspic. Perfect. I put my newspaper under my arm. Right there, in the doorway of the shop, I gripped the clear plastic sandwich box in my fingers. Three or four panicky tugs and the cellophane seal was off. The sandwich practically fell down my throat; it was like dropping a billiard ball down a well.

"Hey, excuse me!"

"Mmm . . . horry."

Mid-morning I went back and got another sandwich.

Egg-mayonnaise on white. Close to confectionery. I sucked it up. The thing is, I should have bought it when I got the BLT, but then I would have had to put it in the fridge and leave it alone for two hours.

By lunchtime, I was hungry. I cooked myself one of my favorite lunch recipes:

You fill the kettle.

While the kettle is boiling, you take a good fistful of three-minute spaghetti.

Snap the spaghetti in half, and put it in the pan on the stove. The pan is still there from yesterday lunchtime, the last time you cooked this meal. It has some white-looking residue on the inside, but that doesn't matter.

Pour the boiling water in the pan.

Oh yes—light the gas.

You can put some salt in the water. But I never do.

Put two handfuls of frozen peas in a sieve.

Pour the rest of the boiling water over the peas.

Wait ninety seconds. The pasta is now ready.

Pour the pasta into the sieve containing the almost-thawed peas.

Shake it about.

Put it on a plate.

Add butter, salt and pepper. I would put grated cheese on, but if there's cheese in the fridge I'll have already eaten it. In my kitchen, cheese is lucky to get to the fridge.

Peanut Butter

Later on, toward dusk, I had a thing with some peanut butter. Afterward I lay on my bed. The sky darkened. The nausea passed.

"I Didn't Enjoy It at All"

I'm feeling guilty because I've eaten too much, and I have a problem, and I need help, but I don't want to talk about it, because I'm a guy, and guys don't have problems like this, and if they do they sort the problems out on their own. My problem is: I overeat. My problem is: I am hungry. I'm hungry for food, but I know it's not really food that I crave. It's something else.

It's everything.

I'm hungry for sex, for drugs, for alcohol.

I want to go out and spend money!

I can't keep still.

If we have a core problem, here in the Western world, I am an embodiment of that problem.

I'm hungry, and I'm out of control. My hunger is emotional, but this is something I find hard to admit. I have a very powerful, top-of-the-range psychological override mechanism, which I use to disengage my emotions. And this mechanism runs on heavy fuel. It needs a lot of food and drink and drugs and sex. To use the technical term, I'm a binger.

And I'm not alone. More and more of us are bingeing. The term was coined in 1959 by Albert J. Stunkard, a professor of psychiatry at the University of Pennsylvania. One day, a patient called Hyman Cohen turned up at Stunkard's practice. Cohen was thirty-seven years old, 5 foot 9 inches tall, and weighed 272 lbs. He was obese. He was a compulsive eater. He told Stunkard he wanted to lose weight "in order to qualify for the position as principal" at the school where he taught.

Cohen told Stunkard he had "no psychological problems." What he needed help with, he said, was his willpower. "Right now," he said, "my willpower just doesn't seem to be up to it. That's where you come in. It's like hiring a policeman to check on me."

Stunkard did check on Cohen, to the tune of weekly sessions of psychotherapy. Cohen began to lose weight. After five weeks, he was 10 lbs. lighter than he had been at the beginning. By the sixth week, though, he was back up to his starting weight.

Something had happened. Cohen described it. He'd gone to the bank to deposit his salary check, and found himself taking $100 out. "And everything just seemed to go blank." He walked into a grocery store and bought a cake, several slices of pie, and some cookies. Then he got in his car and drove, one hand on the wheel, the other stuffing food into his mouth. Next, he "set off on a furtive round of restaurants," staying a few minutes in each restaurant, eating small amounts of food and moving on. He felt in constant terror that he might be discovered. He knew that what he was doing was bad. Later, he went into a deli, bought $20 worth of food—this is the 1950s, remember—and ate "until my gut ached."

Cohen said, "I didn't enjoy it at all. It just happened. It's like a part of me just blacked out. And when that happened there was nothing there except the food and me, all alone."

Stunkard described the Hyman Cohen case in a 1959 report in *Psychiatry Quarterly* titled "Eating Patterns and Obesity." One thing he had noticed, of Cohen, was that, "Almost any kind of frustration, or achievement, could trigger his eating."

Since then, of course, bingeing has grown exponentially. I read books about bingeing all the time. I binge on them. Elizabeth Wurtzel writes about bingeing on drugs, Caroline Knapp about bingeing on alcohol, the former Arsenal and England soccer captain Tony Adams about bingeing on alcohol, William Donaldson about freebasing cocaine, Ann Marlow about heroin, Geneen Roth and Betsey Lerner about bingeing on food. James Frey has written a memoir about his binges on crack and alcohol and cigarettes and self-harm and food. Gus Van Sant has bought the film rights. In his book, *A Million Little Pieces,* Frey says, "It's always been the same, I want more and more and more and more."

And all of these bingers have something in common. There's something hollow, right in the middle of their psyches. Something missing. Something they've spent their lives not wanting to talk about.

Sometimes—every few days, in fact—the *Trisha* show is about people who have been bingeing on food. You should see some of them. They're mostly women. Susie Orbach, the writer and psychotherapist, thinks that a lot of women binge because they can't cope with their sexuality. They can't cope with the sexual demands of the modern world. The sexual revolution didn't solve women's problems—it made them worse. It made them fat. They binge to make themselves fat, to stop guys hitting on them.

Susie Orbach thinks that women get fat because, on some level, they want to be fat. I think this is happening to men, too.

On *Trisha*, bingers ease onto the stage, hunched, bowed, shamed, brave, the Lycra in their oversize clothes stretched to the limit. Sometimes they slowly glide across the stage as if limbless, like galleons moving through the water. Sometimes they are like big trucks trying to maneuver through city traffic. When they come to rest, they park at odd angles, engines hot, brakes tested to the limit. People in the audience whoop and cheer, as if witnessing a miracle.

On the Plane

On the plane I eat a welcome-pack of pretzels and another pack of pretzels and a chicken meal with gravy and wet mash and softish vegetables and a salad with Italian dressing and a bread roll and a soggy cake and, later, an egg-mayonnaise sandwich and a chicken sandwich. I have a feeling about Dr. Atkins and his low-carb mantra—I think it might just be the future. About four years ago, when I was having a really bad time in a really bad relationship with a woman called Sadie, I picked up a book by a Frenchman called Michel Montaignac. The book was called *Dine Out and Lose Weight*. Well, I was dining out a lot, as you do in bad relationships. Being in a restaurant gives you less to squabble about. You eliminate the need to argue about the shopping and the cooking, for instance. And we never argued about the bill, because I always paid it. So there I was, dining out. But I wasn't losing weight. Boy, was I not losing weight.

Still, I wasn't as fat as I am now. I must have been 215 lbs.! It would take me a month of hard gym work to get back to where I was then. This thought flashes through my mind, and I try to push it away, and it won't go, and I grab my pretzel packet and ream my finger around the inside, picking up some pretzel dust, and I rub the pretzel dust on my tongue, a bit like a coke addict rubbing the last little bit of white powder into his gums, and the thought still won't go away, and I think of this fat guy I used to see in the gym, he was a bit fatter than me, looking at him made me perversely happy because I was not as fat as him, and now I am, and I think: I must do something, I must *do* something, and I open my bag and take out a magazine and stare at the cover, and I wonder if it would help if I flipped through the magazine and found something distracting, like pictures of women in their underwear, and I flip a few pages, and I can't settle on any image.

Anyway, I did the Montaignac diet, which is based on the Glycemic Index, or GI. The GI measures the effect different carbohydrates have on your blood-glucose level. Pure glucose has a GI of 100. Hardly surprising. More surprising is that mashed potato has a GI of 91. A bagel is 72. White bread is 70. Carbohydrates, in other words, quickly turn to sugar when you eat them.

That's the science behind the Montaignac diet, which works on the same principle as the Atkins diet. The upshot is that carbohydrate, particularly refined carbohydrate, makes you hungry. When you eat it, glucose is released into the blood, which causes your pancreas to pump out insulin; when you eat too much of it, your pancreas pumps out too much insulin, which eats up too much blood glucose, which gives you a blood-sugar crash, which makes you feel hungry. A vicious circle develops—you eat carbs, you crave carbs. You get fat. You become miserable. You need comfort. You eat more carbs. You crave more carbs. You get even fatter.

And Sadie—she kept telling me I was too fat. Sometimes it was just little hints, funny looks at the dinner table, mean little rolls of the eyeball (oh, that can crush you) and sometimes it was The Frank Discussion. Sadie told me that I was becoming so fat that I was beginning to be unattractive to her. I was only mildly porky when I met her—208 lbs.—but then, somehow, in a horrible, inexorable way, I'd started to get fatter and fatter. I couldn't understand what had happened. "Your weight," she said, "is a problem." And: "Should you be eating that?"

And: "Don't have any more of that."

And: "Do you really need that?"

And: "Come on, why don't you just leave some?"

And: "I told you before, your weight's a problem."

And: "No I'm not sulking."

And: "Why are you always thinking about food?"

And: "I'm just tired, that's all."

And: "I've got a headache."

And: "I know, I know. But I really do have a headache."

And: "Can't you do something about it?"

And: "Would you want to have sex with me if I was fat?"

And: "Have you ever considered therapy?"

Sadie absolutely hated fat, the very idea of it.

I remember one time we'd arranged to go and see Sadie's mother. We had to rush out of the house without having breakfast. We arrived at lunchtime and went out and sat in the garden. It was hot; I was hungover and cranky with low blood sugar. After about twenty minutes, I realized that the reason lunch had not been mentioned was that lunch was not *going* to be mentioned. I looked at Sadie. She looked away. And I asked if I could have something to eat. And I remember what I got—part of a baguette, torn off, with a bit of cheddar. And I realized that the world is made up of two types of people. Those who measure out their lives in terms of food, and those who don't.

In any case, Sadie withheld sex as a motivation for me to lose weight. When we did have sex, she would take charge. I was fat, and she hated fat; in her eyes, I was diminished. So naturally, she felt a need to take charge. She had this one position she favored. I would lie on my back—which, being fat, I preferred anyway—and she would lower herself on top of me, and then tell me to do a specific thing. I felt I had to get it exactly right. When she was finished, she'd give me an opportunity to finish, and then she'd get up quickly, slightly flushed, and put her underwear back on. Afterward she wouldn't talk about it, as if it had never happened. Sometimes I would do the specific thing slightly wrong and she'd be furious—she'd get up suddenly, angry, and put her underwear back on, and that would be that. Once I had to stop doing the specific thing because I got a cramp in my hand.

"What are you *doing*?"

"I'm sorry."

"Well, I can't go on now," she said. Then she got up, put her underwear back on, and walked out of the room.

My Montaignac diet went well. I stopped eating carbs. I stopped being hungry. Every day, I had some fruit for breakfast, and for lunch I boiled up a lot of frozen broccoli and frozen Brussels sprouts, which I ate with salt and pepper and a little butter. The weight dropped off. I lost 10 lbs. in the first three weeks. Still Sadie withheld sex. But she said she'd have sex with me on my birthday.

I didn't know how to feel about this. Girls had said this sort of thing to me before, but that was when I was a teenager. Even so, I had to admit I was excited. I had got thinner. Maybe Sadie felt better about me. Maybe our arguments would stop. Maybe the troublesome hell that was our relationship would get better. On the day itself, we went into the bedroom. I lay on the bed. Sadie closed the curtains. It was afternoon. I kept my shirt on, but unbuttoned it. Lying down, in the shady room, I looked . . . chubby. Not too bad. Sadie took her clothes off, and arranged her trim body over mine, her knees outside my hips. She lowered herself, but not quite the full distance. I started doing the specific thing. From the start, I could tell I was doing it right. After a while, she was finished. But I hadn't started. Then she got up, put her underwear on, and stood in the middle of the room, getting dressed.

I said, "Why did you do that?"

She said, "Oh, come on. I've had enough of this. You said you wanted to go to the cinema. So let's go to the cinema."

When we got to the cinema, there were no films she wanted to see. It didn't seem to matter that there were lots of films I wanted to see. I was too fat. She was in charge. My fat had reduced me to the ranks. Soon after that, I stopped Montaignac altogether. I stuffed myself with bagels, croissants, thick slices of white toast and butter, and bars of chocolate. I started putting sugar in my coffee again. And my drinking took off. If you'd asked me about Montaignac, I'd have said that, sure, I believed in the principles. It was just that, somehow, it hadn't *worked*. I was fat before Montaignac, and fat afterward. It was a diet. It had no palpable effect. So what was new?

Thinking about this makes me feel a rising sense of something bad, a nameless dread, something I don't like at all, and I eat some more pretzels and drink some coffee and ask for more coffee and land at JFK airport and buy a Hershey bar after I get through customs and marvel, briefly, at the way I still buy a Hershey bar when I land in America, even though I could buy a Hershey bar any day of the week in the deli across the street from my flat in London. I eat the Hershey bar, which is not the exciting, semi-mythical experience I want it to be, in three bites.

Carb City

I take a cab across the bridge to Manhattan. Here it is—Carb City, one of the world's great carbohydrate centers. Here, the buildings rise up out of a bed of carbs. Follow each gleaming hive down to the ground and there it is, at the bottom—a starch-crammed deli or diner, a pharmacy groaning with crispy snacks and cookies and breakfast cereal. This is a place where you can get yourself carbed up in any style you want—you can give yourself a blood-sugar spike with doughnuts and bagels and croissants and rolls, with pita breads and flatbreads, with Danish pastries and English muffins and Polish bialys, with potato chips and corn chips, with blinis, fries, pasta, rice, potatoes, noodles. Immigrants from all over the world have brought their carbs here, adapted them, refined them—and enlarged them. A New York croissant, for instance, is exactly twice the size of a croissant in Paris.

It's dinnertime for me, even though it's only late afternoon here, so I sit on a stool at a bar and watch sushi coming toward me on a conveyor belt, and I pick out a plate, two slices of raw tuna on matchbox-sized puddingy sushi rice, and I eat the tuna sushi in five bites, and I pick out, and eat, two slices of raw salmon on rice, and two slices of cooked, flattened prawns on rice, and two chewy strips of octopus on rice. I pick it up in my chopsticks, dip it in soy sauce, and chomp it with robotic, pleasureless vigor, always more interested in the sushi I'm about to eat than in the sushi I'm actually eating. I pick the prawns up in my chopsticks and slide them into my mouth, nipping off the tails with my incisors, picking the nipped-off bits of tail from between my lips with my chopsticks, placing the tails with a flourish on the empty plate. Cool. I hope the waiters are watching. I'm still hungry, or rather not quite satiated, so I order a hand roll, a cone of seaweed filled with the puddingy rice, and also mayonnaise and seafood, and unfortunately I am satiated by the time it arrives, but I eat it anyway, chomping it while I watch bits of salmon sashimi and California rolls buzz past me at the level of my fingers, and I'm filled with nausea and also a sort of greed that borders on the pornographic, and later, a few hours later, I go to a seafood place and have something really healthy, tuna and brown rice, a whole fucking mound of brown rice, and by the time I go to bed I feel painfully bloated, as if someone had cut me open and crammed something large and indigestible into my stomach, and sewn me up really tight, and, just as I'm falling asleep, I wonder if, maybe, starting tomorrow, for a little while at least, I should do Atkins.

The Swimming Pool

I have this memory from the last time I was not at all fat, ten years ago. My girlfriend at the time, Anna, was staying with some friends in a villa somewhere in the middle of France. It was hot. I traveled down on my own, and arrived in the afternoon. It was a fine place, big, with good furniture, a swimming pool, a few girls lounging by the pool, wearing not much. I walked out to the pool in a T-shirt and shorts. I was down to 190 lbs. I'd taken the weight off by playing tennis about 200 times over the course of a year, and swimming, and jogging, and going for long, brisk walks. I had become fixated with exercise. I ate and drank what I liked.

So I'm standing by the pool, chatting away, being introduced to people, and up comes Anna's brother, who is also an old friend of mine, and he's holding a racket and a ball. He's on the other side of the pool. He tells me he's invented a game, which is hitting the ball across the pool to each other, and if you mis-hit the ball, and it falls in the pool, you have to jump in and get it.

"Come on then," he says.

I can feel panic rising in me. I know what's going to happen next.

"You'd better take your shirt off," he says.

I'm wondering how I can get out of this, what diversionary tactic I can use, whether I should just jump in and . . . but nothing would work. I am trapped. I look around me, choked with the fat person's panic at having to reveal your body, and I realize there's only one thing I can do. I'll have to take my shirt off. The girls are watching, mildly interested. And I take my T-shirt off. And I'm trim. Of course—I'm trim. I'm 190 lbs. Waist size 31. I had forgotten.

What Does It Feel Like to Be Thin?

So there I am, standing at the edge of the pool, stripped to the waist, holding my T-shirt in one hand. I'm thin. What does it feel like?

I let the T-shirt fall to the ground. I pick up a racket and play tennis across the pool, and sometimes look at Anna, sitting on a lounge chair in a skimpy sundress and I think no underwear. She is taking no notice of us, talking to a girl called Suzanne who wants to write a novel. Anna herself wants to write a novel, probably about a girl who wears skimpy dresses and no underwear, and has men running around after her.

After a while I dive into the pool and swim up and down, obsessed with the calories I'm burning, feeling high from the exercise, swimming twenty, thirty, forty, fifty lengths, not wanting to stop. I could go on for hours. From my low vantage point I am even more sure that Anna is not wearing any underwear.

She gets up and walks toward the house without saying anything to me. I hoist myself out of the pool and follow her. She walks through the French window and into her bedroom—our bedroom.

"Is this our bedroom?"

"I've been staying here, yes."

We hug. Or rather, I hug her. She stands still, and does not actively resist being hugged.

For a while, perhaps ten seconds, perhaps an aeon, nothing much happens. Then Anna turns away from me. She slips out of her dress, freeing the straps, stepping with exaggerated delicacy out of the ring of cotton on the wooden floor. I walk toward her and place my hands on her shoulders.

"Maybe later," she says.

She had humiliated me when I was fat. Now I'm thin. With her back to me, she steps into her underpants. Then she puts on another dress and a pair of sandals with pointy little heels.

Later that evening, at a restaurant near the villa, I pack away a lot of food—a fried starter, a steak with runny sauce, a couple of helpings of fried potatoes, some vegetables, a tart. The food is great.

I look across the table at Anna. She is tanned. She is not saying much to me. The waiter is grinning, bringing another bottle of wine because I'm drinking so much.

"Cheers," I say, and hold out my glass, wanting more.

That's what it felt like. I wanted more. A snapshot from the trim world. I'm thirty-two years old. Waist size: 31. 190 lbs.

Breakfast

I wake up on the day after the fattest day of my life, and I'm hungry, and I think: "I'll do Atkins," and I think: "I won't do Atkins," and I think: "I'll do Atkins."

I step into the elevator and plummet to the ground, at the expense of no calories, and get outside and walk around, looking for somewhere to not eat carbs. Almost immediately I walk past two mobile carb stalls offering pastries, croissants, rolls, bagels. I am disturbingly hungry. I want carbs. I don't want carbs. I enter a diner on Lower Broadway. There is a big tray full of fried potatoes. Loaves are stacked on the counter. Bagels are stacked. Doughnuts, muffins, pastries are stacked. When I bulk into my seat, the table jolts and makes a scraping noise on the wooden floor. People look up. Fat guy bumping into table.

I look at the menu. It frightens me. Menus always frighten me. Jesus—I can have granola, oatmeal, griddle cakes, bagels, muffins, many types of toast. Maybe I'm not ready for Atkins. Maybe I'm not ready.

"Ready to order, sir?"

"Will you give me a couple of minutes?"

Four minutes tick by.

"Ready to order, sir?"

I go for an egg-white omelete. The waiter pushes me into having toast. He says, "What sort of toast do you want?"

"What sort do you have?"

"White, granary, wholemeal, sourdough, ciabatta, French stick, rye."

"Uh, wholemeal."

Seconds pass. Minutes pass. I pick up my knife and fork.

I look at these objects—first the knife, then the fork. My fingers bend around the knife and fork in a way that is familiar, reassuring. They might almost be parts of my own body.

I stare at my knife and fork. I am edgy. My fork has four tines. My knife has a rounded end. It is sharp along the lower edge and blunt along the upper. I can see my double chin reflected in its glinting surface.

My grandmother, my father's mother (b. 1894), used to tell me that I should not touch my knife and fork before the arrival of my food, that this was rude, a sign of greed, of bad attitude, of bad breeding. Picking up the knife and fork before the food arrives is a sign that you are greedy, that you will be fat. Premature cutlery pickup, she believed, was a model of what was wrong with society in general. Knives and forks exist to promote civilized eating. You sit at a table, upon which your food is placed. As an activity, eating is conducted in the open, transparently. Everything is upright, decent, "on the table." Nothing is furtive. Nothing is "under the table." Everybody can see what everybody else is eating. Everybody's food is distinct from everybody else's. When the food arrives, and only when the food arrives, do you touch your cutlery.

Right now, if it were up to me, I'd chuck the fork away and eat with my fingers. I'm feeling medieval, pre-fork. According to John Beckmann, the historian of inventions, people in England in the Middle Ages regarded the fork as "an effeminate piece of finery." I'd go along with that. Who used forks? The French, that's who. I mean, in the Stone Age, people would use knives made out of bits of flint. They would hack away at meat when they needed to. But mostly they ate with their fingers. People didn't really use forks until the eighteenth century, the age of frock coats and powdered wigs. The fork says, "Look at me! I'm not particularly hungry!"

I am.

When my food arrives, the first thing I want to eat is the toast. So I pick up a slice of the toast, and I start buttering it. My resolve is crumbling already. I know that, to kill it off completely, all I have to do is put this piece of toast in my mouth. Then I'll feel better. I can interview Dr. Atkins, write about him in a knowing, cynical way, go home, and forget about him. As I'm contemplating this, the waiter takes the order from the next table.

"What sort of toast do you want?"

The guy at the next table says, "No toast. We're doing a little Atkins thing here."

I put my toast down. I don't touch it again. I eat the egg-white omelete, fast, as if I am trying to kill it and eat it at the same time. I brandish my cutlery with cruel, slashing precision.

I am d'Artagnan. I am Errol Flynn.

And then I walk through the diner, away from the fried potatoes and the stacked loaves, the English and American muffins, the Danish pastries, the Belgian waffles; away from my religion and out into the cold, carb-scented air of Manhattan.

An Historic Moment

Five minutes later I'm standing on Lower Broadway, looking in the window of a newsstand, and the news is bad for fat people. There's a display of magazines as high as my head, and they're all telling me the same thing.

Breaking news: be thin. Thin is good. If you're not thin, you won't get what you want. If you're not thin, you will not be happy.

This just in: if you're not thin, you don't exist.

I'm looking at pictures of women with thin bodies, the sort of pictures I've been looking at for years, decades, images designed to make women dislike themselves. But I'm also looking at men. Men, stripped to the waist, arms toned, shoulders flexed, pectorals coiled—torsos knuckled like fists. Mostly I'm looking at stomachs. These are magazines *about* stomachs. LOSE YOUR GUT. SHRINK YOUR GUT. FIRMER ABS IN 28 DAYS. GET BETTER SEX. GET MORE SEX. GET HER TO AGREE TO *ANYTHING*.

I don't believe this, of course. But that's not quite true. The truth is: I don't want to believe it. But part of me believes it. Part of me thinks that, if I had a stomach like these stomachs, I could get women to agree to *anything*. With a stomach like this, I would have no fear. I would be . . . a real guy. These stomachs—they are awesome. These stomachs are smooth, shiny, polished. They are sectioned. They are like the bellies of reptiles. They are protective carapaces. Each stomach is a shield, a prophylactic against male vulnerability. They are ripped. They are cut. They are six-packs. Hell, some of them are EIGHT-packs.

Me, I have a one-pack. My stomach looks like dough— after it has risen, before it has been baked. When I saw a recent TV ad for Reebok running shoes, in which a fat disembodied belly chases a man all over town, I had several thoughts in quick succession. The first thought was the ad's slogan, which was "Belly's gonna get ya!" Too true, I thought. The second was that this was an historic moment. For years, we've seen images of women's bodies chopped up into their constituent parts, and now this is happening to men. And the third thought was: That's my belly. That's my belly out there. It looks like dough.

And the fourth thought was: Where can I buy those shoes?

Now I'm looking at the stomach magazines and wondering if I should buy a stomach magazine and thinking that if I bought a stomach magazine I would be fine, fine. And I'm thinking about my own belly, which fills me with a familiar nameless dread, and I want to eat, but I don't want to eat, and I can feel my belly pressing outward against my jacket, straining to get out, straining to get out and chase me through the streets.

And I wonder: how did I get here?

Fat History

I didn't get fat until I was eight years old and my family moved to Canada, and I suddenly started thinking and acting like a fat person. When I tell people this, they say it must have been something to do with the burgers and the fries and the popcorn and the hot dogs. And I say that, yes, the food might have played a role. But what made me fat came from inside my head. When I went to Canada, I was one person; when I came back, I was another. I was fat.

I stayed fat until I was ten. That doesn't sound like a long time, but it was. At ten, I discovered sports, and got trimmer. I played soccer and rugby and cricket. I swam. I got in the school teams. But I still wasn't quite right. I still felt fat on the inside. My weight fluctuated. I had to watch myself around food. Sometimes I binged.

By the time I was seventeen, nobody would have looked at me and seen a fat guy. I was more or less thin. The only person who knew my secret was me. When I went to university, I was still more or less thin. My weight still fluctuated. Sometimes I thought I was getting fat. But this was nothing compared to what would happen later. For instance, at the age of twenty I once got up into the high 190s. Big deal. This was when I was living in a house with some dope-smoking bums. I was one of the bums. Our idea of a good meal was fried "eggy bread"—large doorstep slices of white bread dipped in egg, fried in butter, and covered in brown sugar. We spent our time lounging in odd positions, giggling, listening to obscure rock albums, making rounds of eggy bread through the night. But I wasn't really fat. I looked like a trim person who had become a slob.

After this I lost weight again. I became sexually promiscuous. (This would always happen when I lost weight.) I was trim until I was twenty-six. That's the year I left university. By the time I met Anna, though, when I was twenty-seven, I was 208 lbs.—fat enough to make a difference. She was a princess on the slide; I was her plump provider. I grew into the role. During my time with Anna, I peaked at 220 lbs. At thirty-one, I trimmed down. I was perfectly thin—190 lbs.—at thirty-one and thirty-two. But it didn't make much difference; when Anna looked at me, she still saw the plump provider. Later, when I met Sadie, I was back up to 208 lbs. Weird. Another princess on the slide; another chance to play my familiar role. Except this time things got out of hand.

It was a gradual ascent, but this time it felt inexorable. There were some plateaux and some dips. There were diets. I sometimes lost a pound or two. I joined a gym. That didn't work. I started to use the gym. That didn't work either. I'm making this stupid joke, I think, in an effort to sound jolly. But there's nothing jolly about being fat. As I crept toward forty, I started to worry. At one point I did Montaignac for a while. And, like I said, one day—on my birthday, in fact— the while ended, and I continued my steady ascent.

And now let me put this another way. Getting fat does not feel like an ascent. There is no sense of having a better view, a clear vantage point, or anything like that. Getting fat feels more like burrowing, like tunneling. When you get fat, your view is obscured. Getting fat has a lot in common with burying your head in the sand. Getting fat is like sinking, like being sucked down by quicksand. You panic. You feel hopeless. You are stifled and squeezed, loaded down by a strong force that seems to be outside your realm of control. Your self-hatred grows as you lumber around, grinning, pretending not to notice.

Fat People Are Liars

Fat people are liars. Like I said, when you're fat, you lumber around, pretending not to notice. You try to fool other people into thinking you don't think you're fat. For you, the subject doesn't exist. As a fat person, you would be upset if somebody else started talking about other fat people. But this doesn't make sense, of course, because you're pretending not to know you are fat. A lot of fat people avoid the subject of fat in order to mimic the thin. But it's a poor imitation: thin people talk about fat all the time. I know. I've been thin.

What it boils down to is this. I am fat. I don't want to be fat. And I know how to be thin. But these three things don't add up. Why, then, am I not thin? Somewhere inside my psyche, I am untrustworthy.

I am a liar and a self-deceiver.

This is because I am fat; it is also the reason I got fat in the first place. Deep down, I know I am a liar and a self-deceiver, and that this is because I am fat, and also why I am fat. But every time I remember this, my override mechanism clicks into action, and I put it to the back of my mind instantly.

I don't want to go there.

I like to believe that I am fat, not through my own agency, but through the agency of others. I like to think I'm fat because the world around me is making me fat.

I am looking for a quick fix.

I like the idea of the Atkins diet because I think it might be a quick fix. When I see something that looks like a quick fix, I am capable of trusting it with a faith bordering on the religious. This is because I am a liar and a self-deceiver.

I want a quick fix because I don't want to look into myself too deeply. I am afraid that I might look into myself and despair.

I might look into myself, and despair, and never be the same again.

The Prejudice Is Insidious

Once, during the time I was with Sadie, during my slow, inexorable-seeming ascent, or, to put it another way, while I was burrowing into the mire of pretense and self-deception that became my world as I approached serious fatness, I wondered if it might be possible to live a normal life as a fat person.

I'd heard about the Fat Acceptance movement. Here were people who were fat, and yet who said they didn't mind being fat. I was fat, and I was beginning to despair. And these Fat Acceptance people—were they not despairing too? I imagined that, secretly, they were. I imagined they were lying to themselves and others. I imagined they were untrustworthy.

I was prejudiced.

Of course, I had a reason to be prejudiced. I was fat.

The first person I talked to was Shelley Bovey, probably the most radical campaigner for Fat Acceptance in Britain. At the time, Bovey was 5 foot 4, and weighed 224 lbs. She was fat, and she didn't like being fat. Her campaign was directed at prejudice against fat people, particularly women. So even though, on one level, she did not accept herself as she was, she wanted others to accept her.

Bovey did not fall into line with the Big is Beautiful movement. She wanted fat to be accepted, but not admired. In her book *The Forbidden Body* she writes, "Big is Beautiful puts a forced smile on the face of fat without revealing the depths of unhappiness and humiliation that most fat women experience. It is this that needs to be brought out into the open. It has to be recognised. And it has to be stopped."

At this point, Bovey wouldn't agree to meet me in person. We were talking on the phone. I wondered, perhaps uncharitably, if she wouldn't meet me in person because she was fat. After all, she had written, " . . . in a lifetime of being fat, I have observed that it is those who fear putting on weight who treat my size with the most aggression." And she knew, of course, that I was fat, that I disliked being fat. But what animated me most about Bovey was her level of pain.

Being fat, for Bovey, was intensely painful. She told endless stories about it. She had worked for the BBC, in radio documentaries, but switched to working from home, partly, she said, to avoid the difficulties of being a fat person in an office environment. At the BBC, she was told that her weight was giving the company a bad image. She pointed out that she worked on a radio program. Yes, came the reply, but some of the interviews she did were in the field, where she could be seen. Once, she went to a doctor because she was worried that her year-old child would not eat solid food. The doctor said, "What are you trying to do? Make the child as fat as yourself?"

"I actually feel," Bovey told me, "that prejudice against fat women is the biggest social injustice, bigger than racism, bigger than sexism, bigger than anything else." In *The Forbidden Body*, Bovey describes a fat woman being treated by a thin woman "as though she were a different species."

Bovey believed in the Cannon Conundrum. She believed she had got fat because she had dieted too much. As a fat child, she went through endless starve-and-binge cycles, dieting until she was weak, and then bingeing wildly to keep her strength up. "I've lost thousands of pounds over the years," she told me. She lost 42 lbs., from 182 lbs. to 140 lbs., in the run-up to her wedding, and then put on another 84 lbs. afterward. "If I hadn't dieted," she said, "I would not have been as high as 224 lbs.; I think I would have been about 168 lbs. That would have been fine. I'm sure my natural weight is 168 lbs."

She wrote something chilling: that being fat made her feel like an outcast, and that she worked so hard to hide the pain of feeling like an outcast "that I found it difficult to differentiate what was really me and what was the public face." I began to wonder why, if being fat was so awful, she was so resigned to it. In her work, she was a reporter from the center, the very core, of the fat world. But she was entirely concerned with the consequences of being fat, rather than the causes. I wanted to find out about the causes.

For now, Bovey was concerned with the issue of prejudice. She told me, "Just think about it for a while. Look at how people treat fat women. The prejudice is insidious. It creeps into everything. Once you start noticing it, you'll be amazed."

"I Wouldn't Want You to Bring a Photographer"

Was there anybody out there who accepted fat people unequivocally? Surely somebody did. Perhaps that somebody was a company called 1647, an outfit that designed clothes for large women. The name had been taken from the statistic that 47 percent of British women wore a dress size of 16 or over. The company was run by two women, the designer

Helen Teague (5 foot 6, 154 lbs.) and the actress Dawn French (5 foot 2, but "We don't put out details of Dawn's weight.")

French was extremely upbeat about fat women. She said, "I long for the day of the fatter supermodel." Like Bovey, she was also inspired by anger. She said, "It gets me so angry that sassy, proud girls get stuck in that horrible stuff chain stores think fat women should wear."

French was relentlessly positive. She pushed the angle that fat women are actually very sexy. She posed in skimpy gear in *Esquire*. "Big women," she said, "are told by the men in our lives that we are lovely and good in bed. We're delicious, we're voluptuous. Then everybody else, including the media, tells us that we're not."

Here, it seemed, was a simple dispute. The media—which, as French kept pointing out in the media, is largely run by men—promotes images of thin women, causing endless anguish for fat women. And then there are the fat women who want to fight back by promoting more realistic images—images of themselves, happy to be fat. From where I was standing, it looked like things might be getting better for fat women. French and Teague, for example, not content with producing the 1647 clothes for day-to-day wear, had just launched a new designer range, simply called French and Teague. These were upmarket clothes for large women. Glamorous. Sexy, even.

I met Helen Teague in a bar across the road from the 1647 shop in Primrose Hill, north London. The shop had been designed to make fatter women feel less self-conscious about themselves; it had an air of quiet privacy. For one thing, you could not just walk in off the street—

you had to ring a bell. Also, there were no communal changing rooms. Is this, I wondered, the thin end of the wedge of prejudice that Bovey had described? No, I thought. It's simple sensitivity.

Teague didn't look exactly fat; being moderately tall, her minor bulk made her look statuesque. "Well," she told me, "I am a normal-sized woman." She wore a large, flowing white cotton shirt from the 1647 range, a shirt she'd designed herself. Not fashionable, but certainly stylish. She was planning the launch party for her new designer range, to be held at Liberty. "In midnight blue and sensual chocolate," ran the press release, "a wonderful micro fabric caresses the body. Long trim pants and skirts echo the undercurrents that all women demand, of private pleasures and hidden delights."

We talked about the prejudices suffered by her potential customers. "You're still allowed to abuse fat women," she said. "Society frowns on racism, but not on abusing fat people." Then we talked about the broader picture, about how women's magazines have an economic need to make their readers feel insecure, because they are funded by advertising for products that compensate for this insecurity—cosmetics, perfumes, hair products. And almost all the magazines advertise liposuction operations. Making women feel fat is sound economic sense.

Teague said she believed that all of this was true. "But I don't want to say it in public," she said. "My views are very radical, but they're incompatible with a consumer attitude."

Then she told me about the state of the market in fat women's clothes. The market, basically, was there for the taking. "If you look at market research," said Teague, "you'll see that thin women buy lots more clothes than larger women. A thin woman might have ten skirts. A large woman of the same age will have three. There's no imagery aimed at big women. The images don't work for them; they're not seduced. They can't buy into it."

Teague, therefore, wanted to create images which would seduce fat women, images which, as she put it, "make it acceptable for older and bigger women to send out sexual signals." And this, of course, is terribly difficult. You have to be subtle. If you want women to buy things, you have to make them feel dissatisfied with what they've already got. You have to play with their insecurity. But you have to be careful with fat women. They're easy to scare off. You mustn't remind them that they're fat.

Then I asked Teague if I could attend the launch party for her new designer range, and bring a photographer with me. "You can come," she said. "But I wouldn't want you to bring a photographer. It's a difficult situation. You're writing about fat issues. And I don't really want French and Teague to be associated with all that. I want to keep it separate."

Hold on, I thought. She wants the world to accept fat women without prejudice. She's designed a range of clothes to make these fat women feel glamorous. But she wants to avoid associating her clothes with fatness. So even here, right at the center of the world of Fat Acceptance, fat is a dirty word.

Teague said, "We're trying to sell clothes, not ideas."

Then she said, "Leave the arguments to professional intellectuals. I would never contradict them. But what do they come up with? They're not coming up with anything new. I've been hearing these arguments for twenty years."

Then she said, "What we need is beautiful images. To get resources, you need to be appealing."

The Private Pleasures, the Hidden Delights

I went to the French and Teague fashion show at the department store. It was a big enough attraction to fill one floor of the building with people. Many, but not most, were large-sized women. The women drank champagne and talked positively. It was a great thing that, at last, they could have designer clothes. Here, on racks, were the soft, velvety ensembles in midnight blue and sensual chocolate; they looked like a sultan's pajamas. Here were the long skirts to echo the private pleasures, the hidden delights; a collection, to quote the publicity handout, "which captures all a woman's emotions—the seductress, the feminine, the wife, the lover."

Helen Teague got up on stage and made a speech. Then Dawn French spoke. French was in the sensual chocolate. She looked roly-poly. She said, "Big women are not alienated in this store," which was, at last, true. She went on, "I hope that ultra-skinny people will be green with envy." Then the models took to the stage in the brown and blue outfits, the fluffy, huge-collared opera coat, the diaphanous slip dress. But these women were not fat at all. They were oversized models—tall, beautiful, shapely. I talked to them afterward. One of them was almost as tall as me and weighed 154 lbs. She looked like a fantasy version of Kim Basinger. "I'm just more woman than people like Kate

Moss," she said. If this was Fat Acceptance in action, I could see what Shelley Bovey was on about.

I asked French if she would talk to me—about the politics, the design of the clothes, the fat issues. French looked cagey. She said she didn't know, and referred me to her publicist.

A few days later, Teague mulled over the show's coverage. She felt piqued. She'd watched a TV clip of the show. The TV station, she said, "picked the biggest girls they could see, and filmed them. Some of them were size 36 and 40!"

Dawn French's publicist called me a few days later. Would she talk? "Dawn's done all that now," said the publicist. "She wants to steer away from that. She wants to concentrate on the label, rather than the issue of size."

Staring You in the Face

And that's when I realized that the answer to my question was no. Nobody accepts fat people. Not even fat people. Particularly not fat people. When you are fat, part of you doesn't like yourself, and you wear this self-loathing like an outfit, a clown's suit that tells other people to devalue you. "Above all in our culture," writes the Princeton cultural historian Richard Klein, "being fat means you get no love, because you deserve no love."

Klein relates a telling story: a man asked a fat woman out on a date. All very well, you might think. But then she discovered that he was a Fat Admirer—a "chubby chaser." "She was angry and frustrated," said Klein. "It reinforced her dream of having a man who wants her in spite of her build." She didn't want a man to want her as she was. She was like Groucho Marx, who wouldn't want to belong to a club that would accept him as a member. After all, when you are only pretending to accept yourself, it is unbearable to be loved for the very thing you cannot love in yourself: your fat.

Being fat blots out parts of your mind just as it blurs your outline. Sometimes, as Shelley Bovey says, it's hard to know where you end and where your fat begins.

When you are fat, you are lost in an alien territory, and that territory is you. But it's not you. But it *is* you. It's maddening. And sometimes, you think you can see a way out, and then you look again, and you can't see anything. It feels as if you're searching for something, and you know it's there, it's staring you in the face, and you look again, and it's gone.

Part of the Problem

Reflected in the glass of the newsstand window, my face looks puffy, ill-defined. Should I buy a stomach magazine? Are stomach magazines the solution? Or are they part of the problem? In her book *The Male Body,* weight guru Susan Bordo hints that pictures of muscled, bulky men are history; a new, more feminine aesthetic is beginning to rule. In the old style, the engorged muscleman—the surrogate penis, according to gay theorist Ron Long—stares straight ahead, blank-eyed, ready to fight, unwilling to show weakness. Bordo calls this image "the rock." She calls the new, Calvin Klein–inspired male pin-up "the leaner"—"because these bodies are almost always reclining, leaning against, or propped up against something in the fashion of women's bodies."

Leaners are also like female fashion models in another way—they are leaner. Like women, they are depicted as objects rather than subjects. They challenge the advertising credo, defined by art historian John Berger in the 1970s, that "men act and women appear."

These days, men appear.

Another thing John Berger wrote was, "Men look at women. Women watch themselves being looked at. This determines not only the relations of men to women, but the relation of women to themselves."

We all know what happens when women are encouraged to be self-conscious about their bodies. According to the feminist Susie Orbach, author of *Fat Is a Feminist Issue,* they start to hate the way they look, and then they diet, which leads to a disordered relationship with food. According to the feminist Kim Chernin, author of *The Obsession,* they start to hate the way they look, and then they diet, which leads to a disordered relationship with food. According to the feminist Naomi Wolf, author of *The Beauty Myth,* they start to hate the way they look, and then they diet, which leads to a disordered relationship with food. According to the feminist Caroline Knapp, author of *Appetites,* they start to hate the way they look, and then they diet, which leads to a disordered relationship with food.

So I'm inclined to think that stomach magazines are not the solution. I think they are part of the problem.

Disaster Movie

I walk past a deli and past a diner and past another deli and past a food store with a picture of a cake in the window, a photograph the size of a billboard, a huge crumby cake with red slop on the top, and I'm asking myself the million-dollar question.

Why do I eat too much?

I walk past a place with a neon sign that says "Hot Bagel—we bake freshly every day," and another place with a sign that says "Ohhh that coffee . . . mmmm that bread," and even though it's a bright, crisp morning, a cheerful morning, a toasted bagel sort of morning, I am filled with a nameless dread, a sense that I am in imminent danger, that very soon, any moment now, I will be picked up and hurled into oblivion by terrible, malign forces I cannot control.

I don't know. Why am I getting so fat? Why are we getting so fat? Standing here, panting on these fat streets, in this fat city, having bolted a large plateful of albumen, having passed on the toast, I'm glaring across the street at a mobile bagel cart—a bagel chariot. I want a bagel. I am not satisfied. I want *more*. I want more, even though I know that, by having more, I will want still more. I know that having more will not satisfy me. But still, I want to give it another chance. More is my creed. More is our creed, here in the greedy West. That's all our society has to offer us. More. We are fat, we are getting fatter, and we are not going to stop getting fatter.

I am fat.

I am getting fatter.

Is there any hope for me?

We are, surely, going to get fatter and fatter, until—what? I don't know. But the Fat Crisis is already well under way. The Fat Crisis is rolling. Just the other day, in fact, I was talking about it. I was talking about the Fat Crisis because sometimes it seems there's nothing else to talk about. It's been in the newspapers, on the radio, on the TV. People are beginning to talk about an "epidemic"—"a sudden, widespread occurrence of a particular undesirable phenomenon" (OED). This is how America's Centers for Disease Control and Prevention refer to the Fat Crisis. It is also the term used by the World Health Organization and its younger sibling, the International Obesity Task Force.

Everybody knows the situation is bad, and getting worse. Everybody intends to do something about it. We all have a policy. We all have a diet. The word "diet," derived from the Greek "diaita," means "a way of life." A diet is nothing less than a philosophy.

Oh, everybody has a diet. Dr. Atkins has a diet. Catherine Zeta-Jones has a diet. Sophie Dahl has a diet. Renée Zellweger has a diet.

Kirstie Alley from *Cheers*—she has a diet.

And now we have a diet crisis, a diet disaster. That's what somebody was telling me the other day. It's bad, he said—so bad, in fact, that sixty-five million Americans are overweight. We shook our heads, appalled. Sixty-five million. That sounds bad, doesn't it? And then somebody else said no, you're wrong, it's not sixty-five million—it's 65 *percent*. And I checked, and he was right. Now, that really is bad. According to the World Health Organization, 65 percent of Americans are overweight. That's 127 million. Thirty percent are obese. And get this: ten years ago, 20 percent were obese. And this: according to Professor Kelly Brownell, the director of the Yale Center for Eating and Weight Disorders, "The number of people with very high body weights where disease risk is extreme has tripled in the last decade."

How will this disaster turn out? Will it be like one of those disaster movies in which the terrible threat comes from outside, and can therefore be repelled, like the Triffids in *Day of the Triffids,* or the birds in *The Birds*? Or is this more like one of those movies in which the threat comes from inside, where the threat is not plants from outer space, or winged predators, but . . . us?

At My Age, Brando Was Trimmer than Me

Well, at least I'm walking, rather than what I'd normally do in this situation, which is go back to my hotel room, bagel-bloated, and order something on room service, possibly just a coffee, possibly not, and loll around my bed, fretting and sweating in front of daytime TV. At this hour, 10 A.M., fat o'clock in the TV schedules, I could watch obese people sitting on sofas, with that anti-poise obese people have, talking about how bad it is to be obese, how unfair, how humiliating.

I like watching obese people—it can be a good appetite suppressant. They talk about how they want to get trim, but they can't, they've tried everything, and it *keeps going wrong.* They try to exercise, but they can't fit it into their daily schedule. They try to stop eating fast food, but they crack on Day One or Day Two. I saw one show in which a man was frustrated with his obese wife; she said she'd been on a diet, but she hadn't lost a pound, had in fact gained weight, and one day he left the house, got to the station, then realized he'd forgotten his wallet, and walked back to the house, and let himself in, and there she was, sitting at the kitchen table, in flagrante. Kentucky Fried Chicken. Large bucket. Large fries. He looked at her and said how long has this been going on, and she started sobbing. How long, he said. Eventually, she told him. She'd been doing it *the whole time*. She'd never even *started* her diet. She didn't know how to stop eating. She was "just so hungry." She was "so hungry all the time." She "just couldn't trust herself around food."

Fat people and their excuses. It really makes me angry. They're always whining, the whiny fat pigs. Why don't they just stop whining and do something about it? Why don't I just stop whining and do something about it?

The answer to that question is that I already am doing something about it. I'm on a diet. I've been on the diet for five minutes already, and I'm holding up fine. I'm doing better than that woman, anyway. Look—I'm walking past the bagel cart! No eye contact with the bagel man. I am full of Day One thinking. Such as: if everything goes according to plan, the low-carb way of life might make me thin, and, thin, I might become a better person. I might become my old self, the person I was before I became bloated and weak and self-deceiving. Sure, I got fat because I have problems. But maybe, if I get thin, I'll be able to tackle those problems in a more effective way. I can just see it—myself, in however many months' time, sitting at my desk, thin, paying bills. Myself, in however many months' time, thin, standing in the kitchen, holding a wet cloth. My girlfriend saying, "Oh, you shouldn't have—it was my turn!" Myself, thin, taking my clothes off, slowly, thin-style, before getting into bed. My girlfriend looking at me. Me not minding. Torso like Marlon Brando's in *A Streetcar Named Desire.* (When Brando was rehearsing the original play, Truman Capote went to interview him; later, Capote said that "it was as if a stranger's head was attached to the brawny body." The body was taut and muscular; the head was "so very untough." Ten years later, when Brando was beginning to be haunted by his personal demons, the powerful feelings of self-loathing that live inside the fat person—or, in this case, the future fat person—he told Capote, "Sensitive people are so vulnerable; they're so easily brutalized and hurt just because they *are* sensitive. The more sensitive you are, the more certain you are to be brutalized, develop scabs." Then he said, "Never evolve. Never allow yourself to feel anything, because you feel too much."

Well, that's how he lived his life. Trying not to feel anything. Eating and feeling hungry and eating and feeling guilty and eating and getting fat and feeling bad about being fat, in order to avoid feeling his real emotions. Which is exactly what I do, and I know it. But I don't want to know it. So I don't think about it. I'm fat, and I hate being fat, but there is something else, something I believe is worse than being fat, something I can't bear to think about. What is it?

At my age, Brando was thinner than me.)

Wearing High Heels

I'd like to walk briskly, but my stomach muscles have gone, pushed outward by the blob of churning dough which is my belly, so that the bottom half of my body feels as if it is not quite connected to the top half. I'm not a great walker. I'm a sloucher, a schlepper. I walk at the pace of a woman wearing high heels. Fat, I feel the raw power of the earth's gravitational pull. I move forward discordantly, propelled by the prow of my gut, my feet splayed outward for maximum balance. Whenever I say I'm walking, don't imagine someone actually walking. Imagine effort, discomfort, pain, shame. A long-standing injury in my left ankle has been aggravated by my excess weight. My ankle is weak, but I'm fat, so I don't exercise it, so it gets weaker, and sometimes the ankle turns, just gives way, and I spill over, I fall down with an almighty crash. Falling down is much, much less dignified a thing to do when you're fat than when you're thin. I've fallen down thin, and I've fallen down fat, and there's a big difference. For instance, when a thin person falls down, people turn their heads and look in sympathy. A fat person falling down, on the other hand, is a tragicomic sight. And when I heave myself up, I stand on my bad ankle gingerly, to test it out. And when I walk, I naturally favor my right foot, which further weakens my left ankle, and puts a strain on my right calf. Recently, I had an ill-advised run—the panic exercise of the not-quite obese male as he enters middle age. That morning, I looked at the scales. 230 lbs. I put on a pair of old trainers I had not worn for years. They felt brittle, deep-fried. I donned a tracksuit. I jogged through the park, hobbling slightly, favoring my right leg. After a few minutes,

there was a definite ripping sensation in my right shin—
some kind of string had frayed. Now I hobble slightly on
both legs.

Trying to Kill Me

I take a deep breath. I am covered with a light sheen of cold
sweat. This combination of chilly air and arctic light, glinting from windshields and buildings, makes me want hot
chocolate and custard puddings, red wine and gravy din-
ners, chunky fries and roast potatoes.

Fries!

No!

Chunky fries and roast potatoes. The mixture of starch
and fat, the fries or roast potatoes crumbling slightly at the
edges. Fries heavily salted in the cardboard pack. Eaten
without knife or fork, like a true hunter-gatherer. Except, of
course, when you eat fast food, the hunting and gathering is
minimal, to say the least.

And I'm walking along and I still can't stop thinking
about eating. Putting something in my mouth. Forgetting,
for one glorious moment, my worldly cares. This bright,
chilly day—it's a perfect day for a hot drink and some kind
of tart or strudel. But I won't do that, of course. One thing
you can say for the Atkins diet—it starts working immediately. If you want a snack, you drift instinctively to the nearest snack place, and—you can't have anything. Snacks, it
turns out, are made from refined carbohydrates. It's not an
absolute rule, but it's pretty close. Mostly, snacks are carbs.
On Atkins, you can't have them. Right now, walking up

Lexington Avenue, I only have eyes for the things I can't have. Trays full of baked goods, in a range of flavors. Cinnamon, sesame seed, almond, chocolate, chocolate chip, blueberry. Bright packets with floral colors to catch my eye, as if I were a bee in search of pollen.

I find myself drifting into a deli, a huge, deep deli, wanting things I can't have, possibly a starchy snack flavored with stuff to make it taste like something familiar, cheese, say, or bacon, or beef, or maybe prawns. And here they are, the starchy snacks, not merely arranged, or even stacked, but shelved, a whole shelved wall of them, a library of starchy snacks. I could have cheese-flavored crispy potato snacks or cheese-flavored crispy corn snacks or cheese-flavored cookies or biscuits or Triscuits. I could have full-fat snacks or reduced-fat snacks or low-fat snacks or no-fat snacks. I could have Wheat Thins or Crisps or Bits or Ritz or Hits or Twigs or Snaps or Pops or Chips or Dips or Chewys or Crunchys or Munchies or Lunchies. I could have Frites or Ruffles or Pringles or Singles or Doubles or Mingles; I could have Chunkys or Funkys or Baldys or Garibaldis or Grahams or Lays or Frito-Lays or Newtons, or Cheddars or Cheese-ums, Fritos, Doritos, Cheet-os, Tostitos. A professor of Social Theory at Swarthmore College, Barry Schwartz, recently counted the number of crispy snacks he could buy in his local supermarket. There were ninety-five.

According to obesity expert Greg Critser, research carried out at the USDA Human Nutrition Research Center at Tufts University highlighted "an amazing phenomenon"— the larger the variety of snacks in a person's diet, the more calories he will consume. And, as Critser points out, the number of new snack products launched in America every year is growing exponentially—from 250 per year in the late 1970s to 2,000 per year by the late '80s. And now what? Now what?

Perhaps more worrying still, Professor Schwartz believes that this degree of choice is driving us nuts. This overabundance, he says, "may actually contribute to the recent epidemic of clinical depression affecting much of the Western world." What happens to the consumer's head, Schwartz thinks, is that this level of choice drives up the consumer's expectations, which leads to disappointment, and eventually depression. People are spending more and more time searching the aisles for what they want, and then, when they get it, they find out that it's not what they want. It's just a cellophane bag full of reconstituted starch, flavored with stuff like monosodium glutamate and methyl-2-peridylketone. It's not what they want at all, which makes them feel hollow and empty.

And when you feel hollow and empty, what do you want to do?

You want to eat. Just like the rats in an experiment conducted by Anthony Sclafini of Brooklyn College. Sclafini gave his rats access to foods high in carbohydrates and fat. They ignored more nutritious food, and became obese. The bad food had left them feeling empty, which made them want more of it. Presumably, the fat tasted good, and the carbs made them hungry.

I want to eat, of course, but, more importantly, I don't want to eat, I really don't want to eat. I want to be thin. If I eat any more, I'll be obese, putting myself at greater risk of, among other things, arthritis, cancer, cardiovascular disease, carpal tunnel syndrome, deep vein thrombosis, diabetes, gallbladder disease, gout, heart disease, hypertension, impaired immune response, impaired respiratory function, infertility, liver disease, lumbar pain, pancreatitis, sleep apnea, stroke, and urinary stress incontinence.

So I drift back out of the deli, smiling, hands in pockets, avoiding the evil eye of the man behind the counter who is trying to kill me.

More

According to Dr. Atkins, carbohydrate snacks, quite simply, do not satisfy you. That's why, as a product, the snack is doing so well. Americans spend $32 billion on snacks per year. You eat one, and you want another one. Eat. Want. It's a vicious circle—or, if you're a manufacturer of snacks, a virtuous circle.

Snacks are an advertisement for themselves.

In a time of material abundance and consumer choice, the successful manufacturer must create more than just a product—he must also create a need. Successful products are the ones that make you hungry. In other words, the products that do well are the ones that do not satisfy. Or, to put it another way, in the Darwinistic struggle of the modern marketplace, the ideal product is addictive.

The ideal product is the one that does not work. Like, say, pornography. Pornography doesn't really do the trick. Pornography is an advertisement for itself. The more pornography people have, the more they want.

Carbohydrate snacks make you hungry. They are culinary pornography; they are like *Penthouse* magazine. Looking at pictures of naked girls in *Penthouse* is not exactly having a meaningful relationship with women. Eating carbohydrate snacks is not exactly having a meaningful relationship with food. Fill yourself with snacks, and you'll feel empty a couple of hours later.

In his book *Britain on the Couch*, the clinical psychologist Oliver James writes, "Put crudely, advanced capitalism makes money out of misery and dissatisfaction, as if it were encouraging us to fill the psychic void with material goods." He also writes, "If you are feeling lousy today or in urgent need of a drink or a fix or a fling or a fight, you probably have low serotonin levels caused by the way we live now." Serotonin, of course, is the brain chemical that makes us feel happy. According to the Australian nutritionist Jennifer Alden, eating sugar and refined carbohydrates, such as white flour and crispy snacks, causes the level of serotonin in the brain to rise temporarily and then slump, inducing cravings—similar to the effects of cocaine.

Like Anthony Sclafini's rats, we are hungry for the things that don't satisfy us. We crave the things that make us hungry. I'm thinking of carbohydrates, pornography, promiscuous sex, facelifts, cocaine, credit cards, computer games, and sugar.

What about things that do satisfy us? We're not so hungry for them, are we? Organic cabbage. Broccoli. Brussels sprouts. Jogging. Working at relationships. Here, in the heart of New York City, I am in the global center of relationship angst. This, as Candace Bushnell shows in *Sex and the City*, is a place where people actively repel each other. It is, in the words of the French philosopher Jean Baudrillard, "the anti-Ark." In some ways, it's the loneliest place in the world.

This is the fat society. This is where people come, so they can have exactly what they want. And what they want is . . . more.

The Fat Society

I think the fat society is a lot like the fat individual. The fat society is a lot like me. I'm fat, but I don't know what to think about it. I'm fat, but I don't know what to do about it. I know I have to change my way of life, but I'm looking for a change that is superficial, rather than fundamental. Like me, the fat society doesn't really want to know the truth about itself. Fat people would rather die than know the truth. Fat people would rather eat than know the truth. They would rather eat themselves to death. Like I said, fat people have a complicated relationship with the truth. Fat people are the world's best liars. Never trust fat people.

Golden Arches

It's eleven o'clock, coffee time, time to refuel with a bagel or a doughnut and a cup of something hot, although it feels later to me, more like lunchtime. When you're fat, you live on fat time. Your clock is fat. I walk past a place with a sign that says "Bagel," and past a place that says "Bagels," and past a place that says "LUNCH." Ahead of me I can see the golden arches of a McDonald's, flashing into my field of vision like a warning sign.

Fries!

Not good.

I'd only eat them and feel empty afterward. Fries are pornography. Fries are an advertisement for themselves.

Look at this another way: fries can rely on that excellent ad agency inside your body, the pancreas, which, as a result of eating fries, produces too much insulin, which eats up the glucose in your blood, which gives you a blood-sugar crash, which makes you want to eat more fries.

This is what Dr. Atkins says, and I can feel my belief strengthening. What if he is right?

But hang on—what about the Cannon Conundrum? I can feel my belief in the Cannon Conundrum weakening. Diets make you fat, yes. But surely this is only the case when, by dieting, you reduce your total calorie intake. When you do this, of course, your body, not having evolved since hunter-gatherer times, thinks you can't find food, and switches to famine mode. When you reduce your calorie intake, your body tries as hard as it can to metabolize fat out of every bit of food it gets. And then, when you stop the diet, you put weight on. So Cannon was right. But only in a world in which diets were all about reducing calories.

Calorie-reducing diets, in fact, were just as bad as pornography and cocaine and fries. They didn't work, thus creating demand for themselves.

But Atkins is *not* a calorie-reducing diet, is it? It is simply a *carbohydrate*-reducing diet.

So perhaps it doesn't make you fat.

After the snacks I ate yesterday, my pancreas has been up

all night, sitting at its desk, writing copy. The copy, which is on a crawler strip at the bottom of the screen of my mind, is crude but effective. It says, "Eat snacks eat snacks eat snacks eat snacks eat snacks . . ."

I glance up at the golden arches. There is a pang in the center of my body that feels like hunger, but also like other things—anguish, loneliness, basic misery. A sort of all-purpose craving. The crawler strip at the bottom of the screen of my mind says, "Eat fries eat fries eat fries eat fries eat fries . . ."

I look away.

The Andy Warhol Diet

Perhaps Andy Warhol got it right. The Andy Warhol Diet: you go to an expensive restaurant, and order everything that disgusts you. And remember, this is an expensive restaurant, where some things can be seriously disgusting. When the food comes, it will make you feel sick, so you won't eat it. That's it. That's the Andy Warhol Diet. (Later, he would get the waiter to put the food in a doggy bag and then he'd leave it in the street for homeless people to eat, or feel disgusted by in their turn.)

How Did She Get Like That?

Remember what I said about the obese person's shuffle? Well, I'm walking behind an obese person now. A woman. I'm walking slowly, but she's at crawling pace. She must weigh 300 lbs. The pyramid of her trunk sits uneasily on her hips, which are joined to splayed, bulky legs. As she walks, she rotates slightly from a central axis, hammering pain and destruction downward on her ankles, knees, hips, and lumbar region. Her arms stick out sideways from her body because of the large pannier-sized bulges on the outside of her ribs. Large veinless puffy hands with dimpled knuckles swing outward, high and free, pushed upward by the buttress of the woman's excess flesh, almost as if she's waving at the people she's walking past.

But she's not waving.

And people, in general, do not seem happy to see this woman. Fat or thin, we are not happy to see obese people in public. Just ask an obese person. As this woman walks along, people narrow their eyes or rotate their heads a few degrees away from her. "Yuck!" That's what they're saying. And: "Ugh!"

And: "Jesus."

And: "God, don't let me get like that!"

And: "Poor soul."

Two thin, younger guys catch each other's eye, and their cheeks plump up, their eyes flash. This is: "Whoo!" This is: "Catch that, Dude!" A couple of people walk past, staring straight ahead. This is: "I really don't want to go there."

Looking at people, you can well imagine the stuff that's passing through their minds. Like, "How did she get like that?"

And: "I wonder what it would be like to . . ."

And: "If I could talk to her, just for an hour, I could really help her."

And how do I feel, looking at this woman? Oh, I hate her.

I hate myself for hating her, but like I said, I'm fattist. I hate her because she reminds me that I am fat, that I'm a bit like her. But I think I hate her also because she tells me something about the world. She tells me that we live in a fat world. She tells me that we, the human race, are out of control. She takes away a little bit of my hope.

And look at her *clothes*. For a start, they are frumpy. Seeing this gives me a small frisson of horrified recognition. She's fat, so she is signaling, in a humble sort of way, her very humility. She's saying: I'm not the sort of fat person who is pretending to think I'm good-looking. She's wearing sneakers, but not spiffy, bright, fashionable sneakers. These are *gray*. They look like grandma's shoes; they look like they might smell of house dust and cats and out-of-date cooking oil. She didn't *have* to choose these gray sneakers. Mind you, her hand has been forced somewhat when it comes to her outer layers. Here, she has very definitely Gone Floaty, and wears a swaddling of grays and browns, a sort of protective cladding. She looks like a nomad's yurt that has been ripped from its moorings in a storm.

I'll bet she has an expanding waistband on her trousers. Until recently, expanding waistbands have been associated mainly with children's clothes (because children grow), sporting clothes (they need to be flexible), bedwear (must be comfortable), and underwear (too flimsy to rely on fasteners, must not fall off). But now, expanding waistbands are entering the mainstream. Like children, adults are expected to grow.

And expanding waistbands are a dangerous thing. As Greg Critser points out, research conducted by John Garrow, a British scientist, suggests that tight waistbands inhibit overeating. Garrow investigated a group of formerly obese patients who had lost weight on a calorie-controlled diet. This was a radical calorie-controlled diet: the patients had had their jaws wired. When the wires were removed, Garrow fitted half the patients with cords around their waists. The cords were tight enough to make a white line in the flesh when the patient was seated. The difference in weight gain between the waistband group and the non-waistband group, Garrow found, was "striking." Those without cords gained weight at a much faster rate. And this leads Critser to an interesting point. Elasticized waistbands are the thin end of the wedge. What about the larger-sized chairs being fitted into many restaurant chains?

Will we grow into them?

The Million-Dollar Question

I'm right behind the obese woman, close enough to observe the doughnut of fat she wears around her neck like a brace, like a shameful necklace, and I'm wondering what it's like to be as fat as this, and I'm thinking of Shelley Bovey's heartrending description, "A Day in the Life of a Fat Woman." Interestingly, even though Bovey writes in the first person, she switches to the third person when things get beyond a certain point of horror, when things get really *personal*.

When she wakes, the fat woman feels tired. "She always feels tired, no matter how much sleep she gets." She also feels weak with hunger. She breakfasts on cereal—carbs for a quick energy boost. In the car, "she cannot do up her seatbelt without it digging in so that she can't breathe out." She "drives her car unbelted, breaking the law and feeling precarious and unsafe."

On the train, she is "the focus of many eyes as the train lurches on its way and the cause of irritation to the passengers whose arms she accidentally jogs as she passes them." When she squeezes into her seat, she is "jammed for a few agonising moments as her stomach sticks on the hard rim of the table and she is wedged astride the central divider." In the street, she is jeered at by workmen. At the office, she is desperate for a doughnut, but too ashamed to eat in front of her colleagues.

Later, during a hospital appointment, the hospital gown does not fit—in order to cover her breasts, she must wear it back to front, exposing her bottom. In a clothes store, she is intercepted by an assistant, who says, "I'm afraid we've got nothing in *your* size." On the way home, she visits a supermarket to buy some carbohydrate snacks for her children, because she feels "the working mother's guilt." At the checkout, she stuffs the snacks in the store's plastic bag as quickly as she can. Later still, weary and desperate, she goes home on the train. She is too tired to fight for a seat, so she stands. She wonders: Is it just being fat that brings about this utter dreariness of body and spirit?

Or is there something else, something that *caused* Bovey to be fat? That, of course, is the million-dollar question. It's a question she never answers. It's a question I'd like to put to her.

Ten More Pounds and I'm Finished

Looking at the obese woman in front of me, this lost soul, this woman who I guess must have some terrible problem, who, I would bet, overeats, who almost certainly has a relationship with food which is pretty disgusting, looking at this woman and thinking of her and thinking of myself makes me feel uncomfortable, and I would *much* rather be looking at someone else, thinking about someone else's dress sense. How much longer before I have to upsize? How much longer before I Go Floaty? Because, of course, part of me is still certain, absolutely certain, that Dr. Atkins is wrong, that I am fat and getting fatter and will be fat forever, that all I have to look forward to, as Clive James once put it, is "a lifetime of thigh-chafing misery," that Geoffrey Cannon was right, that diets don't work, that I'll never solve my problems at all, that my girlfriend, who says she doesn't mind about my weight, actually, secretly, does, that my bulk will increase relentlessly, like Robbie Coltrane . . .

Why am I fat?

I'm fat because I overeat.

And why do I overeat?

For a moment, I stop, watching the woman as she walks, haltingly, past the golden arches. Which makes a certain amount of sense. When I have talked to very fat people about fast-food restaurants, they mostly say they never go in them—they're too self-conscious. They don't like the sneering. What they don't like, precisely, is for people to make the connection between their weight and their eating. They do not like people to see the cause and the effect, and make the right connection. Rather, they like to keep 'em guessing.

Yeah, right.

But those clothes—they've made me think. When you're fat, clothes lose their meaning. The messages they were designed to send become warped and twisted. Take jeans. When you wear jeans, you're saying something about being rugged and outdoorsy and fit. When you see a fat person in jeans, your eye computes that image as something different. It doesn't fit. It doesn't work. It looks a bit ridiculous. This is true of other items of clothing, too. I know, for instance, that, above a certain weight (200 lbs.) I can't wear a leather jacket. It really does not work. Somebody recently asked me why I always dress so negatively, why always in black, why always so scruffy. And, in a moment of honesty, a brief meltdown, I said that, well, this was all I had left. Brightly colored, I look like a fool. Smart, I look like a dweeb. I look like a nerd. A fat nerd. When you get fat, your fat drives you away from the image you'd like to have of yourself. Sartorially, it blots out large areas of possible self-expression, until you're left with virtually nothing, and then, eventually, nothing at all. These scruffy black clothes I'm wearing—they're all I have. I am, just, clinging on to an outfit that is the real me. But it's not much. It feels like a life raft. I am bobbing on the waves, clutching my raft, scanning the horizon for a possible means of rescue.

But this woman—she's drowning. Those grim tweeds wrapped around her, around the bulk that she has become, those granny shoes—they're not her. She has lost the *her* she might have had, the *her* I imagine she must yearn for. She's lost it. It's gone.

How long before I lose me?

I'm wearing: a tight black stretch T-shirt by Paul Smith, a tight black short-sleeved sport shirt by Gap, a black corduroy jacket, almost a coat, by Emile Lafaurie, black jeans which say Tommy Hilfiger but I don't believe they really are Tommy Hilfiger, and black suede shoes by Journey. My hair is a tousled mess. I am, of course, still unshaven.

Ten more pounds. Ten more pounds and I'm finished.

What It Means to Be a Fat Guy

Years ago, when I met my friend Michael VerMeulen, future editor of British *GQ*, we talked about men and weight. Michael was a magazine editor. I was twenty-eight years old, living with Anna, getting fatter. Michael was thin. At 5 foot 8, he was 170 lbs. "Yes, but I'm a former fatboy," he said. He told me that he'd been a compulsive eater, and that, at his worst, he'd weighed over 200 lbs.

"Wow," I said, "I can't imagine that."

We talked about the possibility of my writing something about what it means to be a fat guy. I wanted to write the article. But I didn't want to write the article. I didn't want to write it until I wasn't a fat guy anymore. Fat guys terrified me. I began to think about them. Orson Welles had had a strange, difficult childhood, and later tried to blot out his self-doubt with alcohol and food and periods of promiscuity. Marlon Brando had had a strange, difficult childhood, and later . . . exactly the same thing. Ditto Fatty Arbuckle, John Belushi, John Candy. Robbie Coltrane I wondered about. And the same thing seemed to be happening to Chris

Farley, a promising young comedian from Chicago, who was filling out at an alarming rate, hitting the bottle, being spotted around town with escort girls and hookers, dabbling in cocaine. These guys had all fallen into the same hole, the fat guy's hell—you lack some essential thing, some specific, elusive quality, and so you strive and strive, trying to replace the thing you lack with your achievements. You try to be funnier and smarter than the other guys. You succeed. But somehow, the very effort makes you unravel. And then: the food, the booze, the promiscuity, the drugs.

And what about the fat guys who weren't famous? Did they suffer in the same way? Often, they did. They were the guys who laughed the most, sometimes with a kind of forced laughter. They were the guys who partied the hardest, who didn't want the party to end, because they had nowhere to go afterward. (Fat guys who are not famous mostly have to pass on the promiscuity.) I knew fat guys who were incredibly smug and arrogant and brittle, always in on the joke, always quick to the punch, yet emanating a deep sense of unease, of distress. Fat guys who wore big fat rings and finely tailored suits, gangsterish shoes and hats. The fat-guy armor.

Hey, Big Dave!

Drinks are on me, baby!

And I knew about the other type of fat guy, too—the one who wanted to be left alone, the one who'd given up the ghost. This was the person who lived inside the fat-guy armor. Sometimes fat guys tried on the fat-guy armor, and couldn't deal with it, and took it off, and moved around their lives warily, furtively, like peeler crabs.

*　　　*　　　*

A little over two years later, I started getting thinner. How did I do this? I exercised. My diary at the time reads: "40 lengths. Football. Tennis." That's all in the same day. I lived across the road from a tennis club. I hired a coach. Anna had told me that I was too heavy to get on top of her.

Oh, and I met this other woman, and when I talked to her, or thought about her, I felt dizzy. She had pale-blond hair and blue eyes; she looked neat and sane but with something in reserve, sort of like Sharon Stone. We became friends. She was about to get married. There was nothing I could do. Anyway, I started to lose weight. Just to look good at the wedding, I thought, would be something.

I never wrote the article about fat guys. But I noticed something about Michael. He was beginning to get fatter. He put on 10 lbs., 20 lbs., 30 lbs. I remember one particular lunch we had in an Italian restaurant. I had a mixed salad. That was it. Just a mixed salad. Michael had a starter with bread rolls, a pasta dish, a pudding, wine, and coffee. I remember this meal because I had to leave early; I was on my way to France.

"Send my best to Anna," he said.

Later, he broke his ankle in a fall and put on another 20 lbs. One day, he told me that he had decided to write the article about what it was like to be a fat guy. He'd had photographs of himself taken with no clothes on. They looked gross, he said.

Michael told me that he wasn't going to write the article for a while. What he was going to do was this: he was going to lose weight. And then he would write the article.

And Then, Click

When it happens, when the terrible thing happens, it arrives quietly, surreptitiously, like the sort of storm that kills sailors because they can't see it coming. You see the clouds on the horizon; you notice the water getting choppy. But you press on regardless. You press on blithely. Blithe: *showing a casual or cheerful indifference considered to be callous or improper*. It's a pretty good description of the state of mind of the person who embarks on an eating binge.

One minute you're fine, and then, click: you're in a different world. You might be walking along, more or less absolutely certain that you will not have any fries, will not duck under the golden arches, will not walk across the floor, smelling the oil and mechanically recovered meat smell, will not take in the dinky, bright-colored tables and semi-comfortable chairs, will not approach the counter, will not look at the guy behind the counter, will not look up at him and smile. And while you're pretty certain you will not do any of these things, you allow your mind to dwell momentarily on the prospect of it. That's all it is. You sail toward the storm, and there's a moment when you can't quite walk along the deck with your usual assured swagger, because the boat is beginning to pitch a little, to yaw a little. And you tell yourself you're fine. And there's another moment when you have *lost all radio contact*. That's what it's like, inside a binge. It's like losing radio contact. It sounds silly, doesn't it? But that's what it's like.

One minute you're fine, and then, click.

A Time of Great Uncertainty

The first time I had an eating binge, I was seven years old. It was the summer before we moved to Canada, the summer before I came into contact with shopping malls and fast food, with roadside diners and drive-in movies and drive-thru burger bars, with the soft, sugary, oily sensation, in the mouth, of the burger itself.

The burger.

The fries.

Before Canada, food came in two categories—food you had to eat and food you wanted to eat. Canada would make me believe that the food you had to eat could also be the food you wanted to eat.

We were flying out in the next few days. It was a time of great uncertainty. The family was staying in my grandmother's house, talking about what life would be like in Canada. There would be bears. There would be lakes and forests. Snow. I could play ice hockey. I could have skates.

My grandmother always made this same apple pie with very thin pastry. She made it in a large, shallow baking tray, with the thin pastry on the base, about an inch of stewed apple, and more thin pastry on top. You waited for the pie to get cold, and cut it into slices. Then you poured cream on the pie, and ate it on a small, chintzy plate.

I can see myself, sitting at my grandmother's dining table. I eat a slice of pie. Then I eat my traditional second slice, for which I receive my traditional volley of approval and praise. My third slice is not quite as good as my second slice. I take my fourth slice on the quiet, after the pie has been moved into the kitchen. I cut it myself. In the tray is the rest of the pie, not cut into slices. Six of us have eaten half of the pie. Half is left. Nobody will notice. I cut a bit of the pie away. Eat it. Now the pie looks untidy. I chop a bit more off. Eat it. Still untidy.

Chop another bit.

Eat it.

And then, click.

What Do You Think I'm Doing, Mum?

Four years later, I'm standing on a street in a seaside town in Sussex, looking at the shop across the road. I was fat when I came back from Canada, but I'm not so fat anymore. Still, I'm not quite right.

It's mid-morning, and I'm aware that I'm not supposed to be outside the school, but hell, nobody much notices what I do. I wonder what my family are doing, my mother and father and younger brother. They're in Germany. I envy my brother. Even though he's only four years younger than me, he doesn't have to go to boarding school; he's just taking time out, doing whatever. They send me letters. Like the letters are going to improve my situation or something. My father will be at work, probably. It's June, and probably a nice day where they are, which is Konstanz, on the Swiss border, near the Alps.

Later, I've got games, but before that, Math and Latin, both of which I hate, neither of which I can concentrate on. This evening it's bath night, when I will be bathed by Danielle, the assistant matron, French.

What I think about is my mother and brother, probably

going up a mountain in a cable car or something, or taking a boat across the lake, and then later, when my father comes home from work, they'll eat something, and then just more or less do what they want. I got a letter a couple of days ago, and my mum goes, write and tell us what you're doing. What do you think I'm doing, Mum? I'm going for some nice walks around the lake, and sometimes I travel through the dormitory in a cable car.

The best thing, really, is to just think about them for a short time, and then try to stop thinking about them, like they didn't exist or something. I mean, for all I know, they don't. For all I know, they could have been in some kind of accident.

I could just walk across the road here, I have the money, and buy a bag of lemon crystals, which is sugar flavored with lemon, dyed yellow, which you're supposed to dip your fingers in. It makes your fingers yellow, like the fingers of the men who hang around the arcades by the pier. But I don't dip my fingers in it much. I just pour it straight down. It's amazing, it really is. It really sets you up. I could do it now if I wanted, just rush across the street and then just nip behind the wall.

Anyway, I decide not to.

And then, click.

Would You Look at the State of That Cooker

I'm fifteen and I'm at boarding school and it's the middle of winter and my parents are in Canada again and I'm sitting in my study, wondering if this particular prefect is around, wondering if he'll come into my study, wondering what he'll do, if anything, the next time we come face to face. Last week I was sitting in my study with a guy called Templeton, drinking a cup of coffee, when this prefect came in, just burst in, he didn't knock or anything, and he mentioned the fact that there was a ring of milk around the edge of my coffee cup. When I say *mentioned*. He went *wild*. Then he trashed the room.

Coffee's important in this place. We're allowed to make coffee in our studies. We have these things you plug in, like the elements from kettles, and you clip them to the inside of your mug, which you have already filled with water. I suppose they're quite dangerous. And then you put in the coffee, and the sugar, and the milk. Except on this particular day, not every drop of the milk went into the cup.

Templeton, he's an OK kind of guy, except for the fact he was one of the Three, or was it the Four, nobody seems to be sure, who were sodomized by a guy called Guppy who got expelled last term. This is all before my time here. But, see, I knew Guppy, from the school I was at before, and he didn't seem to be that sort at all, the sort who goes around sodomizing people at random. I say random, because Templeton, he's not a bad guy, but not the sort of guy you'd sodomize if you had any choice in the matter.

In any case, I never would have expected it of a guy like Guppy. Of course, you get your frisky types, who will pin you down, say, and try to poke their dick in your eye or whatever. Yawn.

Guppy and Templeton. The whole thing made me curious. So when I asked Templeton about it, just a casual inquiry, this is my first week, Templeton says, hang on a minute, and asks me to step outside in the galley. The galley is where we're allowed to cook some of our own meals if we want. *Big* privilege. We cook Chinese food from dried ingredients, which come in boxes we call Vesta packs. That's the company that makes them. So anyway, I do what Templeton says, I step out into the galley, and he says, would you look at the state of that cooker. And I look, and the next thing I'm on my back, looking up at three or four people. Stevenson and Hughes and somebody else, and Templeton is crying. Hughes told me it's kind of a code of the Three, or the Four, or whatever. If anybody mentions Guppy, they mete out what they call Ultraviolence. Templeton just knocked me out. Just smashed me across the head, and apparently I landed badly, which made it worse.

Anyway, the second bad thing that's happened to me since I got here was this thing with the milk. The prefect just said, and I knew he had this bad reputation, but he just said, you *fucking dirty little bastard*. He put his finger in the ring of milk and wiped a smear of milk across the desk. Then he pulled out my desk drawer, and tipped the contents on the floor, and he emptied every one of my cupboards, again tipping the contents on the floor, all my clothes and the stuff from home, and he overturned my armchair, and grabbed the milk bottle, and tipped the rest of the milk over everything. Then he stalked out, saying he'd send one of the other prefects to inspect me in half an hour, and if the whole place wasn't perfect, I'd be on drill.

This place makes me hungry. Today I've eaten: two rashers of bacon with tomato and fried bread, three slices of toast with marmalade, two more slices of toast and marmalade smuggled out of breakfast folded over in my pockets, two cups of tea, one cup of coffee. That was breakfast. During chapel and the first two lessons I eked out a packet of Mint Imperials. Third lesson was a barren desert. Nothing. At break I had two egg-mayonnaise sandwiches, a cheese roll, a packet of Quavers and a Mars bar. I was too hungry to do what I normally do, which is to put the Quavers, crispy cheese-flavored corn snacks, into the egg sandwiches.

Lunch: sausage, beans and chips followed by chocolate pudding, which we call moonbase, because of the little craters it has in the crust. I had it with not-too-runny chocolate sauce. It's 5.30 P.M. High Tea, in an hour, seems eons away.

And so, just for something to do, I take a teaspoon of this coffee creamer I bought the other day, and eat it. And— God, it's . . . *lovely*. It melts in my mouth. I hold the jar up in my hand. And I stare at the jar. The jar is three-quarters full of this lovely white powder.

And then, click.

Nuances of Hurry

And here I am again, twenty-two years later. 215 lbs. Waist size 34. I'm in a taxi with Sadie, on the way to a station. We are running late. We're sitting next to each other in the taxi, although we do not acknowledge each other's presence. I dare not look at her. Sitting next to Sadie, I can feel her aura, a force field of anxiety and menace. We are not getting on. Outside the station, the taxi shudders to a halt.

Through the window, I look at the station clock. The train leaves in seven minutes. Sadie gets out of the car, a neat exit, and stands on the pavement, cocking her head, smoothing her skirt. For a while I flounder in the quicksand of the taxi's backseat, digging through my pockets, hurting the ends of fingers, my stomach a dead weight in the center of my body. I feel sick. I feel hungry. Things are spilling from my pockets—bright little bits of confectionery wrappers, a blister-pack of ibuprofen, an ibuprofen tablet that has popped out of the pack, a blood-hardened wedge of tissue paper, and finally my wallet, fattened with a dense wedge of restaurant bills. I am slipping, slipping.

Outside the car, Sadie says, "What were you *doing* in there?"

At the ticket machine, we do not say anything to each other. As my turn approaches, I have a vision of myself poking limp paper money at the slot, and the money re-emerging, rejected. But in the event, there is no problem. My money, stiff and crisp, glides in, the tickets and change fall down, and I'm done, with—I look up at the clock—three minutes to spare. I can see Sadie's shape approaching, closing me down.

My blood sugar is painfully low. I cast my eyes around, and see, to my right, not in the direction of the platform, the answer to my problems. A strip of food kiosks. The kiosks are subtly different, catering to nuances of hurry. Sadie moves ahead of me, walking with predatory vigor. I look at Sadie—at the neat skirt, the tights, the sensible boots which also manage to be sexy. And then I look at the food kiosks. Bagelmania. Upper Crust. Burger King.

And then, click.

Peanut Butter

The day before yesterday I opened a jar of peanut butter and ate a spoonful and screwed the lid back on and put the jar back in the cupboard and washed the spoon and put the spoon in the cutlery drainer and walked past the cupboard again and opened the cupboard and decided not to eat any more peanut butter.

And then, click.

Who *Did* This to Me?

Click.

What happens next? You know you shouldn't do it, you know it's not right, you know you'll regret it, but you go ahead, you move forward, because it's suddenly too late. The decision has already been made. As you look at the pie, or the candy store, or the jar of creamer, or the burger kiosk, or the peanut butter, or the golden arches, you may believe you are still in possession of judicial powers. But you are not. At this stage, you only have executive powers. Your status as the master of your own destiny is entirely ceremonial. For all the world, it feels as if you are enacting the orders of a higher authority.

And then you step inside the binge, and, for a brief moment, it's a wonderful place to be. Inside the binge, you are outside yourself. It is as if the air is filled with static. You are in the psychological zone that Shelley Bovey recognizes as neither her public nor her private self. When you step inside a binge, you have waltzed into a gap in your own mind. You have fallen down a hole.

And, for a moment, it's wonderful. Here, objects are sharper, more clearly defined. Your hunger is bigger; the objects of your hunger look smaller. The binge state itself is like a drug. As James Frey in *A Million Little Pieces* says of the binge state, "It flows through my veins like a slow, lazy virus, urging me to do damage." As Don Delillo's character, Jack Gladney, the antihero of *White Noise,* says, "I began to grow in value and self-regard. I filled myself out, found new aspects of myself, located a person I'd forgotten existed." Frey is telling us about losing control and harming himself—actually ripping at his own flesh. "The Fury is within me," he tells us. "Feed it pain and it will leave me," he says. "Feed it pain and it will go away." Delillo is writing about losing control in a shopping mall.

Inside the binge, you are pure hunger—pure aspiration. Nothing else. You have created a time zone more present than the present. You know you shouldn't do it, you know it's not right, you know you'll regret it, you know it will degrade your self-esteem, but none of these things matter, because you are hoping for this degradation—inside the binge, your degraded self-esteem is a ticket to freedom.

The hole you have fallen into is deep.

In this new world, hunger is a state you cherish. You yearn for more hunger. You do not want your hunger to be satisfied. Eating is a response to hunger; eating, therefore, reminds you of hunger. So you continue to eat in the hope that eating will keep your hunger alive. You search for food in the hope that it will make you hungry.

In the deep, dark hole you press on, blindly, full of optimism.

It's always the same. Every binge is like the one before,

and every binge is like the one that will come after. When I had that first binge, at the age of seven, I had fallen into the same hole I would fall into, over and over, for decades—the same "I'll just have another tiny bit," the same "I want another bit," the same false hunger, the same false logic, the same vital miscalculations, the same "just one more slice," the same "just one more drink," the same "just one more snort." The same idea that having a little bit more will solve things. The same "No! Stop now, before you lose control!" The same "What do you mean, before I lose control? I've already lost control!"

And suddenly: "Look, there's not much left."

And: "They'll notice."

And: "Might as well be hung for a sheep as a lamb."

And: "What's the point of putting half a bottle of wine back in the fridge?"

And: "Hell, let's just get it over with."

And: "I'll make a new start tomorrow."

And: "I'll do something about this."

And: "I really will."

And: "I'm feeling sick."

And: "I'm feeling woozy."

And: "I'm feeling wired."

And: "What have I *done?*"

And: "What's the matter with me?"

And: "Fuck!"

And: "Is there anything else to drink in the fridge?"

And: "Is there a place where I can buy a bottle at this time?"

And: "What about the freezer?"

And: "Have you got Leroy's number?"

And: "Maybe I can scrape out the inside of my wallet."

And: "I need help."

And: "I don't need help."

And: "I'll get help."

I'm standing in my grandmother's kitchen, looking at the pie. I begin chopping bits off, the chopping turning into hacking. I know that I will get into trouble. But for the moment, I am in an exhilarating new world; I have banished trouble. I hack, munch, swallow. The apple, which has always had a pleasant mixture of sweetness and tartness, begins to lose its flavor. It is no longer my grandmother's apple pie. It is awesome, terrible, magnetic. I press on. I am like the murderer who, horrified that he has stabbed somebody, keeps on stabbing and stabbing, trying to reach the end of the horror.

The trouble comes after I get into bed. My mother and grandmother, heeding my cries of pain, rush into my bedroom. I am kneeling on the bed, my hands clutching my belly. I am moaning.

My mother says, "Where does it hurt?"

"I don't know."

"Where does it hurt?"

"I don't know."

And I'm standing on a street in a seaside town in Sussex, looking at a candy store. I walk into the candy store and I ask the man for a bag of lemon crystals and I give him the money and I have the exact money in my hand and I walk out of the shop, unaware of anything apart from the bag, unaware even of myself, and I duck into the alley at the side of the candy store and I open my mouth and I pour the flavored sugar down my throat, a quarter of a pound of flavored sugar, the trick is to try to get it all down in two or three gulps, and for a beautiful second my entire mouth and throat are filled with melting sugar.

And I'm sitting at my desk, holding a jar of creamer. I open my mouth. I pour the creamer into my mouth.

And I'm in the station, looking at a strip of food kiosks. I move toward one of the kiosks and I say "fries," and I say "large," and Sadie has turned to look at me, and she is shouting something, she is windmilling her arms, but I am in a tunnel and the air is full of static.

And I'm opening the cupboard in my kitchen and I reach into the cupboard and I take the jar of peanut butter and I take a spoon and I eat a mouthful of peanut butter, and I know everything will be fine if I stop now, but I don't want to stop now, I don't want everything to be fine, and there's a moment when I think I'll eat only half of the jar, but that moment soon passes, and afterward I lie on my bed and look out of the window at the darkening sky.

And now it's the middle of the morning in Manhattan and I'm walking under the golden arches. When McDonald's considered redesigning the arches in the 1960s, incidentally, design consultant Louis Cheskin advised them against it. Cheskin believed the arches had deep Freudian significance. He called them Mother McDonald's breasts.

Under the arches, I'm sliding my hand into my trouser pocket for money, and as I turn into the entrance a large man, obese, angles toward me, and we collide, two big trucks touching bumpers, and both of my stomach magazines, which I'm carrying under my arm, slip downward a notch, and I try to pin them to my jacket with my elbow, but it's hopeless, the angle is too great—my stomach is too big—

and the stomach magazines spill to the floor, falling with a sharp cracking noise on the McDonald's tiles.

LOSE YOUR GUT

SHRINK YOUR GUT

GET HER TO AGREE TO *ANYTHING*

But the obese man isn't looking. He is in his own private world of unwrapping, of removing the outer, inedible paper layer of what looks like a Big Mac. He is two or three seconds away from smelling the fumes, no more than five seconds away from mouthfeel. His salivary glands are already producing a cocktail of enzymes to break down the first bolted bolus of cross-sectional Big Mac—the pure beef patty, the flour, the sugar, the E282 calcium propionate, the E331 trisodium citrate, the wheat flour baked to perfection, with an unchallenging crumb structure and a soft, yielding crust. In three minutes he will be licking his fingers; in four he will want to eat them.

Myself, I'm moving toward the counter with an automatic, jerky gait, the stomach magazines now safely rolled up and stuffed in my pocket, and when I arrive at the counter there are two people in front of me, one a classic Big Mac, fries, large Coke, the other wanting a cheeseburger with fries, but nothing to drink, and, an aeon later, I look at the guy behind the counter, a youngster in a cheerful apron, and I say "fries," and I say "large," and I hand over the money, and the guy in the cheerful apron gives me change, and he turns around to get my fries.

Fries are the most popular food in America and Britain. In America, 25 percent of all vegetables eaten are fries. As a foodstuff, fries are miraculous. Is any food more addictive? With a glycemic index of 75, almost nothing, apart from sugar itself, raises your blood sugar so fast. Fries are strips of starch covered on all six sides with fat; they are like bread that has been buttered on both sides, and around the crusts as well. (With fries, of course, there are no crusts; by the time a potato has become fries, the skin is long gone.)

Fries are made from potatoes with a medium or high starch content, such as Maris Pipers or Pentland Dells or Idaho Russets. The potatoes are stored in vast warehouses, under strict temperature, light, and humidity conditions, during which time some of the starch in the potatoes turns to sugar. This is why, when you fry them, they turn a lovely golden-brown color. This color, according to nutritional scientists, is one of the most desirable food colors on the planet. Fries are strips of starchy tuber which have been fried twice, a process which forces a great deal of the water out of the tuber and replaces it with fat. According to food critic Jeffrey Steingarten, the perfect French fry has deep, even universal, cultural resonance, "like the fear of snakes."

I take the box of fries. The fries are standing up in the box, like a golden-brown skyline.

The air is filled with static. I am huge; the fries look tiny. And I think: Who *did* this to me?

It All Started with French Fries

I could blame the unnamed French, or possibly Belgian, chef who first discovered the process of double-frying potatoes in the 1890s. I could blame the American soldiers who returned from the trenches in 1918 and caused the spread of fries in America in the 1920s, asking their wives to cook

French fries and creating a market for deep-fat fryers. I could blame Henry Ford, who popularized the automobile, facilitating the great suburban sprawl of the 1940s and 1950s, and therefore the roadside diners that became America's original fast-food outlets. The proprietors of these early fast-food outlets sold beef patties and hot dogs and fries, and quickly realized that fries were the most profitable item. It was the profit from fries that allowed these entrepreneurs to expand their businesses, to open more outlets, to sell yet more fries.

I could blame the McDonald brothers, Dick and Mac, who opened a fast-food diner in San Bernadino, California, in the early 1950s. San Bernadino was the epitome of suburban sprawl, and stood at the end of the transcontinental Route 66. Dick and Mac McDonald had an inspired idea: one day, they got rid of everything on their menu that would require the use of a knife and fork. The business boomed. People drove for miles for their hamburgers and fries and milkshakes. They sold so many milkshakes that, in 1954, they ordered six Prince Castle Multi-Mixer machines, enabling them to mix forty-eight milkshakes simultaneously.

I think I definitely should blame Ray Kroc. In 1954, Kroc was a fifty-two-year-old traveling salesman who worked for the Prince Castle company that made the Multi-Mixer machines. Kroc, originally from Chicago, was a heavyset man who had spent his life looking for a big break. He had an insatiable appetite for success; the trouble was, he had never had much of it. Kroc had spent years driving across the country selling paper cups, and now he was doing the same thing with milkshake machines. He was a storyteller, a joker. He was friendly and optimistic. Most of all, he was driven by a primordial hunger: he always wanted more. He once said, "I expect money like you walk into a room and turn on a light switch or a faucet." He called himself "the agitator, the motivator, the never-satisfied type of guy."

When Dick and Mac McDonald ordered six milkshake machines, a light came on in Kroc's head. He sensed that anybody who needed to mix forty-eight milkshakes at the same time must be on to something big. What was going on? Kroc drove to San Bernardino to investigate, and found his answer under the golden arches. Watching from his car, he saw people driving to the original McDonald's restaurant, and then waiting in line for Dick and Mac's burgers, fries, and shakes. The lines were long, and stayed long all day. Kroc made the McDonald brothers an offer: he wanted to buy their name and their methods. He visualized a chain of fast-food restaurants, all the same as each other; he visualzied long lines of people that stayed long all day.

After some initial misgivings, Dick and Mac sold up. And Kroc built an empire—an empire based, you might say, on fries. Fries were Kroc's most profitable item. He called McDonald's fries "the greatest French fries in the world." It was Kroc who perfected the method of curing potatoes in a warehouse, so that some of the starch in the tubers would turn into sugar. According to the great science writer Malcolm Gladwell, he hired men to visit his suppliers and check each batch of potatoes with hydrometers, to ensure the potatoes contained exactly the right amount of water. He hired a former Motorola engineer named Louis Martino to develop a formula for cooking perfect fries. "The French fry," Kroc once wrote, "would become almost sacrosanct for me, its preparation a ritual to be followed religiously."

Or I could blame Harry Sonneborn, Kroc's business partner, a former Tastee-Freez executive, who invented a system that enabled McDonald's to expand fast. Sonneborn realized that McDonald's could open almost endless outlets if they leased them to franchisees and charged a rental fee based on profits. Kroc flew around the country in a light aircraft, looking at the spread of highways, predicting sites of future suburban sprawl. Then he bought land. His empire, based on fries, grew exponentially. Now, somewhere in the world, an average of two McDonald's outlets opens each day.

As well as founding his own empire, Kroc also cleared the way for other franchise-based empires—and, in the end, a whole franchise-fueled economy. Whenever you walk into an outlet that is part of a chain—a Starbucks, a Burger King, a Taco Bell, or a Kentucky Fried Chicken, or, for that matter, a Borders or a Waterstone's—you should understand one thing above all. It all started with French fries.

"I Just Hung On"

And I could blame J. R. Simplot, the greatest potato baron in the history of the world. Born in 1909, Simplot grew up in Idaho. At first, he bought pigs, shot wild horses in the desert, fed his pigs on horse meat, and sold the fattened pigs at a profit. By the time he was in his twenties, he leased 160 acres of potato fields; before he was out of his twenties, he was the largest shipper of potatoes in the West. Later, he also grew onions, and made a vast profit selling dehydrated onion powder to the army during World War Two.

After the war, Simplot became interested in the possibilities of home freezing. He hired a team of chemists to research the concept of frozen potatoes. The big discovery was that French fries, which need to be cooked twice, could be frozen between the first cooking and the second. This, Simplot realized, would revolutionize the fast-food business. Fries no longer needed to be fully prepared on site; they could be frozen, stored on site and reheated according to demand.

In 1965, Simplot went into business with Ray Kroc. At the time, Kroc franchised around 725 restaurants in America. Ten years later, the number was 3,000. Like Kroc, Simplot was hungry for more. "I'm just an old farmer got some luck," he told Eric Schlosser, author of *Fast Food Nation*. "The only thing I did smart, and just remember this—99 percent of people would have sold out when they got their first 25 or 30 million. I didn't sell out. I just hung on."

Wallerstein Was Right

And I could blame David Wallerstein, the great mastermind of supersizing. Wallerstein, a McDonald's executive in the 1970s, had managed movie theaters in the 1960s, and discovered that he could increase his profits by offering people bigger servings of popcorn. As John F. Lore points out in his 1985 book, *McDonald's: Behind the Arches,* nobody wanted to buy two small tubs. But when big tubs were available lots of people chose them. His discovery would be backed up by research conducted at Penn State University in 2001: when volunteers were fed larger portions of food, they ate larger amounts, regardless of the levels of their hunger. When you see more fries, you want more fries. And after you eat more fries, your blood sugar crashes, and you really do feel more hungry. Then, of course, you want yet more fries.

At first, Ray Kroc was not convinced by Wallerstein. "If people want more fries," he said, "they can buy two bags."

"But Ray," Wallerstein said, "they don't want to eat two bags—they don't want to look like a glutton."

In the end, Kroc capitulated. Profits soared. Fries made more money than ever. Portions grew and grew. In 1955, a serving of McDonald's fries weighed 2.4 oz. and contained 210 calories. Now it weighs 4.3 oz. and contains 610 calories.

Wallerstein was right.

People Know What They Like

Who else could I blame? Recently I went to interview a man who had masterminded several advertising campaigns for McCain fries and microwave fries—fries which have been precooked and whose packet-to-mouth time is three minutes. Understandably, the man didn't want to be named: he knew there was a chance I might say something bad about fries. But he needn't have worried—saying something bad about fries is like saying something bad about thin, leggy models in women's magazines. It won't make a blind bit of difference. People know what they like.

We were sitting in a slick, bright conference room. The man told me about the campaigns he had participated in. As he talked, I imagined his face pixilated to anonymity.

The ads were brilliant and daring. In one, a young girl asks herself what she would choose—Daddy or chips. In another, a couple are depicted on a sofa, stealing fries from each other's plates. In a third, black guys force handfuls of fries into their mouths. That's more or less it—black guys gorging on fries. It's wonderful. In a fourth, an attractive man is, somehow, forced to choose between fries and a gorgeous girl.

The advertising executive told me that, according to research, fries are the biggest cause of arguments in restaurants. Couples in restaurants argue more about stolen fries than about their partner ogling members of the opposite sex. "The thing about fries," said the man, "is they taste better if they're not yours. You have to steal them off someone's plate."

The Fries They Ate Yesterday and the Fries They Will Eat Tomorrow

Imagine yourself taking a box of McDonald's fries in your left hand, and picking out a fry, or maybe two or three or four, with the thumb and index and middle fingers of your right. You don't hold them for very long, do you? How long before they're in your mouth? Two seconds? Three? And you don't spend much time thinking about where they come from, do you? But these fries have been on a long journey. Chances are they have been processed by McCain, the world's largest producer of fries. McCain makes fries for McDonald's, as well as other fast-food outlets, caterers, and supermarkets.

Should I blame McCain? One out of every three fries worldwide has been through a McCain factory. I visited the McCain factory in Scarborough, North Yorkshire, but it could have been anywhere; the process is identical wherever you go. The factory is a vast Satanic building, like a huge aircraft hangar bedecked with turrets and chimneys. It steams. On an average day, 1,200 tons of potatoes arrive at one end of the factory, and fries—a mind-boggling amount of them—emerge, packed and boxed, at the other.

Ernie Thompson, a potato man of twenty-four years' standing, told me he was in charge of the liaison between McCain and McDonald's. What, I wondered, was the hardest thing about the job? "Keeping your weight down," he said. But Ernie is lucky. He is tall and thin, and finds time to exercise a great deal. Donning a hairnet, a white coat, and a protective hard hat, and telling me to do the same, Thompson took me on a tour of the factory.

It was extraordinary. I had never seen so many potatoes. On one side of me was a mountain of potatoes. Underneath me was a river of potatoes. Standing on a metal walkway, I followed the potatoes' progress through the factory. They flow into shiny cylindrical tanks that rotate while the skins are blasted off with steam. Then they are shot through "hydro-guns," forced by pressurized water through metal pipes at a speed of over 100 feet per second. At the end of each pipe is a grid of blades. This is the point where one potato becomes ten or more McDonald's fries.

Next, the river of potatoes becomes a waterfall of fries, a Niagara of what potato men call "strips." It is awesome. The strips are whizzed along on a holed conveyor, to ensure that small ones fall through, into the vast netherworld below, the Hades of failed fries, fries that didn't make the grade. Making the grade, Thompson told me, is the crucial thing. Consistency is everything. People who eat fries want the fries they eat today to be exactly the same as the fries they ate yesterday and the fries they will eat tomorrow.

The fries flow past mounted cameras, which photograph any blemishes that might remain; in a breathtaking feat of technology, blades are programmed to pop up and slice off the blemishes. People want their fries to have cosmetic surgery.

When you're standing on a thin metal walkway at the top of a vast factory building, skidding on fat deposits, and looking down into a swimming-pool-sized vat of boiling fat, you understand what people put themselves through to arrive at the perfect serving of fries. You have plugs in your ears to protect you from the noise. "It's a very complex job," Thompson told me. "People think that making frozen fries is the easiest thing in the world. But it's not." Later, the fries are tasted by a panel, some of whom are thin, and some of whom are not. One taster stands still, pushing golden fries into his mouth, small bright eyes darting around his large, pasty face. He is concentrating. He is the size of a black bear. He nods, satisfied, and picks up the next batch. It's thanks to him that the fries taste so good.

I could blame the advertising guy. I could blame Thompson. I could blame the man with the large, pasty face. I could blame the team of food scientists who devised the formula for the cooking oil. When I take a McDonald's French fry, and put it in my mouth, I could blame anybody, at any stage of the process—I could blame the employees, or contractors, who have grown it, harvested it, trucked it, mechanically peeled it, skinned it, trimmed it, brushed it, blanched it, dried it, fried it, de-fatted it, cooled it, frozen it, bagged it, boxed it, X-rayed the box for foreign bodies such as coins or pens, trucked it to one of several distribution plants, from where it is trucked again to the car park or street by the golden arches in your hometown wherever you live in the world, to be re-fried and sold by youngsters in cheerful aprons.

Have a Nice Day

The youngster in the cheerful apron says, "Have a nice day."

I take the box of fries. I nod at the youngster. I execute a swift turn. I push the thumb and first two fingers of my right hand into the box of fries, which are hot but not too hot. I am huge; the fries look tiny. I pick out a fry, and then another, and a third, and a fourth. I push the fries into my mouth. I exit the building.

The fries in my mouth taste of salt and fat and starch: they taste *delicious,* I could eat three or four boxes, they taste of my past, of the person I was when I ate fries and doughnuts and bagels and all the other things that made me hungry.

In what feels like a moment of madness, I walk ten feet and dump the fries in a trash can, and, reeling, confused, I chew my mouthful of fries and I feel the grim tug of dread, and I actually wonder if I should walk back to the trash can and pick my fries out, but I don't.

I walk on. I don't know what I'm doing. A torrent of emotion is passing through me, and I'm trying to dam the torrent with a single mouthful of fries, and before long, the mouthful is gone, and I am left with nothing.

Nothing, that is, except the prospect of being thin.

"I Recommend that You See a Psychiatrist"

I'm trying to remember what it was like to be thin, trying to imagine myself as I was in my early thirties, and, before that, in my early twenties, and I can't fix on the exact feeling, or sensation, of thinness. When I was thin, I didn't eat so much. When I was thin, I was more active. My clothes looked better. Sometimes I had a steady girlfriend; when I did not, I found myself driven by an urge to flirt with women. A relentless, nagging urge. At times I became promiscuous, gorging on sexual encounters in the same way that I had gorged on fries and hamburgers and peanut butter. I was voracious, I was carnal.

I remember one particular day. I was in my early twenties. I was a student. I weighed 185 lbs. Waist size: 30. I was having a drink with a friend. The week before, I had had sex with a girl at a party, in the bathroom, and left the party alone, and a couple of days later I had met another girl at another party and slept with her in her hall of residence, and a couple of days after that I had met the first girl in a bar and spent a night with her, and psychologically, of course, I was a mess, a total mess, and I had a date with another girl the next day. If you'd asked me what I really wanted, I would have said that I was hungry, hungry for flesh. I don't think I fully understood that what I really wanted was not flesh, but something more complex and elusive.

I was in a bar near my parents' house. My parents were not at home—they were thousands of miles away, living in a house I had never seen except in photographs. I was planning to stay in my parents' empty house, and catch the eleven-thirty train to London the next morning for my date, which was for lunch, at first, and then possibly an afternoon and an evening and a night.

My friend said, "Don't you ever worry about your dick?"

"My dick?"

"You know—herpes. Everybody's getting herpes these days."

I felt sick. I knew about herpes; to me, it was a black area of terror locked away at the back of my consciousness. I didn't think I had herpes—but, on the other hand, who knew? The symptoms were awful—painful crusty sores on the genitals. Sometimes the sores didn't arrive for a couple of weeks after transmission, sometimes not for years. My friend told me that, if you looked closely, you could definitely tell. What you had to look for were tiny red itchy spots. This was the beginning. After this, the sores became crusty. Then you were finished. The disease was incurable.

When I got home, I knew I would examine myself, and I knew what would happen if I examined myself. I tried to go to sleep and forget about it, and I tried drinking from a bottle of whiskey, but I still could not go to sleep. I drank more whiskey. I wandered around the house, lay on the sofa, made myself a cup of coffee, drank more whiskey, looked at my sallow, unshaven face in the mirror. My eyes were distant, crazed, inaccessible.

I started examining myself. And there it was—a tiny red spot. Possibly a mole, but possibly not. I poked at the red spot. Was it itchy? Yes. No. I poked a bit more.

A mole?

Or not?

I poked. I drank. The night slipped by in a trance of hysteria, psychological meltdown, insane feelings of guilt and self-loathing. I went to the kitchen cupboard, and found some spaghetti, and decided I did not want to eat the spaghetti, and, listless, tried to put it back in the cupboard, but dropped it all over the floor, and kicked the fallen strands into the sides and corners of the room, so as not to make a mess.

There was a point when I decided that it might be a good idea to see a doctor, just to get myself checked out, and a point, sometime after sunrise, when I began to believe that it was my moral duty to see a doctor. It struck me that there might be a doctor in the neighborhood. I found myself reaching for the telephone book, writing down the number, dialing the number. It was 7:30 A.M. A man's voice answered.

"Hello?"

"Hello. Is that Dr. Rosenberg?"

"Yes. Who is this?"

"Yes. I've just been checking, uh, I was going to, to see you."

"Is this a medical matter?"

"Yes."

"Have you made an appointment? Because . . ."

"I'm a neighbor."

"Is this a serious matter? Are you the patient in question?"

"Yes, I am."

"Is it an emergency?"

"It might be."

"Where do you have the trouble?"

"Where?"

"Which part of the body?"

"My, um, penis."

"What has happened to your penis?"

"Well, you see, I wanted to get it checked out. I just live around the corner. I could come and see you."

There was silence for a while.

Dr. Rosenberg said, "Well, I'm not at my office. I'm at home. This is my house."

"That's fine. I could come and see you now."

"Are you injured?"

"Well, I thought, you see, I could just . . . pop round."

Dr. Rosenberg said, "If you're not injured, it can wait until I get to my office. I have an appointment mid-morning."

"That's too late."

"Are you a patient of mine?"

"Well, you see . . . yes. I am."

"OK. Just turn up at my office. You know where it is. Ask the receptionist for the eleven-thirty appointment. And if she can't fit you in—and only if she can't fit you in—I'll see you at eight-forty-five."

"Could you remind me of the address?"

"It's 54 Castle Street."

"Of course."

I drank some more whiskey, and drank some coffee, and then some more coffee. And then a nip of whiskey, and more whiskey. The red spot appeared to have got bigger. It felt itchy. There was something wrong with me. I put on my shoes and jacket and walked along the early-morning streets. My head was full of static. I was weaving slightly. People were calmly closing the doors of their houses, checking their pockets, opening and closing the doors of their cars.

At the office, Dr. Rosenberg's receptionist told me that I could have an appointment at eleven-thirty.

"Ah," I said. "The thing is, I was talking to the doctor a few minutes ago, and he said it was crucial to see me at eight-forty-five."

"Well, if that's what he said."

At eight-forty, a small dark man walked into the lobby. The receptionist greeted him and he walked through a door, which he closed. The receptionist followed him into the room—his office. I could not hear everything that was being said. One of the things being said was: "But I told him *explicitly*. I told him . . . half-past eleven. I told him *explicitly*."

The receptionist reemerged from the office and sat down at her desk, head bowed.

The door to the surgery opened. Dr. Rosenberg said, "Well, you'd better come in."

I walked in. The static in my head was increasing in volume. I felt a surge of joy, of liberation.

"You're not my patient, are you?"

"Well, yes."

"You're not my patient, are you?"

"Well, not exactly. But I was about to sign up."

"Where do you live?"

"I've just moved into the area." I gave Dr. Rosenberg my parents' address.

Dr. Rosenberg nodded. He moved behind his desk and sat down. "OK. What's the matter with you?"

"I don't know."

"You said it was your penis."

"Well, I just thought . . . I just thought I should get it checked out."

Dr. Rosenberg picked up a pencil and a pad of paper.

"Have you had any discomfort?"

"I don't know."

"Any discharge?"

"Well, not . . . really. Not as such."

"Any itching?"

"Yes. Possibly."

Dr. Rosenberg wrote on his pad. I moved toward him.

"What are you writing?"

"Notes. Now . . ."

"What are you writing?" I moved across to the desk and looked at the pad. In a tiny script, Dr. Rosenberg had written, "Penile itching?"

I could feel my small reserves of self-control slipping away, slipping away. I said, "Penile itching? What does that mean? Is that bad?"

Dr. Rosenberg said, "Now look. You're not my patient. I'm doing this as a favor. I need to ask you a few questions."

"Fire away."

"Have you been having unprotected sex?"

"Yes."

"I can refer you."

"I just want you to check me out."

"I'll refer you."

Dr. Rosenberg walked around the desk, and toward me, ushering me out.

"Just have a quick look."

"No. As I say, I'll . . ."

"Please!"

"No!"

"It will just take a minute!"

Dr. Rosenberg said, "OK! Take your trousers down." He took a flashlight from his desk. He checked me out.

"There is nothing wrong with your penis," he said.

"There's nothing wrong with me?"

"That's not what I said. There is nothing wrong with your penis. But your sex life has led to an extreme reaction. Your promiscuity is causing you mental problems. I recommend that you see a psychiatrist."

A snapshot from the thin world. I was not fat. But I was the same person who had got fat, who would get fat again.

I backed away from the doctor. I felt joyful, unhinged.

"So there's nothing *actually* wrong with me," I said as I backed into the waiting room.

"******* Atkins Diet!"

The waiting room of the Atkins Center is large, about the size of two squash courts, and exudes the bright, hopeful air of the 1970s. High ceilings, low furniture, white walls. The paintings on the walls are the sort of thing a rock star might buy—huge canvases encrusted with jagged clumps of paint. Walking toward the reception desk I'm apprehensive, wondering if I look fat, wondering if people will think I've come to see Dr. Atkins because I'm fat.

A cartoon has been clipped from a newspaper and stuck to the reception desk. It depicts Santa Claus, having come down the chimney, looking at a plate of food that has been left out for him. The caption is, "******** Atkins diet!"

A woman arrives, introduces herself, and tells me that she will introduce me to Dr. Atkins, and for a moment it doesn't occur to me that the unobtrusive, ghostly presence hovering just behind her might actually be Dr. Atkins, so I say something about this being fine, and I nod, and I back away, distracted.

"This is Dr. Atkins," she says.

"Oh," I say.

We shake hands.

"Oh," I say.

Atkins is a seventy-two-year-old man, very pleasant-looking, the sort of old guy who would be the decent grandfather in a heartwarming movie. He does not look at all slick or bombastic or overconfident; he does not look like a diet guru. For a man who has sold several million copies of his latest book, he is not expensively dressed; he is not wearing the celebrity armor of Armani or Prada. His cream shirt does not look like a rich man's shirt made from sumptuous sea-island cotton. He wears a black tie and a stiff dark tweed jacket with long, broad lapels and a single button at the waist, the style popular a dozen years ago. His shoes are spiffy tasseled loafers made from very fine leather, with thin leather soles like pork rinds. He looks to be just under 6 feet tall and around 200 lbs.—not skinny, not thin, but definitely not fat. The jowls around his neck and chin are fairly minimal, signs of age rather than excess weight.

The doctor points me toward the lift, and tells me we'll do the interview in his office upstairs. We walk across the 1970s-looking room, which reminds me that Dr. Atkins, as a diet guru, was originally a phenomenon of the early 1970s, the era when people wanted to believe in hedonism without consequences—Atkins' original "no hunger" Diet Revolution was a counterpart to Erica Jong's "zipless fuck," hippies openly smoking dope in front of the cops at Woodstock, and Timothy Leary saying that LSD was good for us. What Atkins said was that, if you avoided carbohydrates, you could eat more or less what you wanted.

No hunger!

No cravings!

No need for restraint!

Since then, he's fallen into disrepute, and been reincarnated. Over the years, the Atkins diet has been radical, trendy, wildly popular, disapproved of, reviled, buried, resurrected, again radical, and again trendy. Now it's wildly popular again. According to history, a backlash is imminent.

Right now, though, as Atkins presses the elevator button, his diet has good ratings in some parts of the science community. The *New York Times* has recently run an article in praise of fat, entitled "What if it's all a Big Fat Lie?", quoting Richard Veech, a prominent scientist who studied under the Nobel Laureate Hans Krebs, who formulated the Krebs Cycle, a scientific account of how energy is metabolized. Veech says that ketosis, the state in which the body burns fat when starved of carbohydrate, ". . . is a normal physiologic state. I would argue it's the normal state of man."

And Walter Willett, the eminent Harvard epidemiologist, having studied the consistent failure of low-fat diets, says, "The emphasis on fat reduction has been a serious distraction in efforts to control obesity and improve health in general."

Atkins has been enjoying a boom time in the boom-and-bust cycle of the media, too. "Welcome to a city in the throes of Carb Panic," declared a recent edition of *New York* magazine. "Socialite psychiatrist" Samantha Boardman says, "The moment the waiter comes to the table with bread, everyone is like, NO! before he can even put it on the plate. It's almost hostile to serve pasta these days because everyone is on Atkins." Kim France, editor-in-chief of *Lucky* magazine, tells us, "My younger brother is always going on and off Atkins. He refers to Wheat Thins and bread as the white devil."

How long will this mood last? Perhaps the backlash is already beginning. Some people are starting to say that going on a low-carb diet, which dieters refer to as "doing Atkins," is a fad—that it will come and go, like it came and went before, to be replaced by something else, possibly the avoidance of another food group. Nobody will be surprised when a new diet guru tells us that potatoes are the answer, or that eating fish is the answer, or that you'll get thin if you eat lots of fruit, or nuts, or beans. One day, somebody will say that all food must be consumed on the move, and before long a company will invent a tray you can hang around your neck, and everybody will be walking around the park with trays around their necks. One day, the Cabbage Soup diet will make a comeback.

Naturally, Atkins himself does not think that Atkins is a fad. On the contrary, he thinks that low-fat diets—the diets that buried him in the 1970s, and presided through the 1980s and 1990s—were the fad. His scientific reasoning is that low-fat diets don't work—it was during the low-fat decades that we got so very fat. "Nowadays," he writes in the new edition of his book, "the tide is flowing strongly in my favor."

The Only Diet We Knew

Anyway, why should a low-carb diet be a fad? After all, it wasn't a fad for our ancestors, from the Neanderthal era to the Stone Age. For tens of thousands of years, humans ate a low-carb diet. We hunted animals and gathered fruit and some root vegetables, such as sweet potatoes. With an opposable thumb, an upright posture, and a panoramic field of vision, we were designed for walking long distances, throwing projectiles, and reaching up into thorny bushes for berries.

Early humans walked several hours every day, ran and jogged when their prey was in view, and carried animal carcasses on their backs for long distances. To survive, they needed to eat a lot of meat, and a lot of fruit—three or four times as much as we need to eat today. When they didn't die of infectious diseases or trauma, or in childbirth, they lived into their sixties and seventies, and the few senile Stone Age bodies we've found preserved in peat bogs don't show signs of the modern diseases that afflict us—diabetes, osteoporosis, cancer, arthritis, and heart disease.

Ray Audette, author of *NeanderThin: Eat Like a Caveman to Achieve a Lean, Strong, Healthy Body,* tells us that, if you want to lose weight and keep it off, you should do what he does, which is to "eat only those foods that would be available to me if I were naked of all technology save that of a convenient sharp stick or stone." His Neanderthal-style diet, not unlike Atkins in principle, is, he says, what we have evolved to eat. "For the majority (at least 99.5 percent) of human history," writes Audette, "it was the only diet we knew."

There has never been any evidence to suggest that Stone Age people ever needed to lose weight. Sure, they ate a lot of food. Sure, they would gorge themselves after a successful hunt. And, of course, they had evolved big appetites and "thrifty genes"—a love of food and an ability to store fat, in order to survive lean times. They ate a lot, they exercised a lot, their diet was very low in carbohydrates, and they didn't suffer from obesity.

"The NeanderThin rule concerning snacking is very simple," writes Audette. "If you are hungry, eat. Just be sure that your snack foods are within the dietary guidelines— could I eat this if I were naked with a sharp stick on the savanna?"

Fries—no.

Bagels—no.

Steak—yes.

Fish—yes.

Vegetables—yes.

Atkins, of course, is thoroughly pro–Stone Age. He writes about Stone Age man "eating the fish and animals that scampered and swam around him, and the fruits and vegetables and berries that grew nearby." There is no mention of being naked, or sharp sticks.

The elevator arrives and the doors glide open. Atkins steps inside. I step inside. My stomach magazines are safely inside a bag. Atkins presses the button for the top floor. The doors glide shut.

The Seeds of Trouble

Standing in the elevator, I'm thinking about how the seeds of trouble, the trouble with carbohydrates, were sown, quite literally, around 10,000 years ago, when humans started to farm. There we were, hunting and gathering, effectively doing Atkins, and then we started to plant and harvest crops, particularly wheat. We became what anthropologists call "food producers."

Why did we do this? The answer is not at all obvious. As the evolutionary biologist Jared Diamond tells us, "Most peasant farmers and herders, who constitute the great majority of the world's actual food producers, aren't necessarily better off than hunter-gatherers."

Studies, as Diamond points out, have shown that primitive food producers spent more time planting and tilling and harvesting than hunter-gatherers spent hunting and gathering the food for their primitive version of the Atkins diet; archaeologists, furthermore, "have demonstrated that the first farmers in many areas were smaller and less well nourished, suffered from more serious diseases, and died on average at a younger age than the hunter-gatherers they replaced."

Anthropologists disagree about the origins of farming—there are, according to the Oxford historian Felipe Fernandez-Armesto, "thirty-eight distinct and competing explanations of how farming came about." But the smart money is on the most sinister explanation of all: farming might not be good nutritionally, but it's great if your tribe wants to kill people and take their territory.

Farming facilitates war. You can imagine an ambitious Stone Age leader putting it together in his mind. Farming leads to a greater density of human population, because it enables a tribe to settle in one place. Unlike hunter-gatherers, farmers don't have to carry their children around with them, so they can have twice as many. Farming enables members of a tribe to have separate jobs—some men produce the food, while others are free, as Jared Diamond puts it, to "engage full-time in political activities." Farming enables food to be stored, so that fighting men can radiate outward from their original settlements and concentrate on fighting, while their hunter-gatherer opponents must hunt and gather as well as fight.

And farming is, of course, addictive. Farming creates what anthropologists call a "ratchet effect." Once you start, you can't stop. Your tribe grows. Wheat creates a need for wheat. Also, if you belong to a hunter-gatherer community, and your neighbors start to farm, you have two options—run away, or become farmers yourselves.

The advent of farming—it's the most important, not to say the most destructive, revolution in the history of mankind. Early farmers in northern Europe seemed to sense this; they regarded the plowing of fields and the sowing of seeds as an infernal act. Before plowing, farmers invoked the mercy of Odin, god of gods, and planted the skulls of their slain enemies along with the corn. Farming, they believed, was unnatural, a rape of the earth, something they might have to pay for in the end. When the wheat was harvested, the last sheaf was treated like an evil spirit; people jeered it and mocked it, rather like inmates of fat camps putting a hex on pizzas and hot dogs and tubs of ice cream.

Farming led to dense populations, which led to diverse occupations, which led to people having time on their hands, which led to inventions—plows and millstones and knives, and, much later, forks, and the combine-harvester, and the Lamb Water Gun Knife, which shoots potatoes along a tube into a criss-cross network of blades, turning them into perfect French fries. Farming led to the breeding of wild grasses such as emmer and einkorn, which developed into the high-yield wheat we know today, which can be separated from its husk, milled into fine powder, mixed with water, yeast, salt, sugar, chemical oxidants, fat crystals derived from frozen palm oil and emulsifiers made from petrochemicals, fermented at high speed in mechanical mixers, heated, frozen, trucked for hundreds of miles, and baked in a matter of minutes in a supermarket, after which the resulting fluffy and slightly clammy white bread will raise the blood glucose level of anybody who eats it almost as much as a mouthful of sugar. Which will, over time, cause the pancreas of this person to produce too much insulin, which will cause a blood sugar crash and subsequent cravings for more white bread. Which is one of the reasons why white bread, from the manufacturer's point of view, is such a good product. According to Atkins, it's addictive.

Farming was the impetus that caused human beings to

settle down in communities, which became the first cities, which spawned roads and rising land values and, eventually, urban angst and skyscrapers and elevators and fat people riding in elevators at the expense of no calories.

A Bias

The elevator glides upward. I am holding my stomach in. I catch Atkins' eye, and he smiles at me. He is calm, benign, possibly a little frail. His white hair forms a fluffy halo around the top of his head; he's one of those older men who are mostly bald, but who, somehow, do not give off the air of baldness. He is a former ladies' man; when he smiles, the flesh around his eyes crinkles attractively. Atkins is, it occurs to me, one of the most controversial people alive. He is trying to tell the world to stop eating refined carbohydrates. And the production of refined carbohydrates is, economically speaking, the biggest enterprise on earth.

Were diet gurus always so controversial? Almost certainly not. When ancient Greeks such as Galen and Aristotle advocated moderation in everything, they were not damned as faddists. People did not assume, as a matter of course, that their diets—their world views—did not work. Dionysiacs such as Alcibiades might have argued that the moderate man is spiritually lacking, or doesn't have enough fun, but he knew that, if you didn't eat too much, you stayed thin. (We still know this, of course—moderation will keep you thin. It's just not a message anybody in the modern world wants to hear.)

The big thing about early diet gurus, the guys who gave

dietary advice before, say, the nineteenth century, was that they preached moderation. When Luigi Cornaro, arguably the first modern diet guru, wrote his bestselling book *Discourses on a Sober and Temperate Life,* which was published in 1558, he wasn't saying anything scientifically controversial. The book starts in the classic manner, with the author telling us how fat he got, and how dangerous and unpleasant it is to get fat. Gluttony, he said, "kills every year . . . as great a number as would perish during the time of a most dreadful pestilence, or by the sword or fire of many bloody wars."

Cornaro's answer: do not eat "a greater quantity than can be digested." In other words, don't eat too much. Cornaro ate sparingly and lost weight. Another thing he discovered: food tastes better when you don't eat too much of it. "I now find more true relish in the simple food I eat, wheresoever I may chance to be," Cornaro wrote, "than I formerly found in the most delicate dishes at the time of my intemperate life." He lived to the age of ninety-eight.

For centuries, moderation was the main message of the diet guru. In order to lose weight, you had to stop stuffing your face, and never go back to stuffing your face again. Until the twentieth century, a diet was a diet forever, and was based on firm principles that applied to life in general. Cornaro believed that being greedy was bad for the soul. Erasmus preached moderation because it fitted in with his reading of the Bible. Leonard Lessius, the early Belgian diet guru, wrote in 1613 that "Lust knows not where Necessitie ends," paraphrasing St. Augustine. For centuries, the message was the same. Be moderate. Don't stop being moderate. Even the glutton Dr. Johnson believed that losing weight was a simple science. "Whatever be the quantity that a man eats," he said, "it is plain that if he is too fat, he has eaten more than he should have done."

We all know what happened next. People began to have trouble with moderation. The Industrial Revolution brought mass production, steam-powered transport, the mechanized milling of flour, food preservatives, canning, and an increased level of carbohydrate in the diet. Meat was expensive. Carbs were cheap. Being fat, now no longer the exclusive preserve of the wealthy, became more and more unfashionable. One guy who knew this from personal experience was the Victorian undertaker William Banting, who, at 5 foot 5 inches and 202 lbs., had become quite desperate about his ballooning weight.

"No man labouring under obesity," wrote Banting, a Londoner, "can be quite insensible to the sneers and remarks of the cruel and injudicious." It was the same trauma that Shelley Bovey described just over a century later.

Banting had tried various methods of losing weight. He took up rowing, which gave him a big appetite. He traveled to Harrogate to drink the sulfur waters in the hope that the purgative effect of the foul-tasting drink would reduce his weight. He took Turkish baths, hoping to steam his way to trimness. None of this worked. Then he consulted William Harvey, a Fellow of the Royal College of Surgeons.

Harvey told Banting to go low-carb. Having studied diabetes, Harvey had come to the conclusion that eating too much starch and sugar made people fat, and sometimes led to diabetes. Thus instructed, Banting stopped eating bread, milk, sugar, and potatoes, and feasted on beef, mutton, kidneys, bacon, and "any vegetable except potatoes." Over the course of a year, he lost 46 lbs., wrote a treatise, the "letter on corpulence," and became the most famous diet guru of his time. At the age of 65, he told his readers, "I have not felt so well as now for the last twenty years."

For a few years, people lost weight on Banting's diet, and even referred to the act of losing weight as "banting." But then something happened, a fate that would befall Atkins a century later. Banting's diet was buried. In the late nineteenth century, as now, low-carb diets had a crucial problem: it's hard to manufacture low-carb products to support them. When diet gurus such as John Harvey Kellogg and Sylvester Graham, on the other hand, advocated their rival high-carb, low-protein diets, they produced products—Kellogg's cereal and Graham Crackers—to go along with the diets, thus creating a network of corporate allies. But Banting, like Atkins in the 1970s, had nothing to sell, except a message that might hurt food manufacturers.

If you advocate a low-fat diet, the food manufacturers don't mind. People who produce carbs are fine about it. People who produce dairy products might sell less full-fat milk, but they'll make up for it by selling more low-fat milk; butchers sell lean meat at a premium price to make up for the money they lose on fatty meat.

But if you advocate a low-carb diet, the food industry sees you as a problem. Millers and potato farmers work in high-bulk, low-margin industries. If their sales drop by just a few percent, they have to lay off thousands of workers. Low-carb, in other words, potentially harms the food industry in a way that low-fat does not. So if you work in the food industry, or you're a nutritionist, and you say bad things about low-carb diets, or good things about low-fat diets, you'll make a lot of friends.

Atkins himself underlined this point in 1973, when he was interrogated by the Senate Nutrition Committee on Obesity and Fad Diets. When Dr. Frederick Stare, founder of the Department of Nutrition at Harvard's School of Public Health, condemned the Atkins diet, Atkins said, "I think the Harvard School of Nutrition depends on outside funds and this could produce a bias."

Stare's department, it turned out, had received donations from Kellogg's, Carnation, and the Sugar Association.

Two Words That Would Make Us All a Lot Healthier

As the elevator rises, I'm thinking about what always happens to low-carb diets. Eventually, they get buried under a ton of carbohydrates. So far, from the Stone Age to the present day, this has always happened. Carbs are powerful. Carbs have influential friends. Mess with carbs at your peril.

After Banting, low-fat made a comeback. Diets began to change. They got quicker. Around the turn of the last century, people tried one-day diets and three-day diets and one-week diets and one-month diets. Flappers in the 1920s ate eggs for a day, cabbage for a week, or cut out meat for a month. None of this worked; all of these diets fell foul of the Cannon Conundrum. As people began to understand the concept of calories in the 1950s and 1960s, low-calorie diets became the norm. They didn't work, either. As Geoffrey Cannon says, dieting makes you fat because diets change the way your body works. Diets make your body think you can't find food. If you stay on a low-calorie diet, your body turns muscle tissue into fat, rendering you weak. If you stop the diet, you get fatter than you were before.

And of course, after Atkins' 1972 diet, low-fat made another comeback. Low-fat always makes a comeback. In the seventies and eighties and nineties, low-fat was bigger than ever. There were diets which involved counting "fat units," and diets where you would grill things instead of frying them, and diets where you cut the fat off the edge of your steak and removed the skin from chicken legs. Aerosols were used to convey tiny amounts of cooking oil to the frying pan; frying pans themselves were designed with ridges, to enable the fat to run off.

Audrey Eyton had a runaway success with her low-fat F-Plan diet. I did the F-Plan. I understood the science behind the F-Plan. The "F" in the F-Plan stands for fiber. On the F-Plan, you eat a lot of fiber. You become fiber-minded. You develop an interest in husks. You start each day with a bowl of bran. Sometimes you start the day with two or three bowls of bran. You find yourself discussing your bowels in mixed company. Socially, you gravitate toward other people who are happy to discuss the rhythms of their bowels with you. The thing about fiber is that it's supposed to bulk out your stomach, filling you up, and then bulk out your bowels, getting rid of all the putrefying stuff stuck in the crannies, thus detoxifying your body.

The main selling point of the F-Plan diet is that fiber fills you up and then passes straight through you without making you fat. Your body thinks you've eaten something when, effectively, you've eaten nothing. Unfortunately, being bloated doesn't stop you being hungry so you end up eating a lot of things other than fiber, which don't pass straight through you, and which do make you fat.

I did the Hay diet. I understood the science behind the Hay diet. Dr. William Howard Hay was an American surgeon who gained a lot of weight around the turn of the last century. By 1904, at the age of forty, he was so bloated he had to give up his practice. Then he discovered his miraculous diet. On the Hay, you "don't mix foods which fight." It's a catchy idea. The Hay diet had a brief vogue in 1905 and 1907, and made a comeback in the 1980s, popularized in Harvey and Marilyn Diamond's book *Fit for Life*. Harvey and Marilyn were needle-nosed and angular, and told us all about the Hay, which they called "food combining." On the Hay, you treat carbohydrates and proteins as adversaries. So if you eat, say, bread and cheese at the same time, the bread and the cheese fight—they cause a conflict in your stomach. And when foods fight, Hay believed, you get fat.

A woman I knew, a veteran of the F-Plan, and now a food-combiner, put it like this: "You get fat when you eat protein and carbohydrate together because the enzymes you need to metabolize these foods are different. So you have a bad mix of enzymes in your stomach. Which means you don't digest the food properly."

"Right . . . but why would that make you fat?"

"Well, because . . ."

"I mean, surely, if you don't digest your food properly, you get *thin*."

"No. You get fat. Because . . . because the food hangs around your stomach, making you fat."

"OK. I sort of see."

"And then it hangs around your colon. You get all these porky bits in your colon. They can hang around for years."

"No!"

"Yes. *Years*. And then, of course, everything backs up, like with a blocked drain, and the food stays around, sort of rotting and making you fat. *Horrible*."

"Right. Horrible."

"And if I could just say two words that would make us all a lot healthier?"

"Yes?"

"Colonic irrigation."

The Hay, I think, works mostly because when you're on the Hay you have to cook, or at least compose, your meals from scratch. So you don't snack as much. Also, not mixing protein and carbs means you eat fewer carbs. Another thing in its favor might be the fact that you can't eat a fat, lazy diet—you can't have ham sandwiches, bacon sandwiches, cheese sandwiches, hamburgers in buns, or pizza. On the Hay, it's harder to watch TV and eat at the same time. You have to look at your food.

The Veal Conversation

For a while, I was a vegetarian. Vegetarianism grew in popularity in the 1980s, partly as a result of Peter Singer's bestselling book *Animal Liberation*, which exposed horrifying details about meat production. When I was a student, a few people read *Animal Liberation*, but a lot of people had second- and third-hand conversations about it. There was the Veal Conversation, the Factory Farming Conversation, the Abbatoir Conversation, and the Shampoo in Rabbits' Eyes Conversation.

"They keep them in these crates."

And: "They can't even turn around."

And: "They're only three months old when they're slaughtered."

And: "They overfeed them."

And: "They're always perspiring. Always too hot. Singer says they must feel nauseous all the time, what was it, like a businessman after a heavy lunch."

And: "You know how much space each chicken gets?"

And: "They're bred to be obese."

And: "They kill pigs with a metal bolt through the head."

And: "They know they're going to die."

And: "You know what the biggest scandal is? The way they kill turkeys. See, they don't need to slaughter a lot of turkeys all year round. They just have one big glut around Christmas. So there's no point, economically, in actually building a slaughterhouse designed for turkeys. So you know what they do? They kill them with the chicken machines. But, see, the turkeys are much bigger. So when they go past the knives that are supposed to cut off the chickens' heads, they just get stabbed in the chest. And so when they get chucked into the vat of boiling water, which makes the feathers easier to pluck . . . they're still alive."

And: "I'm never eating turkey again."

And: "Just think of the karma."

And: "I'm glad you don't use animal products. I'd feel weird sleeping with a girl who wasn't aware of stuff like that."

I was a vegetarian for years, partly because I didn't like the idea of cruelty to animals, and partly because I had read that, if we stopped farming meat, and instead grew more wheat and pulses, nobody in the world need starve, and partly out of habit, and partly because I thought it was more healthy. But it was a pain. I remember watching *Rosemary's Baby* on TV one night, and being particularly fascinated by the scene in which Mia Farrow eats a steak. She looks so sweet—and yet there she is, eating this bloody steak. I began to fantasize about eating a bloody steak. One day, I went to a dinner party with my vegetarian girlfriend, and we hadn't told the hostess we were vegetarians. And the hostess, who had just got to know us, was really embarrassed, and darted into the kitchen and knocked up a cheese salad for my girlfriend.

"Cheese is OK, is it?"

"Fine."

"I'm so sorry about this."

"No, it's my fault."

"I should have known."

"I should have told you."

The hostess was stirring a large pot on the stove: beef stew. She looked at me. "Oh," she said. "Are you . . . ?"

"Beef stew is fine," I said.

My girlfriend looked at me.

"I couldn't ask her to make another salad," I whispered as we walked toward the table.

I ate the beef stew. Afterward, my girlfriend asked me what it had been like to eat meat again. It had been chewy, and tasted of flesh and blood, and I knew I wanted to eat more flesh and blood, as soon as possible.

"Oh, you know," I said. "Pretty horrible. Chewy."

Around that time, in January 2000, I met Peter Singer. He was teaching philosophy at Princeton.

He had become more notorious; Diane Coleman, the chair of the disabled rights group Not Dead Yet, had called him "the most dangerous man in the world." By now, he wasn't just saying that we shouldn't kill animals; he believed that it was not wrong to kill people, at least if they were severely disabled. He was in the business, as he put it, of "dethroning" the human race—trying to get us to step down from our pedestal.

With his outdoorsy clothes and shy smile, he looked like a genial middle-aged hiker. We had the Veal Conversation. We had the Factory Farming Conversation. He told me about his childhood in Melbourne, Australia; how he had been called "wog" by some nasty kids at a swimming pool because he was Jewish, how his grandparents had died in the Holocaust, how he'd preferred jazz to rock 'n' roll in the early '60s, but had loved the Beatles even more. He'd grown his hair over the years, more or less in accordance with George Harrison's, and he'd grown a 1969 "Let it Be" style mustache, which he'd only recently shaved off.

We had the Shampoo in Rabbits' Eyes Conversation. We had the Abbatoir Conversation.

"Well, I find them pretty disgusting places," said Singer. "They smell dreadfully, for a start. I was not actually able to see the place where the animals were killed. So from the point of view of the moment of killing, I didn't see it. I saw the animals waiting to be killed, and obviously pretty uncomfortable. And I saw the dismembered parts."

I asked Singer about game. What if you were to kill your own food, as it were, in the wild?

Singer frowned. "I certainly think it's better," he said.

The Game Conversation—that wasn't a conversation I had very much, back when I was a student. I shook hands with Singer, and went across the road on my own and ate a salad with adzuki beans and hummus, but I had beef on the plane the next day, and I didn't look back. I reintroduced meat into my diet, and I stopped worrying about it.

As long as it was low in fat.

Ready to Believe

But, of course, avoiding fat did not stop me being fat. And, as Atkins points out, avoiding fat has not stopped us, as a society, getting fat. We eat 15 percent less fat than we did in 1970, and we're 20 percent fatter. So perhaps Audrey Eyton was wrong. Perhaps Hay was wrong. Perhaps Harvey and Marilyn Diamond were wrong. Perhaps Susie Orbach, who says that being fat is all in the head, is wrong.

Perhaps Geoffrey Cannon is wrong.

Perhaps Atkins is right.

I'm ready to believe.

Ping!

The elevator doors open.

"It's this way," says Dr. Robert C. Atkins.

"I Knew I Had Something Wonderful"

Like me, it turns out, Atkins hasn't had lunch, even though it's early afternoon. "I sometimes just eat some macadamia nuts or something like that, when I'm working," he tells me. "That's just something to tide me over until dinner." Macadamias are highly calorific—a handful can contain 250 calories, as much as a handful of chocolate chips. But that's fine according to Atkins, because they're very low in carbs. When you squeeze a macadamia nut between your molars, it pops, and you can feel the fat oozing between your teeth.

We sit down on either side of his desk. For breakfast, he tells me, he ate "Ham and eggs. And onions. Very dark fried onions." Sometimes he has an omelet, sometimes bacon and eggs. He has followed the Atkins diet since November 1963, more than thirty-nine years.

Atkins begins by telling me about his struggles over the decades. He sounds embattled, and a touch weary. Still, the tide, as he has been pointing out recently, seems to be turning his way. "Now," he says, "the evidence confirms what I had noticed in studies that were done forty and fifty years ago. Which is that there's a metabolic advantage to a low-carbohydrate diet. That you actually lose more weight, calorie for calorie, than you do on balanced diets or low-fat diets."

Listening to this elderly man, looking at his pleasant face with the crinkly smile, I can feel something nagging at me, and I'm not sure what it is. Atkins talks on. "And that's been proved by *study after study*," he says, "and all of a sudden, uh, we've reached an era where people are doing these studies, even people who felt that my diet was wrong, and finding out that it is better. And now people are writing about the fact that these studies have been done, and people's minds *have to change*. Because they always said there wasn't any evidence. But now there's an *incredible* amount of evidence, and it's 100 percent consistent with what I had learned about."

When I tell Atkins that I've read articles criticizing him, he looks at me sharply and says, "Whatever it is they're saying, there's nothing to back it up. Everything that we say has backup. There aren't any exceptions. And I'd like to know—what have they said?"

"Well, that your diet doesn't have enough fiber."

"In my new book, we talk so much about fiber."

I nod.

Atkins says, "It's very important to know that here's a diet that is so effective that virtually everyone who goes on it can expect to achieve their ideal weight, and then spend the rest of their lives on a maintenance diet. For instance, in my case, back in 1963, I went on the induction level, and I just lost weight so rapidly. And it felt so much better."

He tells me the story of his own weight loss. It is the familiar diet guru narrative—weight gain, followed by despair, the despair obliterated by a simple, miraculous insight.

"In November 1963," he says, "two things happened. I gained an awful lot of weight from Thanksgiving, and John F. Kennedy was murdered. I was just sitting there watching television, watching all this sad stuff. And I made up my mind. I felt I had to do something. So I went on a diet."

Atkins says, "I looked at a picture of myself and realized I had a triple chin. I was eating junk food. Nobody had ever told me junk food was bad for me. Four years of medical school, and four years of internship and residency, and I never thought anything was wrong with eating sweet rolls and doughnuts, and potatoes, and bread, and sweets."

He was six feet tall and weighed 225 lbs. As a man with a big appetite, Atkins knew he would not last on a traditional low-calorie or low-fat diet. But he'd just read an article in *The Journal of the American Medical Association* about a low-carbohydrate diet. He says, "It was so simple! I hadn't tried a diet before that. It was the only diet that looked like I'd enjoy being on it. I ate a lot of meat, and a lot of shrimp, and a lot of duck, and a lot of fish. And omelets in the morning, and salad vegetables."

The diet worked a treat. The pounds fell off rapidly, and, significantly, Atkins did not feel hungry. His cravings for buns and rolls had gone. He felt perky and energetic. He began to realize that something was happening, something which contradicted general medical opinion. He was eating a lot of calories, and a lot of fat, but he was losing weight. Why was this? He decided to try his diet on patients, to see if it worked on them, too. In the mid-sixties, Atkins put sixty-five overweight patients on a low-carbohydrate diet. All sixty-five reached their target weight.

Atkins looks across his desk at me and says, "I knew I had something wonderful."

Jet Lag

As I look at Atkins and nod along with what he is saying, I realize what it is that's been nagging at me. It's that I want to believe in him. I want him to be right. I want this because, if he is right, I will lose weight. And there's something else, too.

If he's right I won't have to be hungry. True. But that's not it.

If he's right, one day, quite soon, I'll be able to get a haircut and have a shave and wear a suit without looking like a fat nerd or a bodyguard. True. But that's not it.

If he's right, when the weather gets warmer, I'll be able to walk around in a T-shirt. One day, it will be warm, and I'll put a T-shirt on, and just . . . walk around. Again, true. But that's not it.

Yes, I want to believe in this guy. And another thing occurs to me. To an atheist like myself, living in the twenty-first century, it's hard to believe in anything. I don't believe in Tony Blair or George Bush. I don't believe in Gordon Brown or Alan Greenspan. I don't believe in market forces. But then, I never believed in socialism either. And now I'm sitting in an office talking to a man who thinks that he can solve possibly the most serious crisis in the world. And I want to believe him. And he thinks he knows what the problem is. And it's carbohydrates. The problem is carbohydrates.

I mean, I've talked to people with all kinds of ideas. In my work as a journalist, I've encountered a number of gurus. Gurus love journalists. Mostly, I'm pretty skeptical. Once I talked to a guy who said he had the answer to the world's health problems, and it was something to do with taking your blood, and boiling it, and then looking at the result under a microscope. The science, he told me, was incontrovertible. I didn't believe him. But I was perfectly polite. Then he ducked behind some kind of screen and came out with a syringe, and told me to sit down and roll my sleeve up.

He said, "I just need a little bit of blood."

"No thanks."

He walked toward me.

He said, "Just a little bit of blood."

"Uh, no thanks."

"Please. There's nothing to worry about."

He moved toward me, holding the syringe. I darted behind a chair. He was on one side of the chair, and I was on the other.

"You sit down. I'll take some blood. Please. *Please.* It won't hurt."

I backed out of the door and walked briskly away. I never finished the interview.

Soon after this, I met a cult of would-be immortals from Arizona who believed they held the key to eternal life, the answer to everything. The answer was simply not to believe in death.

"But how can you not believe in it? Everybody dies, don't they?"

The man I was talking to, who smiled a lot, said, "See, right now you're being deathist."

"Deathist?"

"Yeah. You should hear yourself. You believe in death, don't you?"

"I suppose so."

"Do you know anybody who doesn't believe in death?"

"Apart from you, no."

"Well, haven't you ever put two and two together?"

"How do you mean?"

"OK. So imagine a world where everybody dies."

"Right."

"And where everybody believes in death."

"Right."

"That's our world. Right here. We live in a deathist culture."

"Uh . . . OK."

"So if you think about it hard enough, you get to understand the real deal. Are you seeing it?"

"Not quite."

"I'll go through it again. Everybody who dies *believes in death*."

"OK."

"And that's why they die. They die because they are deathist. We, on the other hand, deny death."

"Oh. Oh."

"To live forever, you must *deny*."

"Mmm."

"Deny!"

Another time I attended a seminar given by the self-help guru Anthony Robbins. This was while I was with Sadie. I was at a low ebb, drinking and overeating. The seminar, the idea of it, terrified me. I didn't want to be in a conference hall full of people yelling and hugging each other. I wanted to stay in my hotel room, and open a bottle of wine, and watch game shows on TV, and wait for yesterday's hangover to slip away. I dislike game shows. But as the time for the seminar approached, the early game shows were starting up, and they looked great.

One thing I was worried about was the firewalk. Robbins' method was to whip everybody up into a state of rock-hard self-confidence, and then get them to walk barefoot over burning embers. I was certain, absolutely certain, that it wouldn't be dangerous, that he had worked out some way of making the embers safe to walk on. Still, I didn't want to walk on the embers. I wasn't even sure I wanted to possess rock-hard self-confidence. What I wanted was to lie on my bed in my hotel and watch people doing trivial, possibly humiliating things, people who were in worse shape than me. But that was the trouble with game shows. The people on them, the members of the public, had begun to look smarter, fitter. The producers, I thought, must be auditioning dancers and athletes and models. Game shows were definitely less reassuring than they had been. But that night, they still looked great.

In the conference center, Robbins strode on stage and told us stories about how to take control of your life. You had to separate what was good for you from what was bad for you. Stop smoking. Stop drinking too much. Stop taking drugs. He asked us if we thought trying to do a job well was good enough. Then he told us that no, doing a job well was nowhere near good enough. You had to aim for excellent! You had to aim for superb! Otherwise why do it at all?

There were six hundred people in the hall. Robbins, a tall man with the air of Ted Danson from *Cheers,* told us to yell and to hug each other. He played loud bursts of prerecorded rock guitar. The idea seemed to be to lose your inhibitions. Robbins told us he'd built a huge fire in the car park. This was the fire we were going to walk on. After two hours, we all filed into the car park to see the fire. It was just this huge fire, the biggest fire I'd ever seen. You could feel the heat coming right off it. When I got back inside, I sneaked past security and went up the stairs and hid on a balcony.

It's not that I disagreed with Robbins. Everything he said

made sense. To change my life for the better, I should be honest with myself, stop procrastinating, avoid the things that are bad for me. In his book *Unlimited Power*, Robbins had written that his firewalk was "an experience in personal power and a metaphor for possibilities." He said, "The lesson is that people can do virtually anything as long as they muster the resources to believe they can." But I didn't want to muster resources. I didn't want unlimited power. I wanted to procrastinate, to escape into booze and drugs, hamburgers and fries. I wanted fuzziness, not clarity. I wanted to keep a distance from my own inner workings, to hang on to the friendly, familiar clutter of my inhibitions. I was the problem. But I didn't want to look inside, to see what the problem looked like. I wanted to be disengaged.

I watched from the balcony as Robbins mesmerized the other 599 people in the seminar. Later, I sneaked into the car park and watched them line up to walk on the embers. The embers had been laid out on strips of what looked like Astroturf. When people walked on the embers, barefoot, they chanted the words "cool moss!" over and over. Later, somebody told me it was all totally safe—the Astroturf was sodden with water, and the pressure of the sole of the foot lowered the temperature of the embers just enough, so the foot did not get burned. Aha, I thought. I was relieved. I wasn't sure which had worried me more. Not having unlimited power was pretty bad. But the alternative was terrifying.

I've never really wanted to believe in anybody. As a student, I liked certain French philosophers—Roland Barthes, Jacques Derrida, Jean Baudrillard. But wasn't that just because these guys seemed not to believe in anything much themselves? Barthes wrote a brilliant essay about stripping in which he visualized the stripper's G-string as the rock upon which the meaning of eroticism could be built; all else was shifting sands. "Woman," he wrote, "is desexualized the moment she is stripped naked." Barthes, by the way, was gay. He was, I think, saying that as soon as you grasped the reality of something, it wasn't there anymore, at least not in the same way. Or you might say that he had pinpointed, with deadly accuracy, the logic of the market in advanced capitalism—what is valuable is what you do not have. As soon as you have something, it is no longer valuable. Derrida was similar; for him, meaning existed in the gaps between things, rather than the things themselves. Baudrillard, the most elusive and playful of them all, called this "a philosophy of disappearance."

Thinkers were not like this in the past. Plato, with his theory that everything has an ideal version of itself, seemed fairly confident, as did Aquinas and Anselm, who collected together evidence, much of it spurious, to prove the existence of God. Bishop Berkeley had no problem that God existed, simply because he believed the trees in his quadrangle stayed there even when he wasn't looking at them.

Descartes had faith in the self: "I think, therefore I am." But wasn't there a problem with this very thought? When he said the words "I think," was he not positing an "I"—a self—before he had justified it with the latter half of the thought, the "therefore I am" bit? Was he not, in that case, making a false assumption?

After Descartes, it was more or less downhill. By the twentieth century, philosophers had lost the knack of looking for what is true, stymied by the question: "What is truth?" The retreat was on; thinkers began to doubt their own tools. Philosophy began to be about the arbitrary nature of language, and then about the radical uncertainty of the self. Baudrillard said that we had become "obscene" and "obese," bloated with meaningless desires. Mankind, he said, had "become a virus," and might be on course to destroy the world. Well, yes, I thought. He might have a point.

Baudrillard was my kind of guru. For a long time, I suspected that he did not actually exist. Also, I was not sure if I wanted him to exist. Who was he? In the intellectual imagination, he was a fashionable French thinker. He was just about as French as you can get. He had cruised effortlessly past the death of logic and the eclipse of the self. He wrote: "God exists, but I don't believe in him." He wrote: "I feel like a witness to my own absence." He saw the world as a place in which there was no way of knowing what is real and what is fake. We humans, mired in late capitalism, could not see outside the constructions of our own thought. In 1991, he accused the Gulf War of not happening.

I arranged to meet him in the late winter of 1998. The meeting was fixed through a third party. I wanted to find out whether Baudrillard was real or not, and, if he was, whether he was deadly serious, or a joker. Both outcomes would disappoint me. In photographs, he was a bespectacled man in an open-necked, expensive shirt with permanently half-raised eyebrows; he looked as if he was enjoying a joke that nobody else could understand. He once said, "Since the media always make you out to say the opposite of what you say, you should have the courage always to say the opposite of what you think."

I flew to Paris with an address and a telephone number for Baudrillard on a piece of paper. In my hotel, I gave the piece of paper to the receptionist, so she could call a cab. She looked at it and frowned. Then she took out an index of the streets of Paris, looked through the index, and handed the piece of paper back to me.

"*Ce n'existe pas.*"

"What?"

"*L'adresse n'existe pas.*"

Quite, I thought. Baudrillard, who says the world is full of "simulacra," rather than real things, might be a simulacrum himself. He could, quite easily, be a brilliant invention. I was gripped by a sudden panic. Perhaps I was the butt of a joke, and someone would soon arrive and let me in on the secret—that Baudrillard was not, in fact, real. Then, perhaps, I would be invited to join the conspiracy, and pretend to write an article about him.

I called the number. A recorded voice, arch and French, answered and told me to leave a message.

"Hello," I said into the void. "Is that Monsieur Baudrillard? Are you there? If you are, would you pick up the phone?"

A taxi arrived. The driver was actually wearing a beret and a smock. He did not quite look real. I showed him the address on the piece of paper. He frowned. He said, "*N'existe pas.*" He shrugged at me. He looked for the address in the A-Z. Unsuccessful, he put the book down.

I asked the man wearing the beret and smock to call Jean Baudrillard. The hotel receptionist dialed the number and handed over the phone. The man started talking. Someone, anyway, was on the other end. I stood there, slightly paranoid. "*Oui, oui*," said the taxi driver. Then he said, "Come to the car. I will take you."

We moved through the thick, nervy Paris traffic. Baudrillard once wrote, "I detest the bustling activity of my fellow citizens, detest initiative, social responsibility, ambition, competition." On pavements, women were walking to work. "It would be so nice to tear them from the blankness of the morning air and plunge them back into their beds," Baudrillard wrote of these women. He had written that he found women walking to work in the morning "erotic."

Baudrillard's apartment was in Montparnasse, on the south side of central Paris, in a street too narrow to exist on the Paris streetfinder. We moved toward him past famous iconic buildings ("They are not monuments, they are monsters.") One thing I liked about him was that he had a pronouncement for every place, every situation and emotion. Here he is on being fat: "The overweight person . . . says 'I lack everything so I will eat anything at all.' " And on being thin: "The obsession with becoming thinner and thinner is the obsession with becoming an image."

The taxi driver dropped me off at the end of Baudrillard's street. I pressed his doorbell, opened the door and found myself in a large hall with a high ceiling. There was a lift. But I took the steep stairs. Baudrillard was at the top of the building. He once wrote about a girlfriend who "does not take the lift, but goes up the stairs instead and undresses floor by floor—her sweater, her skirt, her shoes, her watch, finally, just outside the door, her knickers; then she rings the bell. When I open the door, she is standing there completely naked, like a dream."

I rang the bell. I felt obscene, obese, totally out of breath.

The door opened. A smallish, compact man, definitely the eyebrow-raiser from the photographs, opened the door and backed away. He was wearing an expensive, open-necked shirt and a V-neck sweater of very fine wool. He looked at his watch. I was, of course, late. Time was short.

The apartment was bathed in light. There was a sitting room, a study, a bedroom. In the study were two book-shelves—one for his books, and another one for books by other people.

He said, "What do you want to talk about?"

"I thought . . . the obscene. Your concept of obscenity. And other things."

We talked about other things for a while. He had recently taken up photography. "When you are a photographer," he said, "you are a keen observer, an ethnographer, a hunter. There is a link with hunting. And also there is a link with traveling. So, for me, photography is a little bit like travel-ing. It's connected with journeys, moving around. But above all, it's connected with objects. There are no human beings."

He continued. He said that photography was "the art of making the object appear, the subject disappear. In other words, me. I try, in fact, to disappear."

He got up from his sofa and went to the desk and picked up tobacco and a cigarette-rolling device. I asked him to tell me about his general worldview. He said, "Where shall we start, then? Obscenity?"

"Yes."

"I often talk about obscenity, but not necessarily in the sexual sense. General obscenity exists in a world where everything becomes transparent, everything is visible, there are no more secrets . . . It's the same thing as pornography, if you like. That is to say that everything that existed before—metaphor, utopia, dream, idealism, everything—is immediately materialized. In pornography, materialized in a body, in a sexual act. But it's like that everywhere."

And for a moment, I could see it. Baudrillard was saying that the Western world had become bloated and pornographic—obese, obscene. We had everything we wanted, in abundance. And it wasn't making us happy. It was making us hungry. He knew what the problem was. It was us. We were a virus. We were nothing but appetite. But was this something I wanted to believe?

I said, "Are you happy?"

"Yes, I think I have succeeded in creating conditions of autonomy and freedom. So if that is happiness, no problem there. I have managed to avoid stress, impatience and all that. Anyway, I have invented for myself a sort of 'jet lag' of a second state in which I can live. Not philosophically. Just a question of existence. I keep a distance from a world which, for me, is not truly real, so the happiness which I can have in it is not necessarily real."

My Kind of Diagnosis

"I knew I had something wonderful," says Dr. Atkins. I look back across the desk at him. The wonderful thing he had, of course, was the conviction that carbohydrates were the problem. Eating too much carbohydrate leads to overproduction of insulin. Overproduction of insulin leads to low blood sugar. Low blood sugar leads to food cravings. Food cravings lead to obesity. And diabetes. And misery on a catastrophic, global scale, legions of miserable people, wave after wave of fat bellies and chafing thighs and self-consciousness and anxiety and deep-seated feelings of not being attractive, not being worthy, not being loved. Women like Shelley Bovey, going through life terrified of public transport, men like Robbie Coltrane who really, really don't want to talk about it.

Atkins and I talk about how insulin works in the body. For the record, I get him to take me through the cycle.

I say: "So, you eat carbohydrate . . ."

Atkins: "Your blood sugar goes up."

Me: "Why does it come down so much?"

Atkins: "Because you then put out insulin. And insulin drives it down."

And we move on to the subject of hyperinsulinism. The pancreas produces insulin in response to carbohydrates, but if you repeatedly overeat carbohydrates, you reach a crucial tipping point, after which your pancreas produces far, far too much—a veritable deluge of insulin, which causes a corresponding low tide of blood sugar, which triggers a cacophony of craving, which leads to an exponential population curve of obesity, an army of overeaters lining up under the golden arches.

What a tempting analysis. The problem is carbohydrates! As Atkins says in his book, "Many carbohydrate addicts could no more walk past a refrigerator without opening it than Venus or Serena Williams could let a short lob drift overhead without smashing it."

"You see," Atkins goes on in his book, "your food compulsion isn't a character disorder. It's a chemical disorder."

That's it! That's why I want to believe Atkins. If Atkins

is right, the problem is not *us,* it's not the human condition. If Atkins were directing a disaster movie about the fat crisis, it would be one of those movies where the threat comes from outside, and can therefore be exorcized. It's just a bunch of spiders! It's just those pesky triffids! It's just the food we're eating! Atkins is saying that there isn't something essentially wrong with us, that there isn't something essentially wrong with *me.* I'm just eating wrong, that's all. And that's a diagnosis I like to hear. That's my kind of diagnosis.

We talk on, as the sky darkens outside his office. Atkins roots around and produces charts, and shows me the results of surveys. He seems tired, but he doesn't want to stop. He makes no secret of the fact that he's not a top-level scientist. He's not a laboratory man. Equally, he doesn't seem like a huckster or a con man. He's a messenger. For three decades, he's been telling us this one thing, this one important fact. "I didn't realize I'd be fighting the whole world," he says. "It didn't enter my mind."

Atkins grew up in Dayton, Ohio. His father was a restaurateur. A restaurateur, in the Midwest, in the 1950s! A vendor of fries! When his parents retired to Florida, Atkins put them on the Atkins diet.

He lives in the shadow of his father. "He was just an extremely likeable person that everybody sort of fell in love with. He was just a very wonderful role model for teaching me to be a nice person."

"Yes?"

"I will never be as nice as him. But he was special."

"What was his secret?"

"He just truly liked people, and you could just tell."

My train of thought goes something like this. So there he was, the son of the neighborhood restaurateur, the man who loved everybody, and fed everybody, a man who soothed the local populace with carbs, and was greatly loved in return. Hardly surprising, then, with food playing such a central role in the Atkins family setup, that Atkins began to overeat. And then he got chubby, and became a chubby doctor, and one day, in 1963, he went back home to Dayton, and ate a huge Thanksgiving lunch with his family, traveled back to New York, looked at himself in the mirror, and felt waves of self-disgust. Here he was, thirty-three years old, unmarried and fat, living in a small apartment, and he'd just visited his folks, these great feeders of people he could never hope to emulate, and he'd eaten this meal, with potatoes and turkey and flour-based gravy and puddings—a meal that, he tells me, went on all afternoon, until six o'clock. And he was filled with self-disgust. And so he became a diet doctor, the world's most famous diet doctor, and, later, when his parents had retired, he put them on his diet. He put his father on the Atkins diet! And what happened? His father followed the diet, and lived to be eighty-four. His mother, who still lives in Florida at the age of ninety-three, "cheats too much. But she tries."

Atkins says, "Oh, I love working, what I'm doing now. Because the relationship I have with my patients is just like a love affair. They're so grateful. It's very gratifying to see them come back and then say, 'Thank you, Dr. Atkins.' It's really incredible. Before I did this I don't think I knew what it was like to have a patient really thank me. But I mean, the emotion that goes into it. It's very gratifying."

Before I go, I have a question—a delicate question. As a

diet guru, Atkins is, in a sense, a living embodiment of his own work. And yet recently, one morning after breakfast—bacon, sausages and eggs, as people have pointed out, sometimes snidely—his heart stopped. He was rushed to the hospital. He was diagnosed as having had a heart attack.

"So do you feel a pressure to be healthy?"

"Very much so," says Atkins.

"And does this make life . . . difficult?"

"Well, whenever I've come down with something, like I've had a few infections that have threatened my health, it's worried me a great deal, because I had to knock out the infections. Some of them were the kind that aren't easy to knock out. But I managed."

"What sort of infections were these?"

"Oh, micoplasma and chlamydia infections that can get involved and infect the heart."

"And how did you come by these infections?"

"Well, as a doctor, I'm treating an awful lot of sick people, and I presume I've been exposed to these infections just because so many different people come into our office."

"I see."

"Now, I still don't know where the infections come from, but unfortunately I do have a kind of infection that you bring under control but you never really eradicate. So that I always have to be extremely careful to make sure that my resistance to these infections is always great.

"Right."

"I have to take lots of vitamins—E and C and A, vitamins which help knock out infections. I have to take about sixty vitamin pills a day."

"Sixteen?"

"Sixty."

"*Sixty?*"

"Sixty."

We leave the office and walk down the stairs and out on to the sidewalk, and outside dusk has fallen, and Atkins tells me he's looking forward to his dinner, which he says will be "fish and about three or four vegetables, plus a salad." Plus, presumably, ten or fifteen or possibly even twenty vitamin pills. Atkins walks east, toward his apartment, and the last I see of him he is on the sidewalk, walking past the spot where, in forty-five days, he will so controversially lose his footing.

And I'm thinking: it's not me, it's the food. I walk to a restaurant and order a large steak with spinach and no fries, and I go to my hotel and pack my bags and call my parents, and I tell my mother that I think I've found the solution to my father's weight problems, which are worse than mine, and mention the name Atkins, and I mention the Atkins diet, which she's heard of but doesn't know much about. I take a cab to the airport, and I don't buy a bar of chocolate or a bagel or a toasted sandwich at the airport, and on the plane I don't eat a bag of pretzels or a second bag of pretzels, and when the stewardess serves me my dinner, beef and vegetables and potatoes, I eat the beef and vegetables, but not the potatoes, and I don't have the croissant for breakfast, or the toast, and after the plane lands I move along the moving sidewalk feeling lighter and more optimistic than I have in ages, and at the station I walk through the big, crowded concourse, swiftly past the snackpoints and mobile eateries, the bagel kiosks and baguette hatches, and I get home and later I buy some bacon and eggs and tomatoes and broccoli, and for dinner I eat another steak and a tomato salad, and my girlfriend is not sure about the Atkins diet, not sure at all, and I go to sleep feeling less bloated than usual, and when I wake up I feel hungry, but not so desperate as before, not quite so empty, and I go into the kitchen and I don't make myself any toast and my girlfriend is sitting on the sofa, smoking her second cigarette of the day, and I don't say anything about it. That's her affair.

It was the food. The food was the problem. I put some butter in the frying pan, and wait for the butter to melt, and put two rashers of bacon in the pan. Then I put another rasher in the pan. As the bacon sizzles, I take an egg out of the carton, and break the egg on the side of the pan, and slide the egg into the sizzling mixture of butter and bacon fat, and watch the transparent albumen as it gets denser, cloudier, more opaque.

A Creeping Sense of Dread

Over the next few days, I find myself repeatedly standing over my kitchen sink, squirting detergent into my frying pan, running hot water over the cooking surface, watching the waxy deposits of fat melting and dribbling away.

Fat.

I hate fat.

No, I don't. I hate carbs.

I brush the pan clean, using circular motions, and put the pan straight back on the stove. The frying pan is no longer "one of the pans." It's "the pan." I no longer bother, between meals, to hang it up on its old hook alongside the saucepans and the wok.

The first week is fine. In the mornings I have bacon and eggs, or maybe an omelet, and for lunch I have an omelet, and for dinner I have steak and salad, or fish and salad, or maybe an omelet with salad. I get better and better at making omelets. I put three eggs in a bowl, and add some grated cheese, and fry onions and tomatoes, and pour the eggs into the pan, and after a few minutes I put my plate over the pan, and flip the omelet into the plate, and slide the omelet back into the pan, to cook the other side.

I keep discovering new omelets. Omelet with wilted spinach leaves. Omelet with wilted salad vegetables. Omelet with cheese and wilted salad vegetables.

My hunger subsides. After a couple of days, I stop thinking about food all the time. After a week I only think about food a couple of hours a day, at mealtimes. And I must say, not being hungry all the time is a strange feeling, strange and slightly disconcerting. As I get less hungry, I find myself with more time on my hands. One day, after about a week, I'm sitting at home, trying to write something, and I get up to take a snack break. I walk into the kitchen, and it's as if something is amiss—I'm not hungry. Temporarily, I am without a purpose. So I pour myself a glass of water from the tap, and drink half of it, and sit back down again at my desk, suffused with a creeping sense of dread.

Maybe I should have some macadamia nuts. No, I've run out of macadamia nuts.

Maybe I should have some bacon and eggs. But I don't want bacon and eggs. I'm not hungry.

And I realize there's something I miss, more than bread, more than potatoes, more than fluffy white rice or pasta. Don't get me wrong—I do miss these things. I miss the rush of blood sugar I used to get after eating a few slices of toast or a flapjack or a bagel, and I miss the crunch of cornflakes and bran flakes, and I miss twirling a bunch of spaghetti in the tines of my fork, the elasticy feel of undercooked spaghetti, the farinaceous pasty sensation of chewed spaghetti. I miss the crispy outsides of fries and the starchy, comforting gravy sponge of mashed potatoes on my plate in the evening, a hot, bland pile I can lose myself in.

Most of all, though, I miss being hungry.

My Clothes Are Looser

Still, I'm losing weight. I lose about three pounds in the first week and three pounds in the second week, and I definitely feel less puffy, less tight around the face and neck. My clothes are looser. After two weeks, I look in the mirror, and there it is—my jacket no longer hangs like the skin of a snake. It's beginning to hang like a jacket.

And, as the weeks go by, I stop craving carbohydrates. In restaurants, it's easy—I just have a salad instead of the fries, or the mash, or whatever. When I want a snack, I eat macadamia nuts. I keep buying these packs of macadamia nuts, 2.5 ounces, which is slightly too much for a quick snack, but I tend to tear off the corner of the pack and pour them all into my mouth, and they're great, and I love them, and they hardly make me feel sick at all, but sometimes I look at the information on the pack, and it scares me. One hundred grams of macadamia nuts, it says, contain 748 calories. So a pack is 560. And that's just a quick snack!

But then I remember that it's not calories I should be

counting, but carbs. And macadamia nuts are very low in carbs. And I'm losing weight. And my clothes are looser.

My Fat Self

I'm talking to a friend over the phone, somebody I haven't seen for a while and who is overweight, has always been overweight. I mention Atkins, and the overweight friend says that he or she, I have agreed not to identify the person even by gender, is also doing Atkins. So we have an Atkins conversation, and this person is definitely less enthusiastic than me. About a week later, this person calls again, and tells me that he or she has stopped doing Atkins, even though it had been working, even though being overweight had been the biggest problem in his or her life.

"Why have you stopped?"

"I don't know."

"Did it stop working?"

"No, it's not that."

"So why did you stop?"

"I don't know."

Soon after this, I go to see this person, and we have dinner, and I explain my interest in diets, and this person agrees to talk to me about diets, about his or her history of diets.

We talk for hours, and I realize that, even though we've known each other for years, we've never talked about weight or diets, and, toward the end of the evening, we're talking about how magazines are full of thin people, the usual stuff. I remember a feature in a glossy magazine about how fat people dread the summer, particularly going to the beach. This is an article written by a woman, and it's full of pain and despair; in the article the author says the beach is a no-go area for overweight people. The piece is illustrated with a picture of a woman on a balcony, wearing sunglasses, looking mournfully down at the beach. And the woman—get this—is thin. No, she's actually *thin*.

The person I'm talking to, the overweight person, lets out a little yelp, a yelp of actual pain. And we talk about what it's like to be fat, and what it's like to buy clothes when you're fat.

I say, "It's enough to make you want to . . . eat."

"Yes. Right."

And somehow, aware of how hard this will be, I steer the conversation around to the subject of compulsive eating, and this person says that, yes, he or she is a compulsive eater.

"Can I talk to you about it?"

"OK. But I don't want to be identified."

"That's fine."

We talk for a while about compulsive eating. He or she says that he or she compulsively eats only when alone. In the evenings. Pizzas, pasta meals, avocados with mayonnaise, oven fries, tinned shellfish.

"Elton John had a thing for tinned shellfish."

"Yes, well."

"I can't do tinned shellfish myself."

"Oh, when you start you can't stop. A jar of cockles . . ."

"Why did you stop doing Atkins?"

"I don't know."

"Is it because you actually like being hungry?"

"What?"

"Is it because, you know, deep down you sort of actually want to be, you know . . ."

"What?"

"Well, you know."

"No, I don't know. Want to be what?"

"Well, overweight."

"No."

"Susie Orbach says . . ."

"That's stupid."

"Well, when I started doing Atkins, I . . ."

"That's rubbish! And when you write this, I don't want to be identified at all. No identifying details. I don't even want you to say if I'm a man or a woman."

"OK. Fine."

We look across into the corners of the room. There is awkwardness, a depth of embarrassment and shame. I nod my head, trying to look serious.

We catch each other's eye. And for a moment it's like looking at myself. My fat self.

A Thursday Morning in February

It's a Thursday morning in February and I'm drinking a glass of water, something you're supposed to do on a low-carb diet. Atkins, for instance, recommends drinking eight glasses of water a day. And every day, somebody—a news-paper columnist or a nutritionist on the radio or somebody I meet in the street—tells me that I should be drinking more water. One of our big problems is that we're dehydrated—partly, I think, because we are obsessed with consumption, and drinking water doesn't quite feel like consumption. Somebody told me something very interesting about water the other day. I wish I could remember what it was.

Is my memory going? A friend of mine, an Atkins skeptic, told me that cutting out carbohydrates adversely affects the memory. We were sitting in a bar.

I say: "Have you read this?"

"I heard it somewhere."

"So it might not be true."

"Well, I wouldn't take the risk."

"But you're drinking beer."

"So?"

"Well, we know that beer destroys brain cells."

"Yes, but . . ."

"But what?"

"But . . . this is just *beer*."

This morning I had a cup of peppermint tea and some blueberries, which are low in sugar, and a very tart cup of sugar-free cranberry juice. I made that up. Actually I got out of bed and had a talk with my girlfriend and when she went to work I walked down the road to a café and ordered a full English breakfast—two sausages, bacon, a fried egg, and a fried tomato, which felt like quite a lot, almost too much, although I got through it. Soon I will be able to leave food I don't want on my plate.

As I'm sipping my water, which is from the tap, and has a metallic aftertaste, I'm thinking about the talk I had with my girlfriend. She wants to quit smoking, and she's waiting for "the right time." I told her that if she wants to quit smoking, she should quit smoking.

I said: "I stopped eating carbohydrates."

"Smoking is different."

"Not really."

"Oh come *on*."

"Carbohydrates are addictive."

"They are so not!"

"They are! They give you a buzz! They make your blood sugar go up . . ."

"Not this again."

"Well, it's true."

"It's not the same."

My girlfriend took a cigarette from the pack, put it in her mouth, clicked her lighter, sucked on the cigarette, a sharp tug, and sucked on it again, removed it from her mouth, and looked at the end, put the cigarette back in her mouth, and tugged on it again, and removed it from her mouth again, sucked down a ball of smoke, held the smoke in her lungs, tilted her head upward, and blew the smoke out in a narrow stream, a rhythmic procedure, complex, automatic.

"It *is* the same. I was addicted to carbohydrates."

"Look. I've been smoking, apart from twice when I quit, which, added together, is about two weeks—I've smoked every day of my adult life. I don't know what adult life is like without smoking."

"Well, I ate carbs every day of my adult life. And my childhood too. I mean, I probably ate carbs every day of my life after the age of, I mean, even when I was a baby."

My girlfriend sucked on the cigarette again and removed it and inhaled the smoke, and held it and tilted her head and blew it out, a long, steady stream. She said, "Yes, but smoking is connected to my emotions. If I can't smoke I feel all these emotions welling up. And that's why it's so hard to quit."

"Once you've got through the first couple of weeks, you'll be fine."

My girlfriend sucked, removed, inhaled, held, tilted, blew.

She said: "It's not just a physical thing. It's an emotional thing."

And I wondered if addiction to carbohydrates might also be more than just a physical thing. My girlfriend left for work. I tried to imagine what would be a really healthy low-carb breakfast. I could have strawberries, blueberries, raspberries, or rhubarb, as long as these fruits were unsweetened. I could have a salad with cold cuts. I had an idea: I would buy a chicken—a free-range, organic bird—and I'd roast it, and not eat it there and then, but wait for it to go cold, cut it into slices, and keep it in the fridge, and eat it over the next few days. The thought made me feel optimistic, non-compulsive. I had, I realized, never cooked anything, *anything*, and not eaten it on the spot.

And then I walked down the road, sat down in the café, and the waitress came up to my table and said, "Full English breakfast?"

And now I'm sitting on the sofa, sipping my water. After this, I only have seven more glasses of water to drink, and I will have fulfilled my day's quota.

And then I remember the interesting thing about water. People are not drinking more tap water, but they are drinking more bottled water. This might be because, with bottled water, they feel like consumers. That's what this guy was saying. And the interesting thing is this: the higher the price of bottled water, the more people drink.

That's a relief.

My memory is not going.

A Bowl of Fries on My Plate

I keep having to explain to people how a low-carb diet works. I explain about the blood sugar. That's the first thing. How carbs make you hungry. The addiction angle. I tell people to look at the facts—in a society where more than half the adult population is overweight, and where these adults are eating less fat than ever, you have to look elsewhere for a culprit. Sugar, sure. But what are we eating a lot more of? Carbohydrate.

I say, "Look, it's *because* we've spent thirty years trying to avoid fat. And it's because food companies can easily re-move fat, or make things without fat. And when people see that something is '99 percent fat free,' or whatever, they don't mind eating it."

And sometimes people get testy with me. They ask me about eating a low-carb diet, and I explain it, and they say, "But what about bread? Huh? Are you telling me I shouldn't eat bread?"

"I'm not telling you you shouldn't eat anything."

"Yes you are. You're telling me I shouldn't eat bread."

I have a lot of conversations like this. People say to me, "Look, how can it be healthy to eat sausages and bacon all the time? And cheese?" And I tell them I don't eat sausages and bacon all the time, which is sort of true, or at least could be true if I were less lazy. I mean, I could have berries for breakfast, with soya milk, which is really healthy, and a few slices of, say, chicken breast or turkey breast and a salad for lunch, and then fish with green vegetables in the evening.

I'm always making the same point, which is that, conducted properly, a low-carb diet is not about eating more meat, or more fat, or more cheese, or more cream—it's about eating less carbohydrate, for God's sake. It's about taking away something bad. It doesn't have to be about taking away one bad thing and replacing it with another.

But the trouble with the Atkins diet is that, although in the book Atkins goes on at length about fiber and the beauty of eating lots of green vegetables—he once said he ate more vegetables than a vegetarian—in practice, you tend to eat the same old things. Bacon. Eggs. Steak. Cheese. This is because, in your past life as an eater of carbohydrates, you were absolutely spoiled for quick, easy snacks. I mean, when I ate a lot of carbs, making toast seemed like a struggle. I was used to eating on the hoof, just darting into a newsstand or a snack bar, and grabbing a sandwich or a filled bagel. As a low-carb dieter, you are haunted by memories of convenience.

So you do the best you can. I had a kebab the other day. But I didn't eat it in the usual style. Normally, the recipe for a kebab is simple—you just take a quantity of alcohol, and pour it down your throat, and repeat the procedure for a while, and eventually, there you are. The kebab seems to materialize in your hands. You can eat it on the move, because the kebab itself—the slices of reconstituted lamb, the fiery chili sauce, the creamy garlic sauce, the raw onions, the shredded lettuce—all of this is encased in a carapace of pita bread. I was sober when I ordered my kebab—I'm still not drinking—and I sat down at one of the rickety little tables in the kebab place, and ate the kebab on a plate, without the bread.

"Without bread?"

"Yes. That's right."

"Large kebab. Without bread?"

"Uh-huh."

And that's another thing. I keep having to tell waiters to bring the meat, and hold the carbs—to bring the burger and hold the fries, and replace the fries with a salad. This worries me. One day, I realize, the waiter will bring the burger and forget to hold the fries, and they'll be there, on my plate, invitingly presented in one of those little bowls—and I'll have to pick my way through the burger and the salad and stare at the fries; I'll have to stare them out.

When the day comes, I'm sitting in a French-themed café with three other people. I've ordered a steak, and the waiter has fussed over me in the way they do when you order the steak. There has been steak banter, some nodding, some respectful movements of the hand, some approval of my judgment, and the waiter has taken away my silly, blunt, round-ended cake knife, and replaced it with a real knife, jagged and pointy. And the steak arrives, and there is more nodding, the waiter and I looking at the color of the meat, the oozing blood, and everything is all set . . .

And there is a bowl of fries on my plate.

"Could you take these away, please?"

"Hein?"

"The fries. Could you take them away?"

"Of . . . of course."

And then somebody says, "Hang on a minute. I don't mind picking at them."

And that's what he does. He picks. He has about three. A thin guy. He dips them into the dinky little tub of tomato ketchup. He eats one every three or four minutes. He's having mashed potatoes anyway. And I eat the steak, and stare at the fries, just like I used to stare at people's drinks a few months ago, although that phase has passed now. Of course, when it comes to booze, the hardest thing will be starting again. Starting again and not going overboard. Because I don't think you've truly beaten alcohol if you just give it up, like a sissy. No, you must get back on the horse, and not try to kill the horse with your spurs.

And one day, I'll be able to pick at fries again.

Later, I go home and devise the healthiest low-carb meal I can imagine; a kind of low-carb elixir. I fry some onions and garlic in a saucepan, spice it with a teaspoon of turmeric, which aids digestion, some grated ginger and some fennel. Then I add a fistful of turkey mince, two organic zucchinis, a head of broccoli, and a little shredded cabbage, both also organic. Then I make a salad of arugula and tomato. Olive oil. White wine vinegar. A pinch of sea salt. White pepper.

Adventures with Carbohydrates

I'm losing more weight and I'm not drinking alcohol and I'm not snorting coke and I'm not taking painkillers, hardly any painkillers, and I find myself smoking cannabis every so often, and then more than every so often. The painkillers were a problem when I was drinking a lot and eating junk food, both of which increase your levels of pain. I would take ibuprofen, two or three or four at a time, several times a day, and sometimes I would take combinations of ibuprofen and codeine, which made me feel temporarily calmer and steadier, and sometimes I drank a soluble mixture of codeine, paracetemol, and caffeine.

So now, if I've been smoking dope in the evening, I might take a couple of painkillers in the morning. Nothing more. I read a news item somewhere claiming that painkillers, ordinary over-the-counter analgesics, are addictive, that they actually give you headaches. They take away your problem and give you another one. Just like carbs, food that fills you up and makes you hungry again. And just like pornography, cocaine, cigarettes. Addictive products, advertisements for themselves, spreading like viruses in the Darwinian modern marketplace.

I'm preoccupied with painkillers.

This is what I'm thinking on a Sunday in March as I wake up, slightly headachy. I'm thinking about painkillers. I'm thinking that these days, these painful days, painkillers play a different role, a new role. When I was a kid, in the '60s and '70s, the painkillers were kept in a glass bottle in the bathroom medicine cabinet. When you had a headache, you would wait until you got home and then open the dusty bottle and shake out two powdery discs, and you'd swallow them with a glass of water, they'd taste bitter, and you'd put the bottle back in the medicine cabinet, and not open it again for ages. The bottle, which contained fifty pills, would hang around for months, even years.

And these days, when you feel a headache coming on, you pat your pockets or, if you're a woman, check your handbag. The time between pain and treatment has shrunk to almost nothing. These days, painkillers do not come in glass bottles, but in blister-packs in bright, shiny boxes. I'm thinking of the colorful boxes, of the sensation of popping a pill through the foil sealant, of the pill's sugar coating, which makes it taste like an M&M. This is what I'm thinking as I open my eyes and squeeze them shut against the glare.

I'm not at home. My girlfriend and I are staying with friends, another couple, even though we're not getting on particularly well, not getting on well at all. My girlfriend says she still can't find the right moment to give up smoking, and she's smoking a lot. I've never seen anybody smoke so much. We go into restaurants and sometimes the person at the door, the greeter or whatever, says there's no room in the smoking section, but we can have a choice of tables in nonsmoking, and I say yes, that's fine, and my girlfriend says hold on, no, that's not fine. And we have to find another place. And I say can't you go for a little while without, I mean after all this is a meal, we've come here to *eat,* and she says no, she can't—not smoking around mealtimes is one of the hardest things. Particularly after the meal. Like she always lights up when she has a cup of coffee, and when she picks up the telephone. It's linked to all these other activities.

And so at the restaurant we say sorry, we'll look for somewhere else, and we walk off, silent for a while. And she'll say, where do you want to go, and I'll say, no darling where do *you* want to go?

It's ten o'clock by the time we get up, and there are no painkillers at my friend's house—he's anti-pill—and I don't have any breakfast, just a cup of coffee. I'm not a slave to meals anymore. One thing is that I can look back at my former self, the person who sat in Sadie's mother's garden, desperate for carbs, begging for a bit of bread, and I don't blame Sadie or her mother for thinking how awful I was—how fat and weak, how *unattractive*. Now I'm sitting at my friend's sunny kitchen table, drinking coffee, and my friend's wife says do I want toast or anything, and I say no, I think I'll just wait till lunch. Last night we had a roast, with several vegetables and roast potatoes, and I ate everything but the potatoes, and we discussed the fact that I was on a low-carb diet, but I didn't make a big deal of it, and my friend's wife has either forgotten all about it, or she hasn't made the link between toast and carbs—some people don't—or maybe she's just being polite.

And when somebody offers you toast, you don't say, "No, but can I make myself an egg-white omelet?" You don't say, "No, but I wouldn't mind a few slices of last night's chicken." You don't ask for a bowl of berries. You just say you're not hungry. When you're at somebody else's house, and they ask you if you want something to eat, you should only ask for carbs, or something carb-based. It's etiquette. It's engrained, deep in the culture.

So I'm keeping the low-carb thing low-profile. People quite often ask me if I'm doing Atkins, and I say, "No, not really," or, "Well, sort of." The trick is only to use the word "carbs" in certain company. When you say "carbs," you're definitely saying that you think carbohydrates are bad. You draw raised eyebrows, and some people won't let go of the subject until they feel they've discredited you.

Meanwhile, the Fat Crisis gets worse, and whenever politicians or nutritionists talk about it, they say the problem is we're eating too much fat. Sometimes it's too much fat and sugar. And sometimes it's too much fat and sugar and salt. It's like a mantra. Nobody official will mention carbs in public; it's as if they've all signed a pact or something.

The morning slips by and my friend's wife starts preparing lunch, and we go for a walk, something that would have been unthinkable on an empty stomach just a few weeks ago. Sure, I'm beginning to get hungry, but my hunger has a steady, smooth progression, is almost pleasurable. We walk through the woods and breathe the fresh, cold air. I haven't seen my friend for a while and, last night, just as I was getting ready for bed, he caught sight of me in this T-shirt that I haven't worn for years because it was too tight, and now it hangs quite nicely, and he said, my God you've lost weight. And it's true—I've lost about 15 lbs. Some people, I'm told, get all testy when people compliment them on their weight loss; they feel insulted on behalf of their former, fat selves. It's as if somebody is treading on the grave of the fat person they used to be. But I didn't feel bad about the compliment. I felt fine—a good sign.

The weird thing happens when we get back from the walk. My friend's wife has made lunch—and it's risotto. I tell my girlfriend there's no way I'm going to eat it, and she tells me I can't not eat it, and my friend's wife overhears the conversation, the hissing, and says, "Oh, sorry. Of course! I forgot," and I say it's fine, I'll eat the risotto. There's a whole big bowl of it. It tastes like a forbidden pleasure from the past; as soon as I touch the first mouthful I could eat the whole bowl in two minutes. Starchy grains of rice soaking up the flavor of the mushrooms and seafood, covered in gloopy starch paste and when you mill it with your back teeth the grains of rice have these uncooked kernels of pure killer carb. And of course, I have a second helping, it's like drinking wine, one glass leading to another, and I'm hungrier at the end of the meal than I was at the start, and I'm hungry in the car on the way to the station, and I get even hungrier on the train, hungry like I used to be, craving, wretched, unable to concentrate. My saliva is full of amylase, the starch-digesting enzyme, and I can't seem to swallow it all, and my blood is full of insulin, and the insulin has gobbled up all the glucose in my blood, and I'm crashing, crashing.

And when we arrive at the station, I find myself staring at a display of pies, and I know I could eat three or four pies in as many minutes. My blood is raging. The pies look tiny, in the same way that a drink looks tiny to an alcoholic. How do they make them, these miniature pies? I know the pastry would be crunchy on the outside and gummy on the inside, starchy, starchy. But I walk away, and fill the hole with macadamia nuts and cheese, stuff I really shouldn't be bingeing on, and in the evening I have a big fat steak and green vegetables, and I don't drink any alcohol or snort any coke or take any painkillers, and when I wake up the next day I don't feel too bad, not too bad at all.

It Was the Bread and Potatoes All Along

My mother calls me and tells me that my father has lost weight, more weight than he's ever lost before, and she's pleased.

But she's also a bit worried. He's losing weight, but he's

still eating a lot. He bought the Atkins book and read it, cover to cover, and felt he understood the principles behind the book, even went to the library to find more reading material. For years he's had the same breakfast every morning, which he insisted on making himself—a double-decker bacon and egg sandwich, with three thick slices of bread, the middle one fried in the bacon fat from the pan. Sometimes, like on Sundays, he'd add mushrooms to the sandwich.

And now he has everything except for the bread, and possibly a sausage or two, or a slice of black pudding.

And he's lost more than 10 lbs. in less than a month.

My mother says, "Do you think it's safe?"

"Well . . . probably," I say.

"He's eating so much fat. So much meat. So much black pudding."

"But he's not eating bread? Or potatoes?"

"No, he's very strict about that."

I say, "Remember you used to think he was overweight because he ate so much fat?"

"Well, yes."

"And it was the bread and potatoes all along."

Complex Rather Than Simple

I'm beginning to think like a conspiracy nut. I'm in a bar, ranting at a friend of mine who happens to be a diabetic.

"So you see, it's the carbs. The carbs that make us hungry."

"And you're sure about this?"

"Given the facts, any economist could have plotted the graph of today's obesity epidemic. Look, technological advances lowered the cost of refined flour; manufacturers increased the amount of refined flour in food products. Bakers, right . . ."

He looks at me, takes a sip of beer.

"Bakers, yeah, began to put larger amounts of white flour in brown bread. So people got hungrier. And now, as a population, we've hit a tipping point, a sort of insulin watershed, and people's hunger for junk food is out of control."

I take a sip of San Pellegrino. I'm still off the booze, and I'm beginning to sample different types of water, I'm starting to like the weird shapes of the bottles, the labels.

"And no government anywhere can think of a solution. Politicians are stymied. They don't mind telling people to eat less fat or sugar, because the people who produce fat and sugar are used to abuse in the media. They factor it in. But politicians won't say anything against carbs."

"Why?"

"Well, can you imagine? Carbs are the biggest thing in food. Can you imagine the panic? The idea that carbs are bad is not a message anybody wants to hear. And yet carbs are the cause of obesity and, and . . ."

"And what?"

"And, well. And diabetes."

I look at my water bottle, twirl it around in my fingers. My friend says, "I'm confused here. My doctor tells me I should eat carbohydrates. Complex carbohydrates."

I'm ready for this. "Yes, well first of all, what he means is complex rather than simple. Simple carbohydrates, refined stuff like white bread, fries, pastries, certain types of rice, as far as your pancreas is concerned these things might as well be sugar. You should be eating stuff which hasn't been refined, stuff like brown rice. The carbohydrates which have the least effect on your blood sugar. In other words, the carbohydrates which behave least like carbohydrates."

"But . . ."

"It's like a doctor might say, if you're going to drink, have wine rather than whiskey. He's not saying, go ahead and drink as much wine as you like. He's not telling you that alcohol is good for your health *per se*."

"OK-aay."

"So you shouldn't go around saying, 'My doctor told me to drink.' What he told you to do was to go for the least harmful option. In this case, wine."

"So you're telling me that brown rice is sort of the wine of the carbohydrate world?"

"Right. And white bread is the whiskey."

"And doughnuts?"

"Doughnuts are like high-proof vodka. Chocolate is . . . chocolate is absinthe."

"So telling me to eat complex carbohydrates is like saying, if you must drink, stick to wine."

I'm nodding. I'm beginning to rant. I'm sipping at my water, automatic little sips from the bottle, and the water is fizzing at the back of my mouth, bubbling up into my nose, and I'm thinking about the analogy between wine and brown rice, and I'm thinking about wine, what it would be like to drink a glass of wine, just one glass.

I say, "Stick to wine."

"Hi, Fatboy."

It happens on a Saturday evening in March, and I've lost something like 20 lbs. I'm wearing a brown corduroy jacket, blue jeans, brown shoes, a blue shirt, and the jacket is hanging just so, or rather not quite just so, but almost just so. I'm walking differently, picking my feet up, I've lost my apologetic slouch, and my knees hurt less when I go downstairs, soon I'll be able to do normal things, such as run, and I'm standing in a doorway at a party, holding a bottle of San Pellegrino, I wish I could say San Pellegrino 1996 or whatever, but they don't put the year on the bottle, with water the year is immaterial, and someone I know spots me and nods, and that's when it happens.

He says, "Hi, fatboy."

I'm getting somewhere.

Happy

Meanwhile, the world is getting fatter. In her book *The Hungry Gene*, obesity expert Ellen Ruppell Shell explains that people are getting fatter wherever "Western-style commerce" thrives. Fifty percent of people are obese in Brazil, Chile, Colombia, Peru, and Uruguay. In India, overweight and obesity are "endemic" among the fast-Westernizing middle classes. In China, a country that has Westernized faster than anywhere else on the globe, obesity increased "sixfold" in the 1990s.

According to *National Geographic* magazine, "supermarkets stocked with processed food" accounted for 20 percent of Latin American food retail in the 1980s. Now the figure is 80 percent. Snack foods are up 25 percent in Europe in the last five years. In some parts of Africa—Africa for God's sake—obesity rivals malnutrition as a health concern. In America, 41 percent of people who believe they are "underweight" or "about right" are actually overweight. Also, a growing percentage of people who are underweight believe themselves to be overweight. Many of them will develop eating disorders such as anorexia nervosa or bulimia, or cut themselves, or binge on diet pills or cocaine or cigarettes.

Around the world, obesity is concurrent with the increased incidence of these things: TV, mobile phones, cars, multi-storey buildings, computers, pornography, credit-card use, cocaine use, binge drinking, celebrity gossip, images of extremely slender female models, images of male models with six-pack stomachs, media driven by advertising, depression, increased consumption of serotonin-enhancing drugs such as Prozac and Seroxat, increased incidence of self-harm, shopping malls, painkillers in bright, shiny packets, and supermarkets with upward of 20,000 products under the same roof.

But as March progresses, I'm happily losing weight. I'm beginning to refine my diet. The ideal breakfast, for me, is a handful of low-carb macadamia nuts, a slice of turkey breast, and a couple of plums. The ideal lunch: a huge bowl of steamed vegetables. Mid-morning I walk to my local greengrocer and buy cabbages, broccoli, Brussels sprouts. I then steam them, using two sections of the steamer, for four or five minutes. I eat them with butter, a bit of salt, and a lot of white pepper. I binge on the pepper. In the evenings I have fillet steak with three or four tomatoes. I'm slightly obsessive, a little unhinged, but I'm losing weight and I'm not hungry and I keep telling people the same thing, over and over.

"It's not about eating more meat. It's about eating fewer potatoes."

"But don't you get hungry?"

"It was the potatoes that were making me hungry."

"Huh?"

"Look," I say, and then I rant on, trying to find an analogy that will fit. I find myself sitting at a table, at a dinner party, telling people that carbohydrate foods such as white bread and pasta are more dangerous than chocolate, because "everybody knows chocolate's bad. Right? Everybody knows chocolate is about indulging yourself. You know that ad with the lizard? Where the woman is in the bath? And the phone rings, but she doesn't answer the phone, she just gets the bar of chocolate and, you know, slides it into her mouth, and as she's sucking on the chocolate, the phone's still ringing . . ."

"What do you mean, 'the lizard'?"

"There's a lizard. There's a lizard on the wall. It's to tell you she's somewhere hot and, you know, sensual."

"OK."

"Well, you know, she's not answering the phone, and you're supposed to think it's a man calling her, but she'd rather be sucking on the chocolate, because the chocolate . . . it's her, you know, her indulgence."

"Now I remember the lizard."

"OK. The lizard. But see, my point is, right, we all *know* that chocolate is sinful. But then you see ads for really bad white bread, and it's all about, you know, families, health, kids running around in the garden. That's the real problem."

I keep saying the same things. "My point is," and "What I'm trying to tell you is," and "See, that's just where you're wrong," and "I'm not saying Atkins is right about everything," and "But Atkins has really put his finger on something," and "It's not about fat," and "It's about carbs," and "Carbs are the problem."

And people say, "But doesn't Atkins say you shouldn't eat fruit?"

"No! Well, yes he does, sort of, but that's only for the first two weeks of the diet. People are always confusing the *induction* phase, that's the first two weeks, to get you going, you know, to break your addiction . . . with the *maintenance* phase."

"How long is that?"

"The rest of your life."

"So you can't eat fruit for the rest of your . . ."

"*Certain* fruits. And you can eat fruit, anyway. The thing is, to be *aware* that fruits contain sugars, simple carbohydrates, and if you eat too much, you could get a sugar rush, and a crash that makes you feel hungry. So just . . . be aware. Be aware."

"Is that what Atkins says?"

"No. That's what I say."

The world is getting fatter. Unlike the world, I'm getting thinner. Catherine Zeta-Jones is getting thinner. Sophie Dahl is getting thinner. Jennifer Aniston remains steady. Kirstie Alley, on the other hand, is still gaining. Kirstie Alley is keeping pace with the world.

I eat one-third of a cabbage per day. For every cabbage I

eat, a branch of McDonald's opens, somewhere in the world.

Now, 25 percent of household pets are at risk of obesity.

Experts, we are told, believe that the current overweight generation of children is the first who will not outlive their parents.

Cocaine use in Britain is growing. Of 450 men who went to St. Mary's hospital in West London complaining of chest pains, a third tested positive for cocaine. In London, cocaine deaths have "soared" 600 percent since 1997.

One mobile phone user in three is "said to be addicted."

Across the Western world, people, particularly young people, particularly young women, are increasingly engaged in "binge drinking."

Something, something pretty fundamental, is not working. We want more, and then we want even more. We want more, and we want it faster. The plots of soap operas are changing; murder and sexual assault in soaps are growing at the same rate as obesity in the outside world, although not as fast as cocaine-related death. An academic study of pop songs finds that they are no longer about yearning, but about sex; they are cutting to the chase.

Meanwhile, an automatic iron is about to go into production. Sales of robot lawnmowers are increasing exponentially. People are getting more materialistic, more compulsive, lazier. People want quick solutions; the liposuction graph looks like the obesity graph, which looks like the graph describing mobile phone use, which looks like the graph describing the growth of labor-saving devices such as dishwashers.

My mother tells me she can't imagine how she managed before she had a dishwasher.

A new version of the Cabbage Soup diet is published.

One day in late March, I'm walking through the park, and I hear a strange, buzzing sound behind me, and I momentarily freeze, and a fat guy buzzes past me on a kid's scooter. But this guy is not a kid. And the scooter is motorized.

Another day in late March, U.S. and British forces invade Iraq, a country rich in a resource which has enabled us to cut our journey times, to expend fewer calories, to watch more TV.

And although all these things worry me, I'm happy, because I have, I believe, located my central problem. My problem is carbohydrates. I'm a recovering carbohydrate addict. I eat meat, vegetables, eggs, and nuts. I am planning to reintroduce fruit into my diet, and I'm still not drinking alcohol, and I'm happy, I think I'm happy, and I'm losing weight, and of course I'm not entirely happy, because I want . . .

I'm not quite sure what I want.

To lose more weight, I suppose.

Keeping the Faith

Take a slice of Emmenthal or Leerdammer cheese. Place a slice of turkey breast on the cheese. Then cut a beefsteak tomato into fine slices. Place the tomato on the cheese and the turkey. A smear of mayonnaise on the tomato, or, if you like, a couple of drops of olive oil, a drop of vinegar, and a bit of basil. Then put another slice of the Emmenthal or the Leerdammer on top of that, and you have a low-carbohydrate sandwich.

This is what I make myself for lunch on a day in early April, and I'm walking through my apartment, and I pick the sandwich up as I'm walking, and the tomato slice begins to slip out of the sandwich, and I squeeze the edges of the sandwich to halt the slippage, which is my instinct, which is what I'd do with bread, but in this case, my instinct is wrong, and the tomato slice shoots out of the side of my sandwich, slides along the plate, falls to the floor. A big, fat tomato slice, lying on the dirty floor, soaking up dust and carpet fluff.

And I think to myself: you can't really have sandwiches without bread. Just like: you can't really have pies without pastry. When you use cheese instead of bread, you can't control the sandwich in the same way; it's like trying to write with a pencil while wearing gloves.

But maybe, as a low-carb dieter, I shouldn't be sandwich-minded. I feel slightly guilty, like a Communist yearning for personal wealth, or a vegetarian who buys "cheatin' chicken" or soya products tricked up to look like bacon. Anyway, I walk back into the kitchen, put another tomato slice in my sandwich, and I begin to eat the cheese, tomato and turkey combination with a knife and fork, and . . . it's not bad, really not very bad at all.

And when I sit down, I tell myself, that, yes, I have definitely lost weight, and, yes, this weight loss is definitely a good thing. I feel perkier, lighter, less bulky. I fit my clothes better. When I walk along the street, I know I do not compute in people's eyes as "fat man," and this subtly alters my status, it affects me in a million tiny ways, all of which are positive.

And yet . . . can bread be bad? Can pasta be bad? And

rice and potatoes and pastry and couscous? Can I go through life as an unbeliever in these things, these pillars of our culinary society? The answer, I think, is this: too much carbohydrate is bad in a sedentary society. Refined carbohydrate is bad, period. And look at the Italians. They have small platefuls of pasta, a little course before the meat and vegetables. We, on the other hand, have vast mounds of it, and we overcook it, which makes the starch molecules convert to glucose in a shorter time . . .

I sit there, during this brief crisis, recapitulating low-carb science in my head; I'm like a religious convert repeating a mantra or fiddling with a string of beads. I'm thinking that, yes, carbohydrates definitely have an effect on insulin production, which means that they can be classified as addictive. So if you cut them out, you are less hungry. I'm thinking that, yes, addiction specialists, such as Robert Lefever, a doctor who runs a recovery center in west London, have known about carbohydrate addiction for a while; it's accepted in the literature of bingeing. Addiction specialists talk about "trigger foods"— foods that make you want to binge—and addicts nearly always list pizza, bread, toast, sandwiches, bagels, doughnuts, and fries, as well as chocolate and other sugary snacks. They rarely list broccoli, cabbage, or Brussels sprouts. Never lettuce, chicory, raddichio, arugula. Never turkey breast, tomatoes, and thinly sliced cheese.

Eating my sandwich, which is slightly slimy, I begin to calm down. Carbs make you hungry, I'm thinking. Carbs make you hungry. They do. They *do*.

I'm keeping the faith.

But what about the contention that, if you avoid carbohydrates, you can actually eat more food and still lose weight? This appears to be happening to my father. He's eating a lot of bacon, sausage, steak, and black pudding, as well as some green vegetables, but he's losing weight quite dramatically—faster than me, in fact. And he'd never lost weight before, ever.

How can you eat high-calorie food and lose weight? This is the low-carb mystery. It's what Atkins calls the "metabolic advantage." Atkins says, "The metabolic advantage is there. It can't be disguised, evaded, put down to water weight or wished away." It boils down to a simple idea— that the body extracts less energy from a protein calorie, or a fat calorie, than from a carbohydrate calorie. That a greater proportion of the energy derived from fat or protein is burned up in the metabolic processes of the body.

That, in short, not all calories are equal.

Which might be true.

After all, nobody has proved that calories derived from protein have the same metabolic "exchange rate" as calories derived from carbohydrate. To assume they did would be to make a groundless assumption.

So there's nothing to say that Atkins is not right.

Whether he's right or not, I'm thinking, as I eat the last of my slimy sandwich, I'm not so interested in food as I was before; my drive to eat is no longer turbo-charged with low blood sugar. Food is no longer an addiction.

And, therefore, no longer a source of escapism. I don't *want* to binge anymore, at least not on food.

Which is a good thing, right?

I'm sitting on the sofa and I'm not hungry, not hungry for food, and I believe I'm doing the right thing, eating this low-carb diet. It's ten minutes past one, and I started making my lunch at one o'clock precisely, and I'm done, sated, and I wonder what to do with the rest of the lunch break. I'm staring out of the window.

I'm keeping the faith.

A Day in Early April

I'm having lunch with a woman, an old friend, and things are looking up, I'm 205 lbs., waist size 34, and soon I'll be size 32.

Walking toward the restaurant I remember that I have two pairs of jeans in my wardrobe, jeans I bought in 1994 and held on to, hoping I'd be able to wear them again, clinging to them through several moves. The jeans are comforting. This week I tried on a beige three-button jacket in Agnès B, and it didn't look terrible, it did not pull into ugly shapes around the shoulders. I didn't buy it, but still. Beige. I'm pleased with myself. It makes me happy that I have beaten the odds, that I've spent several weeks not giving in, not doing what the nagging voices all around me are telling me to do: consume more, have more, escape reality, buy more stuff, hate yourself.

I also feel pretty pathetic that this is all it takes to make me feel happy. Last week, my hairdresser said the word "carbs." I was startled. She told me she was trying to lose weight, she'd heard about Atkins, and she was looking into this thing about "carbs." That day, waiting in the salon, I saw a picture of Justin Timberlake, stripped to the waist, and he looked great. I also saw an episode of *Friends* in which Joey has a shower, and he's a little chunky, but not bad, and I looked at him and thought: maybe in a month or two. Maybe in a month or two I'll be at that stage.

Lunch starts off well, with fizzy water, and when the waiter comes with the bread basket I wave it away confidently, and the woman I'm with says, "You're not into this low-carbohydrate nonsense, are you?"

"Well, I'm sort of going easy on bread and stuff, yeah."

And she looks at me, and what I see in her eyes is a mixture of confusion and anger, much more than simple disagreement.

"But it's so stupid! It's so faddy!"

"Well, I don't know. What about people who don't eat fat?"

"Well, that's fine. That's been proven. But bread! How can you be against bread? Bread is important. Bread is one of the most important, nourishing things, and it has been for thousands of years, and now! Now some stupid fad diet tells you not to eat it, and everybody's going along with it, oh I don't eat bread these days, oh, I'm low-carb these days . . ."

"But what if, you know, fat is not so bad after all?"

"Oh, come on! How can you fall for that?"

"Well, you went for food-combining in a big way."

"Yes. But there was science behind food-combining."

"And you gave up meat."

"Meat causes cancer."

The waiter appears with the menus. My companion and I look at each other, still sparring. That's when I realize that low-carbohydrate diets are in for a rough ride, a rougher ride than I'd thought. People have an emotional, not to say economic, link to carbohydrates. Any politician who came out against carbohydrates would instantly make himself un-popular. If I was a politician, and I absolutely knew for sure that carbohydrates were the cause of the obesity crisis, I'd keep quiet about it, or at the very most, try to break the news gently. If I was a newspaper editor, depending on ad-vertising revenue from food companies, I'd say nothing. I'd do what everybody else is doing: I'd blame fat and sugar and salt.

I order a steak with green vegetables and a side salad. My companion orders a risotto.

She says, "I mean, what would I tell my children? What would I tell them about sandwiches and baked potatoes and pasta and rice? All these healthy things? What would other people think of them at school? What would I put in their lunch boxes?"

After a while, we change the subject. Later that after-noon, a woman from the obituaries desk at the *Guardian* calls me.

"Would you write an obituary of Dr. Atkins?"

"Is he dead?"

"No, no. We just like to get things done in advance."

"Oh, I see. Yes, of course."

"Well, he has had a fall."

"A fall?"

"He's in hospital. Probably under observation. But could you do it by tomorrow? Just, you know, in case?"

At 9:15 A.M. New York time, just about when I was or-dering my steak, Atkins lost his footing in the street.

One school of thought, dominated by those who believe the obesity crisis is the result of eating too much fat, will suggest that Atkins fell because his heart failed.

Those who believe that the obesity crisis is the result of eating too much carbohydrate, on the other hand, will say that Atkins fell because the weather had been unseasonably cold, because he stepped on a patch of ice, and slipped—those spiffy tasseled loafers with thin leather soles!—and cracked his head on the sidewalk.

Addressing a group of firefighters, New York's mayor, Michael Bloomberg, will say, "I can't believe that bull that he dropped dead after slipping on the sidewalk. Yeah, right."

Bloomberg will cast a mischievous glance upward, and continue, "The guy was fat. Yeah. He was a big guy, but heavy." Bloomberg had met Atkins at a reception hosted by the doctor at his house in the Hamptons.

"And the food was inedible. I took my appetizer and had to spit it out in a napkin."

Denial

In his groundbreaking book *The Structure of Scientific Revolutions,* published in 1962, the Harvard physicist Thomas Kuhn explained that science—the study of the natural world through observation and experiment—does not move in a straight line. Science, in Kuhn's words, "does not develop by the accumulation of individual discoveries and inventions." Instead, scientific disciplines move forward in a jerky manner, punctuated by revolutions. For a while, scientists believe one thing, and then someone comes along and demonstrates that everything they thought was wrong, and they have to tear up their calculations and start again.

This is known as the "paradigm theory." Kuhn describes a paradigm as "an accepted model or theory." For instance, at one time everybody believed that the earth was flat. That was a paradigm. At another time, everybody believed that the sun revolved around the earth. That was another paradigm. In the nineteenth century, scientists believed that God had created the world, the planets, and the stars. Another paradigm. Of course, Galileo caused a revolution in astronomy, with the eventual result that everybody came to believe that the earth revolved around the sun. And Darwin, with his theory of natural selection, caused the scientific world to doubt the existence of God.

One of the most important things about scientific revolutions, though, is how scientists react to them. Basically, they hate them. Well, wouldn't you? As Kuhn says, most scientists spend their lives engaged in what he calls "normal science"—conducting experiments to prove the existence of the paradigm. Mostly, scientists behave like those old-time clerical philosophers who spent their lives trying to prove the existence of God. Remember Bishop Berkeley? The trees existed because God existed. God existed because the trees existed.

Normal science, says Kuhn, is "an attempt to force nature into the preformed and relatively inflexible box that the paradigm supplies."

A paradigm, then, is more than just a scientific model— it becomes a focus for shared beliefs, a social club, a political stance, a bonding tool, a springboard for economic interests. It's a boat that doesn't like being rocked. And when somebody rocks the boat, what happens? At first, they are ignored. Next, they are contradicted. Defensive research is produced to discredit their position. Often, like Darwin, they are vilified or smeared. Sometimes, like Galileo, they are thrown into jail. And this, of course, is completely understandable. How would you like it if you spent your life believing in a scientific theory, had written books and academic papers and conducted research and received grants and delivered lectures in its service, and then someone came along and started to make people doubt you?

You'd hate him. You'd say he was dishonest and stupid and wrong. You'd call him a con man and a huckster. At the very least, you'd make the point that your rival was less experienced, less eminent, than you were. This is what happened to Crick and Watson, the Cambridge researchers who discovered the double helix, a breakthrough in genetics that eventually led to the mapping of the human genome. And actually, the people who pointed out their lack of eminence were right, as they usually are in these circumstances. "Almost always," says Kuhn, "the men who achieve these fundamental inventions of a new paradigm are either very young or very new to the field whose paradigm they change."

The history of science is littered with revolutions. And also with denial. Sometimes, and of course much more than we can ever know, the establishment is successful in its attempts to stifle revolutionary thought. As Max Planck, the founder of quantum theory, said in his *Scientific Autobiography,* "A new scientific truth does not triumph by convincing its opponents and making them see the light, but rather because its opponents eventually die."

This is what I'm thinking as Atkins lies in a coma in a

hospital in New York. I'm thinking about death, about paradigms, about scientific revolutions. Is low-carb a scientific revolution? For thirty years, the nutritional establishment has had the same paradigm—fat is bad, carbs are good. Cut down on fat. Eat a balanced diet. Watch your intake of sugar and salt. A healthy diet is a low-fat diet. We're fat because we eat too much fat and sugar. Cut down on sweets. When you buy food, check the labels for fat content. That's the paradigm. And we've had thirty years of normal science to back it up. During those thirty years, vast economic interests have clustered around the paradigm, too—supermarkets and farmers and bakers and producers of breakfast cereal. Naturally, the political establishment has fallen into line, making sure the boat is steady, protecting people's jobs, enhancing revenue, collecting taxes. And the media, whose job is to sell readers and viewers to advertisers—they are believers, too.

And Atkins came along and rocked the boat. In the 1960s, when he started his low-carb diet, he fitted Kuhn's model perfectly. He was in his early thirties. He was a cardiologist, rather than a nutritionist. He hadn't discovered his low-carb diet—he'd read about it in a medical journal and tried it on himself. He was an outsider. He was not eminent. He had nothing to lose.

In the obituary, I say that, just over a year ago, Atkins suffered a heart attack, "but, as he pointed out, this was caused by an infection and had nothing to do with the Atkins diet," even though I do not know this for sure. I quote him from one of his last appearances on *Larry King Live,* on which he said, "Carbohydrate is the bad guy."

When Atkins dies, on April 17, having been in a coma for

just over a week, my obituary, like many articles on Atkins, is illustrated with a picture of the doctor looming over a huge chunk of meat, holding carving tools in the air, posing, grinning.

My first thought is: no! The Atkins diet is not about eating huge amounts of meat! It's about avoiding carbohydrate!

And I think about Thomas Kuhn, about the paradigm theory, about denial. Was Thomas Kuhn, the expert seeker of denial, himself in denial? Because the paradigm theory is, of course, itself a paradigm. And when you base your scientific or intellectual world on a paradigm, you do not see it as a paradigm—you see it as the truth. As Kuhn says, "What a man sees depends both upon what he looks at and also upon what his previous visual-conceptual experience has taught him to see."

Well, my visual-conceptual experience has taught me to see that I've lost weight. And I believe that carbohydrates were my problem. If you asked me, that's what I'd tell you right now. It was simple. Carbs were my problem.

And I don't see that as a paradigm. I see it as the truth.

A Simple Mistake

When I quit alcohol, on New Year's Day, it was easy. It didn't even take any willpower. I drank a lot on New Year's Eve, of course, and woke up the next day, as usual, feeling fuzzy and nauseated, and the day after that I felt fuzzy and nauseated, too. For a few weeks, having drunk nothing in the evening, I would wake up, and my first thought would be, "Jesus! How much did I put away last night?" and I'd get out of bed, my head throbbing, and then I'd go into the bathroom, and look at myself in the mirror, and only then would it hit me: I hadn't drunk any alcohol at all. And then, after about five minutes, my head would clear, and I'd feel strangely hollow and shaky. Being hungover every morning, of course, had been awful. But waking up without a hangover was no picnic, either.

This was something I had not factored in. Walking along the street, with a clear head, you find yourself assailed by all kinds of unfamiliar emotions. To remove hangovers from your life is to open a door somewhere in the deep recesses of your mind. As you go about your daily business, you have no idea what might come through that door. Like a teenager, you feel sudden bolts of joy, and dark waves of creeping confusion and terror. This is a very vulnerable state; sometimes you feel like a released prisoner yearning for the comfort of his cell. Like a fat person who, having lost weight, feels naked.

Early spring has turned into late spring, and I'm still losing weight. I'm not eating carbs, I'm not drinking alcohol. Incidentally, I'm not getting on especially well with my girlfriend. Giving up alcohol was easy, although it made me binge on carbs. Giving up carbs was just as easy. I don't think I'll go back to bingeing on carbs again—or any food, for that matter. But I never intended to give up alcohol forever. What I wanted, what I always wanted, was a sensible relationship with alcohol. I wanted to have a couple of drinks, every now and again. And, yes, to get drunk once in a while. But I didn't want to be smashed out of my head every night, and I didn't want to feel fuzzy and nauseated every day.

The funny thing is that I miss the hangovers more than I miss being smashed.

One morning I'm walking past a French wine shop, and the guy who runs the place walks into the doorway and waves at me, and we exchange greetings, tradesman to former customer, and I walk on, and the thought occurs to me again, yet again, that you haven't truly beaten alcohol if you just give it up. That's the easy option. And that's the moment I know that, sometime in the near future, I will visit the French wine shop again, and say hello to the guy again, and buy a bottle of wine, and try to have a sensible relationship with it.

My girlfriend's away somewhere, and I go home and try to do some work. I can't settle. I look out the window, and get up from my desk, it's the middle of the afternoon now, and I put on my jacket and ten minutes later I'm back at home, with a bottle of wine, with which I believe I can have a sensible relationship.

I'll open it at seven o'clock.

I'll open it at six-thirty.

Six o'clock.

I have a very clear memory, from the time when I drank a lot, of an evening, six or seven years ago, when I had arranged to meet some friends and go to see a play. At the time, my habit was to start drinking at lunchtime, have a couple of vodkas and some wine with my lunch, and maybe a brandy or two afterward, and then stop drinking and work through the afternoon, getting progressively sober, and then start drinking again in the early evening. On this particular day, I arrived at the theater bar at seven o'clock, feeling bleary, inflamed, toxic, and slightly feverish—not too bad, in other words. I sat down, ordered a drink.

"Oh," I said, to one of the people I had arranged to meet, a woman who had just arrived, "would you like a drink?"

"Ooh, thanks. I'm dying for a glass of wine."

I ordered the wine.

She said, "I just love that first glass of wine in the evening. Don't you?"

And I thought, my *God,* no, absolutely not, I *hate* the first glass of wine in the evening. Right now, my hangover's just kicking in, and the wine I'm about to drink will be a grim, painful experience. It will taste thinly acidic, and I'll have to force it down, and it will affect me like a mild sleeping pill and a bash on the head. No, the first glass of wine in the evening is my enemy, because it stands between me and my friends, the fourth and fifth glasses of wine, the cocktails, the shooters and shorts I will consume in the early hours.

I said, "Yes, the first glass of wine." I laughed, shook my head slowly. "The first glass of wine."

And then the wine arrived, and I paid for it, and I watched the woman take a sip, and then a gulp, and I had an inkling of what it might be like to have a healthy relationship with alcohol.

And now I'm looking at a bottle of wine, and the evening is approaching, and I fully intend to enjoy a glass or two of wine, just like the woman in the bar. I'm confident that I'm going to pull this off, to have this healthy relationship. I'm absolutely determined. Nothing will stop me.

Of course, just about everybody who has ever written about having a drinking problem, or talked in public about it, has said that the best solution, the only solution, is to stop drinking altogether and never go back to it. I once interviewed Billy Connolly, a former alcoholic, or probably recovering alcoholic is how he would rather define it, and he said he believed that if, as an alcoholic, you quit drinking, and then start again a few years later, you do not pick up where you left off, in terms of addiction, but *where you would have been* if you hadn't stopped. I'm not sure I agree with that, but I've heard other people say it, too.

Former alcoholics—they're always warning you off. In her book *Drinking: A Love Story*, the late Caroline Knapp wrote, "Liquor creates delusion . . . A single drink can make you feel unstoppable, masterful, capable of solving problems that overwhelmed you just five minutes before. In fact, the opposite is true: drinking brings your life to a standstill, makes it static as rock over time." Knapp quit drinking because she changed her mind about one thing in particular. She had spent her adult life, she wrote, believing that she drank because she was unhappy. And then she thought, *"Maybe, just maybe, I'm unhappy because I drink."*

But isn't there a third possibility—a third way? What if Knapp drank because she was unhappy, and became even unhappier when she drank? And what if she had looked deeply into herself, and sorted out why she was unhappy in the first place, and become happy? What would happen if she drank when she was happy? She once wrote that her mother, worried about her drinking, had taken her for a walk on the beach, and said, "This is very serious. It's more serious than smoking." In the end, her mother might have been wrong; Knapp quit drinking, but died of lung cancer in 2002, at the age of forty-three.

Yes, they always say the same thing. Get off it, and stay off it. In his memoir *A Million Little Pieces,* James Frey, a former alcoholic and crack addict, describes what happened to him after he drank and took drugs for the last time. He woke up on a plane, with absolutely no idea how he had got there. "I look at my clothes," he tells us, "and my clothes are covered with a colorful mixture of spit, snot, urine, vomit, and blood." In the book, Frey is being taken by his parents to a rehab center. After his parents leave, he tells us, "I am lost. I am completely fucking lost." His response:

"I scream.

I piss on myself.

I shit my pants."

When he leaves rehab, Frey walks into a bar and orders a whiskey. But he doesn't want to drink it. He wants to stare it out. In a passage that reads like the script of a gunfight, Frey describes the struggle between the part of himself that wants the whiskey, and the part that absolutely does not want the whiskey.

"I stare at the glass. The Fury rises from its silent state it screams bloody fucking murder it is stronger than it has ever been before. It screams you are mine, motherfucker. You are mine and you will always be mine. I own you, I control you and you will do what I tell you to do. You are mine and you will always be mine. You are mine, mother-fucker. I stare at the glass."

Frey doesn't drink the whiskey. And he makes an inter-esting point—the problem is not the whiskey. It's himself.

And my problem was not drink, is not drink. It was overeating, caused by hyperinsulinism due to the overeating of carbohydrates. Which made me fat. Which made me unhappy. Which sucked me into a fat, unhappy mind-set, which meant that, when I drank, I drank too much.

I walk into the kitchen and open the kitchen drawer with its knives and forks and spoons, all messed up in their tray, no particular order, the knives with the forks, forks with spoons, which, I'm sure, says something about my attitude to food, and I pick up the corkscrew, my old "waiter's friend," which I used to think was the best corkscrew design in the world, it's roughly the shape of a wrench, with fold-out tools for prying and penetrating and levering, and an ingenious pull-out mechanism for slicing the thick foil or sharp plastic at the top of the bottle. Just *holding* the corkscrew makes me feel heady and weak.

Is this what Caroline Knapp referred to as "the dark fear" experienced by the drinker the moment before drinking?

Possibly.

And I remove the cork, and pour myself a glass of wine, and take a sip, and sixteen hours later I wake up, in my own bed, alone, feeling fuzzy and nauseated, and a flock of images—streetlights and taxis and bars, assignations made on my mobile phone, more bars, a kebab shop, friends and strangers in my flat who stayed until God knows when—these images are all rattling on a door deep inside my brain. But I feel terrible, laden down with heavy pain, and I *will not* open the door. I move my head, trying to get more comfortable, but then I learn that it is better not to move at all.

It was a simple mistake, a mistake anybody could make. I know I've made it many times before. And I'll clear up all the mess and drug paraphernalia later on. I can't face anything right now.

Luckily, though, I don't have any obligations to do anything. I have a hangover to deal with.

Broken Heart

"Do you mind if I smoke?"

"No. Not at all."

Stretching out on his bed in a London hotel room, James Frey says, "I feel great. I don't really smoke. I don't smoke when I'm at home because it drives my wife crazy, but I'm smoking now because I'm stressed out. But I feel great. My body's in pretty good shape. Luckily, the liver is the only organ in the body that regenerates itself, and that's where the most profound damage was. So I feel great. I'm in great shape."

We are talking about addiction. Frey was addicted to crack and to alcohol. Crack, he says, is like "powder cocaine," but it's "a much dirtier high. Have you ever sniffed glue?"

"Well . . . when I was at school we used to sniff solvents."

"Smoking crack is like a combination of snorting the strongest powder cocaine you could ever have, and sniffing glue at the same time. One way I've described glue—it's like that Pink Floyd song."

Frey begins to hum "The Great Gig in the Sky."

"OK."

"The first couple times you smoke crack, when you take the hit, you have this moment of . . . *perfection*. Perfect confidence. Perfect understanding. Perfect orgasm. Perfect pleasure. So you're always chasing that initial moment, and it diminishes over time."

Of crack, Frey says, "It's still the only thing I can't be around comfortably. It still freaks me out to this day. There are weird triggers for it. Like, the last time I had an urge for it, I was sitting in a bar waiting to meet somebody. I had a pack of cigarettes, but I didn't have any matches. So I asked the bartender if he had a light. He pulled out a lighter, and it was a butane lighter. Flip, click—just the hiss of the lighter ignited just this *fucking crazy urge*. Because that hiss is something I very much associate with smoking. Every time I hear a butane lighter, it's immediately what I think of. I don't always have the urge, but at that time . . . you know, I didn't feel very good, I was emotionally not very happy at that moment, and the combination of not feeling good, and the sound of that hiss, and the association of those two things with crack—knowing what that does, knowing how it could make it all go away, makes me want it. I think: oh, wouldn't that be great!"

"Say people were to capture you and tie you up and put a gun to your head and make you smoke crack. What would happen? Would you be addicted again?"

"I would definitely have to go through the process again, yes. I don't believe that I could ever use anything again, recreationally or in any way whatsoever."

Frey believes that, "The source of addiction is emotion. And I think over a long period of time, I have associated, internally, certain emotions and certain feelings with the use of chemicals."

He grew up in a stable, wealthy background. His father was a lawyer who spent a lot of time abroad. As a child, he suffered from what he calls "infant ear infection," which went untreated, and, he thinks, might be the source of his troubles.

But he hates the idea of blaming his parents. "For me," he says, "it was very important to accept the blame. To take full responsibility. If I went back to using, it wouldn't be because I had infant ear infection. It wouldn't be because my parents couldn't get me to the right doctor. It wouldn't be any of those things. It would be because I, in an immediate moment, made a decision to reach for something, pick it up, bring it toward me, tip it . . . and swallow it. That's a process of decision making that I am responsible for."

"And you'd never consider drinking again?"

"It's no issue at all. I know what the repercussions would be if I started drinking again, and it's not something I wanna do."

"Like, if you stepped out into traffic, you'd get hurt. And so . . . you just don't. So why do it, unless you want to get hurt?"

Frey says, "Right. That's a great analogy."

He started drinking when he was ten. "My parents were very sociable. I always watched people drink. There was alcohol everywhere. I noticed that when people drank, they changed. People who were in a bad mood, if they drank, they were in a good mood. Everyone seemed to be having a great time while they were drinking. And neither of my parents had a drinking problem. They were recreational drinkers. I can't remember any time in my life when I've seen my father or my mother drunk. I've never seen either of them slurring their words or stumbling—any of that. Anyway, I was fascinated from a young age with alcohol. So one night, when my parents were out, the babysitter fell asleep, and I went to the drinks cupboard and took a big sip of vodka. It was awful. But a couple of minutes later I noticed it made all that shit that I felt go away. All the anger. All the rage. All the confusion."

So Frey started drinking more and more heavily, and then moved on to drugs. Oblivion, he says, was always his goal.

"Have you ever drunk for enjoyment?"

"No. My goal was always to get fucked up. I don't know the pleasure of a nice glass of wine. Or a beer on a hot afternoon. That was never anything I understood. I understood that I used things to get fucked up. To achieve oblivion. To achieve a state of no emotion. And when I think about drinking, even now, it's always when I'm in a heightened state of emotion—either very angry about something, or very upset about something. And I don't think about having a drink. I think about having a lot of drinks. I think about having enough to drink so I don't have to feel what I'm feeling at the moment."

"And so . . . how do you deal with everything? The drinking, the not drinking?"

Frey stops to think for a moment. He lights another cigarette. He says, "Have you ever had a broken heart?"

"What?"

"Have you ever had a broken heart?"

"Millions of times. Well, you know. A lot of times. Well . . . we all have, haven't we?"

"Do you know what it feels like?"

"Well . . . yes."

"You can draw on that if you so desire?"

"I suppose . . ."

"But do you carry it around with you? Does it affect your every waking moment?"

"Um . . ."

"In this immediate moment? Right now?"

"Not . . . really."

"And that's how the rage lives within me now. It's something I know very intimately. It's something that is a part of me. It's something that I have experienced and remember."

"Right."

"But it isn't something that affects how I live every day."

Appenzell

I can have avocados, and steaks, and chicken, every kind of meat, every kind of fish, particularly oily fish, which, as nutritionists are beginning to say, contain fats that are good for the heart, now that's not something you thought you'd be hearing, fats that are good for the heart, and I can have tomatoes, zucchinis, asparagus, garlic, cottage cheese, all kinds of cheese in fact, although I don't like the idea of going overboard on the cheese, "the corpse of milk," I remember somebody calling it, and I also remember getting very animated and anti-cheese at one point, this is when I was with a girl who was vegan, or who was considering taking the step from vegetarian to vegan, and I remember saying, "You just have to look at it, don't you? You just have to look at it to realize it can't be doing you any good."

But I have cheese every couple of days. I like cheese, I like the taste, although I can't help feeling that cheese is sinister in a way that, say, bread isn't. I didn't like cheese when

I was a kid, when sweet things were my goal, and savory things, in contrast, were burdens to be borne—my first experience of food was suffering the ham, the eggs, the cheese, with the apple pie or chocolate mousse or whatever as a reward afterward. As people get older, they want increasingly disgusting things—anchovies, rare steak, inhaled smoke, oyster sauce, whiskey, powder that stings the nasal membranes.

I'm sitting in my apartment. My girlfriend has left me. Emotionally, I am numb. Of course, I knew the relationship was not working out. But perhaps I wanted to be trapped for a bit longer. Now I am free. Now I can do what I like. We were in a restaurant when it happened. We had ordered food—I'd ordered lamb shank with cabbage and something else, and she'd ordered some mess of carbs with bits of stuff in it, spaghetti with tomato sauce probably, something crowd-pleasing and unhealthy anyway, and the exact sequence went something like this: she lit a cigarette, the woman at the next table complained, loudly and rudely, tears sprang to my girlfriend's eyes, she slid her hand across the table, reaching for mine, my mobile phone rang, and I picked up my mobile instead of her hand.

That was the start.

And now she's gone, this was yesterday, and I'm sitting here alone, and I feel a powerful urge to leave the premises and go somewhere and flirt with, and possibly kiss, and possibly have sex with, women. Maybe it's just like Billy Connolly says—these urges continue to grow inside you, even during the abstinent period. It's the excitement of going out, the challenge of catching someone's eye, the first touch of hands, the first suggestive thing one of you says to the other. The sex itself I can take or leave. Waking up in the morning afterward? No thanks. And then the guilt, the feelings of emptiness and hollowness, the worries about what you've caught, what you've passed on. I think about this, but I manage only to think about it for a moment, a second, and then it's gone.

I've been to the deli a lot recently, sampling all sorts of cheeses. Today I tried Jarlsberg, and Gruyère, and Appenzell, which is creamy and slightly foul or mildly rotten at the same time, seductive and punitive, and therefore rather addictive, and my mother called and said, "Oh, Appenzell, we had that when we lived in Germany, and you liked it, I think," and I remember seeing photographs of us, myself at ten and my brother six, in Appenzell, by the Rhine waterfall, but I can't remember the cheese. I think they must have had the cheese on another occasion, probably after I had flown back to England to go to boarding school.

And I can have tomatoes and raspberries and blueberries, and tuna stir-fry. My girlfriend, or rather my ex-girlfriend, liked to stir-fry. She would chop vegetables, peppers and zucchinis and eggplant, I remember, and broccoli, and fry these things with chunks of chicken, not organic, and therefore worryingly battery, possibly full of injected hormones and fed on ground-up bits of animal protein, and suggestive anyway of bad karma, and she would sprinkle soy sauce on top, and have it with rice.

I of course have it without rice, and with chicken that is organic and free range. I can have cauliflower, mushrooms, onions, and vodka, as long as I drink the vodka with a sugar-free mixer.

Girls

And over the next few days, the next few weeks, I meet girls, and I talk to them, hold their hands, kiss them, whatever, and the worst of it is that one day I'm walking along the street with a woman I've slept with, and will sleep with again later on, and I look up at a poster of another woman in her underwear, and I can't stop looking at it, I can't stop looking at it, the woman is holding herself in a certain way I find very appealing, and the woman I'm with notices and I make a joke about it, but I'm not sure, in the end, if the joke is good enough.

Revenge of the Killer Carbs

Research published in the *New England Journal of Medicine* appears to demonstrate that people on the Atkins diet lose more weight than people on low-fat or low-calorie diets. In one study, conducted by the University of Pennsylvania's Weight and Eating Disorders Program, sixty-three middle-aged people were divided into two groups—an Atkins group and a low-calorie group. After twelve weeks, the Atkins group had lost an average of 14.5 pounds; the low-calorie group, on the other hand, had lost an average of 5.75 pounds. In the second study, conducted by the Philadelphia Veterans Administration Center, 132 obese men and women were divided into two groups—again, an Atkins group and a low-fat group. The low-carb group lost around twice as much weight.

Time magazine, a significant cultural beacon, reports

something equally important: "What was perhaps more interesting—even baffling—was that the group on the Atkins low-carb diet showed lower levels of the blood lipids that contribute to arterial disease."

Time magazine also says, "Of course, the mere suggestion that the Atkins diet and others like it are worthy of scientific attention still makes many experts bristle. Yet it is also clear that the low-fat paradigm has developed some cracks in its façade."

Yet more research, published in *Metabolic Syndrome and Related Disorders,* a journal devoted to the bodily process of metabolizing food, seems to solve an important Atkins riddle: Why do people lose more weight on a low-carb diet than on a low-fat diet *even when they consume the same number of calories?* For Atkins, this "metabolic advantage" was the holy grail. For a while, the scientific community has begun to grudgingly accept Atkins' other main claim, that carbs make you hungry. OK, they say, some carbs, maybe refined carbs, might make you hungry. OK, they say, the Atkins diet might work, therefore, because when you feel less hungry, you eat less. So really, they say, the Atkins diet is a low-calorie diet of sorts. Which means that actually, they, the advocates of low-calorie diets, were right all along.

The paradigm is cracked, but remains in place.

But here, in *Metabolic Syndrome and Related Disorders,* in an article by Dr. Richard Feinman, a biochemist from the State University of New York, and Dr. Eugene Fine, a clinician from the Jacobi Medical Center in New York, is something radical. In the article entitled "Thermodynamics and Metabolic Advantage of Weight Loss Diets," Feinman and Fine explain why the theory of Metabolic Advantage has not been refuted, "but rather largely ignored." It's been ig-nored, they say, because it apparently refutes the laws of thermodynamics, which state that energy generated by one type of calorie must be the same as energy generated by any other type of calorie.

"In this review," say Feinman and Fine, "we show that there is no such violation of thermodynamic laws." Of course! It's so simple! Protein calories and carb calories ar-rive as energy in the body via different pathways! And the protein pathway is longer and more complex. The body, therefore, needs to expend more energy in the process of metabolizing a calorie of steak than it needs to metabolize a calorie of bread. Carbohydrate, as one doctor puts it, is like local currency: you get a big bang for your buck. Protein, on the other hand, is like foreign currency. An exchange rate applies. When you change foreign currency, you leave a lit-tle bit behind at the bureau de change. Fineman and Fine conclude by saying, "There is no theoretical contradiction in metabolic advantage and no theoretical barrier to accept-ing reports describing this effect."

Now, the paradigm is toppling.

Slowly at first, but with deadly inevitability, the Atkins backlash, like some complex piece of machinery, comes into being. Politicians and the media—loyal, as always, to the manufacturers of products that make the most money—come out against Atkins. We read in newspapers that Atkins dieters suffer from constipation, bad breath, narrowing of the arteries. Those that have done Atkins, and suffered set-backs, are given a sympathetic hearing, even if the setbacks cannot be scientifically attributed to the diet. Meanwhile, corporate giant Unilever, the owner of Slim-Fast diets, reports a 4 percent decline in sales for the first quarter of 2003. Slim-Fast products, which are based on radically cutting fat, are staying on the shelves; Chairman Niall Fitzgerald admits the slowdown is due to the popularity of the Atkins diet. A company spokesman explains that Unilever had "taken its eye off the market."

Susan Jebb, head of nutrition and health research at the Medical Research Council, damns the Atkins diet, claiming that a diet high in fat and protein, and low in carbohydrates, is a "major health risk," and based on "pseudoscience." Later, it emerges that Jebb accepted a £20,000 grant, on behalf of the MRC, from the Flour Advisory Bureau, the lobbying arm of the National Association of British and Irish Millers.

In America, nutritionists accuse government health officials of issuing "groundless" warnings against the Atkins diet. Official guidelines drawn up by the Department of Agriculture recommend six to eleven servings of carbohydrates in school and hospital diets, with one serving equivalent to a slice of bread. Senator Peter Fitzgerald says that, "Putting the Department of Agriculture in charge of dietary guidelines is like putting the fox in charge of the henhouse." Harvard Professor Walter Willett adds, "Looking at some of the recommendations from the Department of Agriculture gives the idea that they've forgotten that we are feeding people, not horses."

In Britain, as the weather heats up, Dr. Sarah Schenker, a dietician working at the British Nutrition Foundation, warns that the Atkins diet may be harmful in hot weather. "The body has to work harder to metabolize protein than other food types," she says. "This means that on a really hot day, people on the protein-based diet who are facing, say, the Underground could have problems. My advice would be to avoid the Atkins diet in hot weather."

A cartoon in the *Daily Telegraph* depicts a brace of grouse hiding from a man with a shotgun. One of the birds is saying, "I have some very bad news—we're recommended as part of the Atkins diet."

William Bush, an Atkins dieter from Rockford, Illinois, is rushed to the hospital with chest pains. He blames the Atkins diet. The *Sunday Times* points out that Bush had never dieted before. "It's dangerous," says Bush. "I really took to it in a big way. It was like, 'Oh, man, steak and eggs at every meal.' "

Audrey Eyton, the author of *The F-Plan Diet*, says, "The Dr. Atkins diet achieves weight loss because it reduces total calorie intake and much of his own explanation for why it works is total hogwash."

In the *Daily Telegraph,* the Atkins diet is described as "the cream, steak, and mayonnaise regime."

A spokesman for Slimming World, a low-fat diet enterprise, says, "We would be concerned about any diet that excludes or limits essential food groups such as carbohydrates, fruits and vegetables."

Real Story, a television documentary series, follows the progress of three Atkins dieters. A worry about the diet, the narrator tells us, is that it makes you burn lean muscle tissue. This is not true. One of the dieters is Dr. Maurice Gleeson, who does Atkins, but also boozes pretty heavily and eats large amounts of chocolate biscuits. Later, he is rushed to the hospital with a blocked bowel. Has the Atkins backlash found its sacrificial victim, its Leah Betts? Not quite.

Gleeson survives. When Atkins spokesperson Colette Heimowitz points out that he was not actually doing Atkins, was not following the program, the *Daily Mail* publishes an article under the headline "Cheating on the Atkins can damage your health."

The media message is becoming crystallized. Atkins works, but might be dangerous. Atkins works, but there is a price to pay. Atkins works, but is unnatural. "Welcome to the weird world of the Atkins diet," says the narrator on the BBC's *Horizon*, "a world where fat food makes you thin." Brian, an Atkins dieter, is described as "sticking to food high in protein and fat." Green vegetables are barely mentioned. The First Law of Thermodynamics, we are told, "underpins the cosmos," and is the "foundation stone of chemistry and physics." How could Atkins have the temerity to defy it? After all, a university professor points out, there is no such thing as perpetual motion. In which case, how can the Atkins diet possibly work?

Interviewed on television, Susan Jebb tells us that there is no long-term evidence of the effects of low-carbohydrate, high-protein diets, failing to mention the fact that the human race lived on a low-carbohydrate diet for most of its history.

But people are listening to the backlash. The tide appears to be turning against Atkins. Catherine Zeta-Jones, one of the most-cited celebrity Atkins devotees, threatens to sue anybody who links her with the Atkins diet. Her lawyer tells the media, "According to publications around the world, the Atkins diet has been derided by nutritionists and other health officials for decades. By stating that Ms. Zeta-Jones uses and or endorses the Atkins diet, those publications are falsely representing to the average reader, including many young women who look up to my client and admire her beautiful appearance, that Ms. Zeta-Jones would recommend this diet to any person looking to lose weight."

The lawyer continued, "My client is being made to look as if she is more concerned about her outward appearance than she is with serious health concerns. Nothing could be further from the truth." The statement came a few days after Zeta-Jones and her husband, Michael Douglas, were awarded damages against a celebrity magazine for publishing unauthorized pictures of her wedding. She sued partly because she claimed the pictures made her look fat.

I get an impression people think Atkins was too good to be true, that he was a snake-oil merchant. People absorb this notion with what appears to be a sense of relief. Maybe the truth is that, at heart, we are disturbed and disoriented by a diet that works; it upsets the natural order. We don't want diets to work in the same way that we don't want facelifts to work. Time marches on. Calories make you fat. If you overindulge, you must pay the price. These are the simple truths we live by.

At last, a mini-scandal. Colette Heimowitz, speaking on behalf of Atkins, says Atkins dieters are not recommended to eat large amounts of fat. The media pounces. The story is: even the Atkins organization is anti-Atkins. "The diet," says the *Sun* newspaper, "was designed to let followers feast on fatty foods. But now Colette Heimowitz, the director of research and education for company Atkins Nutritionals, has told dieters to cut back on saturated fat."

"Good evening," says Sir Trevor McDonald, standard-bearer of sensible thinking and host of *Tonight*. "It always did seem just too good to be true. The Atkins diet told us you could eat fat and get thin. But last week, the organization came forward with a bombshell announcement—that too much fat could be bad for you."

A Cooked Breakfast

An editor at the *Evening Standard* calls me and asks me to write, as an Atkins dieter, about the Atkins backlash. A photographer is arranged. I speak to a woman at the picture desk. "We'll just want a picture of you and a plate of bacon and eggs," she says.

"Yes, but this is not about bacon and eggs. What I'll be saying is that Atkins is not all bacon and eggs, steak and so on . . ."

"Fine. Well, you just tell the photographer about it."

When he arrives, the photographer says, "I just want a picture of you sitting over a plate of bacon and eggs, sausages, full English breakfast sort of thing."

"Ah yes. I talked to the picture desk about this. What I'll be saying in the article, you see, is that Atkins is not just about bacon and eggs and sausages."

"It's not?"

"No. It's about the avoidance of too much carbohydrate."

"But you eat lots of bacon and eggs, don't you, on Atkins?"

"No. Well, some people do. But that's not what it's about."

We walk to a local café. The photographer negotiates a compromise; I will be depicted over a plate of bacon, sausages and eggs, but I will be frowning, as if to say that I do not like them.

"You can make a face," says the photographer.

The bacon and eggs arrive. I am in the position of being hungry, and on Atkins, but unable, for tactical reasons, to eat bacon or eggs. I am making a political statement. In any case, I cannot eat the bacon or the eggs, because they are part of my photographic backdrop. The bacon and the eggs will stand on the table; I will sneer at them. But what about afterward? Would it be possible to eat the bacon and eggs then? Nobody would notice. Yes, they would. The photographer would notice. I must remain pure—I must sneer at the bacon and the eggs, to make my point.

The session begins. The photographer says, "Can I just get a couple of you sitting normally?"

"Not making a face?"

"Right."

The photographer snaps away.

"Shall I start making faces now?"

"OK."

I hunch over the bacon and eggs, sneering and scowling. I try to appear disdainful of the bacon and eggs, scornful, sickened. I shrink theatrically away from the bacon and eggs.

"You could, like, make your knife and fork into a cross."

"A cross?"

"You know, like in *Dracula*. As if you're warding off evil spirits."

For a while, I am Van Helsing, warding off the evil spirits of the bacon and eggs. The photographer shoots hundreds of frames. The café is beginning to fill up.

"You hate them."

"I hate them."

"Good. Lovely."

"They are evil."

"Great. Great."

"I curse you!"

"Perfect."

The session ends. I am hungry. The photographer says, "I'm hungry. I could do with some of this food. You don't want it, do you?"

"No, no. You have it."

"Do you mind?"

"Not at all."

In the meantime, I formulate a plan. I will wait until the photographer has gone, and then I'll order some bacon and eggs for myself.

In the article, I write, slightly self-righteously, "As an Atkins dieter, or at least as someone who tries to limit my intake of bread, pasta, rice, cakes, and biscuits, I'm used to scare stories. Almost every television program or newspaper article on the subject tells me the Atkins regime is bad. Recently, I watched a documentary telling me the Atkins diet was 'against fruit and vegetables.' People often ask me if I'm worried that I might give myself a heart attack. But actually, I don't think that avoiding fries, mashed potato, bagels, croissants and chocolate is likely to give me a heart attack."

"This diet," I explain, "is not just about eating bacon, sausages and steak. It's about avoiding too much carbohydrate."

The article appears the next day, illustrated with a picture of me sitting over a big plateful of bacon and eggs. I am not scowling. I am not sneering. I am not warding off the bacon and eggs with my cutlery cross. It is one of the early pictures. I look as if I love the bacon and eggs, as if I want the bacon and eggs. In a way, it is a true picture, because I did want the bacon and eggs. But I am disappointed. I wanted to look as if I did not want the bacon and eggs.

The picture is captioned, "Chewing the fat: writer William Leith tucks into what is considered to be a typical Atkins meal—a cooked breakfast."

The Sacrificial Victim

During the Ecstasy panic in the British media in the 1990s, Ecstasy took on a new meaning. In reports, it was no longer merely a drug, but a super-drug, a killer drug. It was the product of pure evil. If somebody died of a heroin overdose, he or she might be reported in the papers if there was something very peculiar or newsworthy about the incident—if the victim was the progeny of a peer or a top politician, for instance. But Ecstasy was different. All you had to do, to get on the front page, was take Ecstasy and lose consciousness.

Reading the reports, one sensed a huge gathering force, a primitive need for bad news. Certainly, people took Ecstasy and died occasionally, but mostly when the drug was taken in combination with other drugs. And yet reporters routinely gave us the impression that Ecstasy was the most dangerous drug in the world.

What the media craved was a sacrificial victim, and several attempts were made to create one. Ecstasy victims were granted column inches according to their youth, their looks, their gender, their academic promise, and the class status of their parents. When Leah Betts, who was a teenager, a pretty girl, a bright student, and the daughter of a policeman, died after taking an Ecstasy tablet—her first, it was suggested—editors knew that this was their moment. This was the best they were going to get, and they ran story after story, and a charity was organized, and huge posters were printed with a picture of Leah's girlish face, taken years before her death, and for months newspaper headlines bristled with the story.

Now, at the heart of the Atkins backlash, a similar search for bad news is in progress. Atkins dieters, we are told, are "at risk of a sharp rise in cholesterol," and the Atkins diet "could cut chances of pregnancy." When Rachel Huskey, a 230-lb. sixteen-year-old from Missouri, dies of heart disease after six weeks on the Atkins diet, there is a flurry of headlines:

DID THE ATKINS DIET KILL THIS GIRL?
And: ATKINS ALARM
And: NEW ALARM OVER ATKINS DIET
And: ATKINS DIET CAN TRIGGER DISEASES
And: ATKINS DANGER "OFFICIAL"

Rachel's mother, Lisa, was wary, on behalf of her daughter, of "crash diets," but, "after reading reports about Atkins"—before the backlash, of course—she "allowed her to go on it." Huskey did Atkins, reportedly complained of nausea, lost 15 lbs. in six weeks, and collapsed during a school history lesson. The coroner's report ruled that the cause of death was cardiac arrhythmia. Lisa Huskey blames the Atkins diet, and says, "I want people to know you can die doing something as stupid as this."

But Rachel, for whatever reason, does not have what it takes to be the media's sacrificial victim. She was obese. She died of heart disease. The media want something more.

They get what they want when Neal Barnard, a vegetarian activist who once said, "Meat consumption is just as dangerous to public health as tobacco use," publishes the New York City medical examiner's report on Atkins' death. Barnard was sent the report by Richard Fleming, an anti-Atkins cardiologist, who simply wrote to the authorities requesting it. What the report says is that Atkins had a myocardial infarction, hypertension, and congestive heart failure—typical conditions, one might say, for a seventy-two-year-old American whose father also suffered from congestive heart failure.

What the report also says is that Atkins, who had spent nine days in a coma in intensive care being pumped with fluids, had swelled to 258 lbs. His wife, Veronica, would later say that she couldn't bear to look at his swollen hands, which were "like ham hocks."

There is a flurry of headlines:

FATKINS

DR. FATKINS

DIET DOCTOR WAS OBESE

Eat Right, Live Longer

Neal Barnard's book, which promotes the virtues of a high-carbohydrate, vegetarian diet, is called *Eat Right, Live Longer*.

Flares

I wake up naked, I think alone, and there's a buzzing sound which, it turns out, is not my alarm clock but coming from inside my head, and I get out of bed, walk into the bathroom, and look at my body in the mirror. Not bad. It turns out that I am alone. My torso, which used to be square and bloated, is definitely taking on the beginnings of a V-shape; the shoulders are much broader than the waist. I weigh myself, looking closely at the poundage, pressing my feet into different areas of the scale. 203 lbs. Not bad. In the most advantageous position, I can get 201. But I'll stick with 203. Ten more pounds, I'd say, and I'll be fine.

Walking over to the mantelpiece, a towel around my waist, hungover but not unpleasantly so, I study a picture I took of myself more than a decade ago. I stood in front of a full-length mirror and used a Polaroid camera. In the picture, I am wearing tennis shorts, white socks, white sneakers, and nothing else. My belly is flat, and there is some definition; the middle part is separated from the edges. I can almost, but not quite, see the muscles. I cannot, however, see my face, which is obscured by flash.

Fifteen more pounds and I will have the beginnings of muscle definition in my stomach. And has losing weight made a difference to my life? In many ways, yes. For a start, the clothes I wear look more or less like they do on the mannequins in the windows of the stores where I buy them. Seams are not pulled out of shape. The clothes will last longer, too. I once had a girlfriend who told me that certain people, mostly fat and bulky people, wear clothes out quickly; their bodies are hard on the seams. Well, I used to be hard on seams, and now I'm not. And when I try clothes on, I no longer have to look at them purely in terms of minimizing bulk; I buy them if they look good.

I pop three ibuprofen tablets, which I know I shouldn't be doing, but I drank too much vodka last night, but at least I had it with Diet Coke. Which makes me think of the Diet Coke ad in which a group of office girls rush to a window to get a good look at a builder with a perfectly toned body. Now that I'm not so fat, I think the ad is good, funny even, and I can admit something to myself that I would not have admitted before—when I was fat, ads like that made me uneasy. Not because the man is being sexually objectified, but because the man is thin and toned, and I was fat, and the message, that women would not find me attractive unless I had a great body, made me feel uneasy.

People are always saying that women don't really want men to have a great body, that what they want is a man who will make them laugh, or a man who will take care of them and make them feel special, but I don't think that's the point. When you don't have a great body, you behave differently around women—you behave like an insecure person. If you're fat, women do not respond well to you, not because of the fat itself—or not only because of the fat itself—but because of the fat mind-set that accompanies the fat. I've noticed, for instance, that I walk differently now that I've lost weight, and this is not only because I'm carrying less baggage physically. When I was fat, I slouched and shuffled partly because I felt, in a deep, almost instinctive way, that I didn't deserve to carry myself with any elegance.

And now, when I see myself in mirrors, in windows, on CCTV cameras, I see a normal person. When I take my shirt off at home, my eye does not slide instinctively to the window to see if anybody is looking. My posture, in general, is no longer defensive.

Yesterday I tried on the jeans I've been saving for the last ten years, and they fitted. I can wear my old jeans!

Unfortunately, I don't want to.

When I went into the cupboard, and took them out, I thought that, by wearing these old jeans, the jeans I last wore in 1993, I would be able to erase a decade of bad living. I thought that, by wearing my old jeans, I might be able to reenter my life as it had been, to think the thoughts and feel the feelings of my former thin self. I unfolded the jeans. I put them on. They fitted perfectly. And yet they looked . . . wrong. They looked strange. Ugly, even.

What was going on? The old jeans are subtly, rather than dramatically, different from the jeans I wear now. They are slightly baggier around the knees, slightly tighter around the calves. And yet they look completely wrong. Did I walk around in jeans that looked like this? Yes, I did. At the time, I thought they looked good.

Ten years ago, these jeans looked right.

Something has happened to the way I look at things, and I have had no control over it.

These days, I wear trousers that are almost . . . *flares*.

Flares, as an aesthetic choice, have crept up on me. I hardly noticed.

Of course, I wore flares as a kid. I loved them. We all did. They just felt . . . *right*. Like long, frizzy hair, and slightly chunkier models on magazine covers. The guys you admired in those days were different, too—more solid, with broader shoulders and less muscle definition. The girls had rounder thighs and bottoms, bigger breasts. Back in the seventies, flares looked fine, and the bodies you saw, in magazines and on the television, in parks and on beaches, did not vary so much as bodies do these days—there were not so many obese people, and not so many skinny people. When you thought of male film stars, you thought of them with clothes on. I don't think I would have been able to conjure up an image of what, say, Clint Eastwood's stomach looked like. All those spaghetti westerns, and he did not leave an identifiable memory of abs or pecs. Now, when I think of Clint Eastwood's stomach, I think of the vaguely sagging flesh of the Clint character in *The Bridges of Madison County*, a movie made in the more body-conscious 1990s.

I can't remember James Stewart's stomach, or John Wayne's, or Gary Cooper's, or Gregory Peck's, Henry Fonda's, or even Robert Mitchum's, although I must have seen them. The camera looks at men differently now. I can tell you about Brad Pitt's stomach—rippled, tan, moist-looking like connective tissue. And Dennis Quaid—he's cut into panels, but skinnier and whiter, like a hard guy from a poor background. And Jack Nicholson I think of as surprisingly flabby, but only because he didn't show his body much in his earlier films—or rather, it wasn't presented to us for inspection. Like Eastwood, he's had the misfortune to be pored over in his later, fatter years. John Travolta was a perfect V-shape in *Saturday Night Fever,* and then muscled up for the forgettable sequel, *Staying Alive,* and was slightly fat in *Pulp Fiction.* He loves burgers and fries, he says, and has a huge appetite and loses weight by exercising. Like a shark, he must keep moving—the moment he stays still, he bloats.

And Joey from *Friends* is chunky, with inflated pecs, and Chandler, like me, has yo-yo weight, he can have quite a double chin, and, like me, he has had trouble with drink and painkillers.

After I loved flares, I hated them, and now I don't hate them as much as I thought I did, in the same scary way that I probably like slightly skinnier women than I did before, with slightly higher, firmer breasts, smaller bottoms, and a pubic hairstyle of some kind, it's hard to remember how it used to be, but in the past, right through to the mid-eighties, women just let their pubic hair grow, and now a full thatch is the exception rather than the rule, most women I know are getting waxed and plucked, buying trimming tools, reading about different pubic hairstyles on the beauty pages, and this, of course, will happen to men.

"Beckham shaves," I was told the other day, with some authority.

"Beckham shaves?"

"You know. Down there."

As a teenager, I felt naked without the reassuring weight of my flares on my feet. Not feeling it, not experiencing the billowing flutter every time you took a stride, would have seemed . . . distasteful. Revealing *the whole of your shoe*— it was something old men and tramps did; it was bad taste, like having food stains on your shirt. I remember an older boy making a joke at the expense of straight trousers. The punchline was about Communists. Straight trousers were something you wore in the fantasy totalitarian world of your bad dreams, a world that harked back to the fifties, to shaved backs of necks, narrow lapels, no spliffs or pop music or casual sex.

In those days, things moved so *fast*—from bootcut to baggies in *three years,* 1972 to 1975; the cuffs moved outward across the shoes in three deft movements—from the middle of the shoelaces to the edge of the shoelaces; then out to the toe, and then, the final frontier, to beyond the edge of the shoe. The middle stage was awkward—the front edge of the trouser cuff didn't quite cover the shoe, and so had to be longer than the back edge, which meant that, for a year or so, everybody's trousers were too long at the back. The material picked up mud and other filth, and then it became frayed and split, so even when people took their shoes off, long tendrils of, at worst, dogshit-marinated denim left brown streaks all over the carpet. Indoors, with your shoes off, you manipulated your front trouser-cuff with your toes; outdoors, you leaned against walls and bus shelters, looking downward, casually flipping your cuffs over your shoes.

And then I turned against flares. Why? I can't remember. But members of my generation had a particular grudge against flares, because they were all we had known, and somehow, in 1977 and 1978, we were persuaded to spurn them for straight trousers. We were made to *hate* flares. Straights were our first major conversion, our Damascus, and the new religion was tough at first—skirmishes with the older boys, still clinging to the last shreds of hippie; walking into rooms, hyperaware of your feet.

So I never thought I would even consider wearing flares again. I remember having conversations—

"*Never*! I just . . . can't see it."

"Right. It's like you made a mistake in the past, and you won't make the same mistake again."

"Exactly. I can categorically state that I will *never*, ever wear flares. Not even *slightly* flared trousers."

But here I was, looking at myself in the mirror, and these jeans from 1994 looked awful, and so I took them off, and put my slightly flared—or, rather, bootcut—jeans back on again.

And now I don't know what to do with my old jeans. Shall I throw them out? I pick them up, and run my fingers over them, feeling uneasy, feeling a creeping sense of dread, and I decide not to put the jeans on again, and I go and look at myself in the mirror again, my torso almost V-shaped but, I can see now, still too chunky, too fat. When I looked at it earlier, I must have had exceptionally good light. Weighing myself again, the scales say 205. I shuffle my feet on the scales, looking for a better reading. There, 204. Not too bad.

So today I put my bootcuts on, and a shirt, and look at myself in the mirror in the shirt, and relax a little—I don't look too bad in the shirt. I look again at the picture of myself in the tennis shorts, and have a momentary worry—is that muscle definition, or a flaw in the picture?—and I decide it's OK, it's muscle definition. And then I notice something in the picture. My sneakers. A box-fresh pair of Reeboks, pre-Belly's-gonna-get-you era, shoes I bought in 1989. And then I look at the sneakers on my shoe rack—a pair of Diesels, a pair of Nikes, a pair of Reeboks—the same pair! And they're slightly battered, frazzled, but still wearable.

Jesus! No wonder I got fat. My tennis shoes have lasted me for nearly thirteen years.

And I pack my bag, leave my apartment, hail a taxi and head for the airport; I'm flying to New York, where there is a slight chance I will be able to meet Elizabeth Wurtzel, the former addict, and talk to her about addiction. I try not to drink at the airport, but fail, and I try not to drink on the plane, but fail, and on the plane I reread Wurtzel's book *Prozac Nation,* and also an article headlined "Prozac 'found in tap water,' " which tells me that so many people are taking Prozac these days—six million Britons—that tap water might contain toxic levels. I also read an article telling me that the Atkins diet causes depression, and the article is illustrated with a picture of two girls, one saying, "Really? Well, gimme thin and grumpy any day!"

As Shelley Bovey says, the word "thin" is beginning to replace the word "trim." Thin used to mean "too thin." Now it means "just right." And as Laura Fraser says, the difference between the average weight of models and the average weight of women gets bigger every year. No wonder there's Prozac in the tap water, I think as I try not to drink on the plane, and fail, and when the plane lands I get a taxi and get out and try not to drink on the way to my hotel, and fail, and after a while I stop trying not to drink, and end up drinking vodka with apple juice, which I really shouldn't, because it has carbohydrate in it, and, later, when I meet Elizabeth Wurtzel, she's not the naughty, drug-seeking girl of *Prozac Nation,* the Ritalin-snorting reprobate of *More, Now, Again,* but a thirty-something woman with a sweet face, who has, for now at least, renounced all artificial stimulants, although she has started smoking cigarettes instead. We go to a party, where she smokes, and I drink. She's been deeply marked by 9/11 and would rather talk about world politics than addiction, and we end up going back to her apartment, where she smokes, and I drink, and we take her new puppy for a walk in the small hours, and when we get back the puppy bites me with its needly teeth, but I don't mind, because I'm not sober, and I'm not sober when I walk out into the night, and I'm not sober when my plane takes off the next day, and I'm not sober when it lands.

The Experience

Back in London, as the world gains weight, the illusionist David Blaine hangs above the Thames in a Perspex box, getting thinner. Every day, we look at him, and there is less to look at. People hate him. They throw eggs at the Perspex box, and stand on nearby Tower Bridge, training laser flashlights at his head.

I'm in Starbucks, drinking coffee, not relaxed, waiting for my mobile phone to ring. My weight has "plateaued" at a touch over 200 lbs. I should do more exercise. I hardly do any exercise. Five years ago, when I weighed 214 lbs., when I was gaining weight at an alarming rate, I joined a gym. I went four times a week, then three times a week, then two, then, panicking, back up to four. I averaged three sessions per week, at roughly one hour per session, which means forty minutes' exercise. My favorite machine was a rotational jogger, which minimized impact injury to the knees.

I didn't mind going to the gym. I plugged in my headphones and jogged while watching daytime TV, sometimes jogging while obese people bulked into view, telling the daytime hosts about their failed diets, their new resolve. I watched MTV. When you are exercising aerobically, your music tastes change. At home, I listened to the Beatles and

Thelonious Monk. Jogging, I yearned for Bryan Adams or Oasis; I wanted power chords, lamenting voices, slashing, venegeful guitars. During my gym year, early January to late December 1998, I exercised aerobically for just over a hundred hours. I weighed myself throughout the year. My weight hardly fluctuated. At the end, I weighed 215 lbs.

The gym had not made me thin. But it had slowed down my rate of expansion, my Coltrane trajectory.

Still, in four months of low-carb dieting, I've lost 30 lbs. Low-carb works better, for me, in terms of pure weight loss. On the other hand, going to the gym made me *feel* better; exercise, as everybody knows, produces endorphins in the brain, feel-good drugs. Merely being less heavy does not. It just means you look better in clothes, hold yourself with more elegance, are able to have more sexual contact with strangers. Getting thin pulls you into the world of surfaces and appearances and snap judgments. You are less ashamed of your body, but more self-conscious. When you lose weight, you begin to understand how frightened you were, as an overweight person, of the body-conscious world outside. How frightened, and how skilled at hiding your fear from yourself.

I'm drinking a "double-shot cappuccino," a frothy coffee with two shots of espresso, trying to savor the coffee, wondering if it tastes good or bad. Should I have had a latte, a macchiato? Or the Starbucks "coffee of the day," which won't be the same tomorrow? My favorite is the espresso Double Shot, a cold drink, or beverage as they say in Starbucks, a cold beverage made with espresso, milk, and sugar. But I am anti-sugar, just as I am post-sandwich, post-pasta, post-rice. I do, however, drink coffee, even though it stimulates the adrenal glands, and this, in turn, has a negative effect on insulin production. But you have to draw the line somewhere.

Why is my phone not ringing? I'm glaring at it in the same way I glare at a half-boiled kettle, in the same way I used to glare at my toaster. But I no longer use my toaster; these days it is packed away in a cupboard. I no longer toast, no longer partake of the cheerful ritual, and I feel a gap in my life, possibly a spiritual gap.

My phone is silent, still. Academic research tells us that mobile phones make us feel more connected, and yet less connected, with other people. They encourage a state of being that sociologist Kenneth J. Gergen calls "absent presence." You are here, and yet not here. Part of you is in cyberspace, waiting for messages, instructions. The average cell phone user talks on his cell phone for seven hours every month. But how many hours is he in its thrall? In an experiment at Rutgers University in New Jersey, a group of students was asked to switch off their cell phones for forty-eight hours. Some of them saw the world as a different, more hostile, place. One woman said, "I felt like I was going to get raped if I didn't have my cell phone in my hand."

Certainly, I feel naked without my phone. Without my phone, I feel edgy and disconnected. With my phone, I feel edgy and disconnected. I am aware that one of the things making me feel like this is the phone itself; having a phone makes you feel the need for a phone, a need to connect that you were unaware of until you had a phone. In an important sense, mobile phones cause a lack of confidence, a vulnerability.

But at least I've got my phone on me. (Why isn't it ringing?) Just before I leave my apartment every day, I check my pockets: keys, phone, wallet. Oh, and painkillers. I've just taken my last two painkillers, two sugarcoated ibuprofen tablets which taste like M&Ms, with my cappuccino. On the table in front of me, on either side of my coffee, are my phone and my now-empty painkiller packet—bright, silver objects that look good on the table of a café, objects that have evolved hugely in the last few years, objects that, in fact, look very similar to each other. I am looking at the phone, waiting for it to light up. The painkiller packet already looks lit up. The brand name, Nurofen, stands above a fiery orange target. Nurofen, claim the manufacturers, "targets" pain.

It is early evening. I sip my coffee, read my papers, wait for my painkillers and mobile phone to do their respective jobs. The papers, once again, are full of the obesity crisis. Government officials and obesity experts are bristling with enthusiasm for the battle ahead. They cite the villains: fat, sugar, and salt. Carb is off the agenda. In my *Guardian,* Susan Jebb, we are told, "called for the government to act and set real targets for bringing obesity levels down." At the International Obesity Task Force conference, President Philip James says that the well-being of children is "systematically undermined by the intense marketing and sales of foods high in fat, sugar and salt."

Meanwhile, the Institute of Physics has been studying the diet of Homer Simpson. "We watched lots of *Simpsons* videos," says the Institute's Michelle Cain. Analysis reveals that Homer consumes an average of 3,100 calories per day, including 4.5 ounces of fat. His body weight, which is remarkably steady, is 239.8 lbs. Nearly 4 lbs. heavier than me at my fattest, at least when I positioned the scale correctly. "Homer's current lifestyle is putting him at risk of coronary heart disease," comments Deborah Allen of the British Heart Foundation. There is a picture of Homer eating a doughnut. The picture's caption is: "Homer Simpson: eats too much fat."

Barry, an overweight character in *EastEnders,* is trying to lose weight. He's exchanging cooked breakfasts of bacon, egg, and sausages for something apparently healthier—cereal.

The paradigm is solid.

I flick through newspapers, magazines, waiting for my painkillers to kick in, waiting for my phone to ring. Sophie Dahl's weight is still decreasing. After several years as a token "oversize" model, Dahl's career briefly flourished as a normal-sized model, and now she is conspicuously thin. Her greatest moment was a much-maligned perfume ad in which a beautifully proportioned Dahl was depicted on her back, legs spread, apparently being ravished by invisible forces. And this, I guess, is how she must have felt as an oversize model—supine, ambiguous, trapped. Anyway, she is now famous for being thin, for having shed the bulk that defined her, which means that she is, of course, still defined by bulk, or rather its absence, which, in turn, drives her to shed yet more pounds.

I'm looking at a picture of Sophie Dahl, and I'm thinking of Cyril Connolly's phrase: "Inside every fat person there is a thin one wildly signaling to get out." And that's what this picture of Dahl looks like—the thin person wildly signaling to get out. In the picture, Dahl is thin. But look into her eyes, and what do you see? The eyes of a fat person?

Jennifer Aniston—steady. Cameron Diaz—steady. Kirstie

Alley—still gaining. Alley is puffing up like Robbie Coltrane. I happen to know that her diet, the diet she recommends, involves fasting. Dolly Parton does this, too. I once interviewed Parton, and she told me that fasting made her feel cleaner and more clearheaded; being empty physically makes her feel less empty spiritually. In the case of Alley, though, I can imagine what might have happened. Fasting led to hunger, which led to bingeing. In pictures, she is beginning to take on the pyramid shape of the truly obese.

Was that . . . ? No. Just somebody with the same ringtone. My hand is clutching at my phone, stroking it. Academics studying mobile phone users recently referred to phones as "electronic pets." People leave buildings to take their phones for a walk, to check messages, rearrange settings. I saw an ad the other day in which people were trying, fruitlessly, to describe a sporting moment. The solution? Send a video clip of the moment to all your friends. The messy business of talking is replaced with the very thing you want to describe. Every day, we are more connected. Every day, we are less connected.

This morning, my homepage had an article about celebrity eating. There was a picture of Cameron Diaz eating an unidentifiable piece of food, possibly a burger.

"Cameron: how does she stay so thin when she obviously loves her food so much?"

The answer comes from Lucy Liu, Diaz' co-star in *Charlie's Angels*. Liu describes Diaz as "a genetic freak because she can eat whatever she wants without piling on the pounds."

Liz Hurley was eating fries. Renée Zellweger was eating either fish or scampi. Sarah Jessica Parker "didn't do anything, honest" in order to lose weight after giving birth. "I'm just one of those people who doesn't gain weight."

Renée Zellweger, it is reported, did Atkins after gaining weight for her role as Bridget Jones, but did not slim down enough to prevent *Harper's Bazaar* from dropping her as the cover girl "for being too fat."

Elsewhere: the woman who plays Kat in *EastEnders* has been told she is too fat to play romantic storylines, and so must slim down. Jennifer Aniston says, of her youthful plumpness, "I wasn't really fat. I was just Greek."

Maybe that was my problem all those years. Maybe I was just Greek.

My painkillers are beginning to take effect. Interestingly, even though aspirin was discovered in 1899, nobody knew how it worked until the 1970s. It works by fooling the brain, by messing with the signal that tells the brain something is wrong. When you take a painkiller, you are treating a symptom rather than a condition. You're still in pain, but you no longer know it.

Are painkillers a bad thing? We're certainly spending more money on them than ever before. In 1997, the British painkiller market was worth $595 million. In 2001, it was worth $767 million. Is this because we are in more pain? A pain specialist, Dr. Raj Munglani, told me he believed that our society tolerates pain less well than before. So we're not in more pain. On the other hand, "Pain is what the patient says it is." So we might be in more pain.

These days, our expectations are higher. We want fast-acting pain relief in the same way that we want fast-acting diets, fast food, speed elevators, speed-dialing on our mobile phones.

One thing about painkillers is that they are more widely available than they used to be; in 1996, the government relaxed restrictions on ibuprofen, allowing it to be available in supermarkets, newsstands, and corner stores. This was part of a drive to save money by taking pressure off doctors and pharmacists; as citizens, we have been taught to be self-medicating when it comes to pain. Now, when we are in pain, we are no longer in the hands of the doctor—we are in the hands of the marketing man.

My painkillers might, and might not, be working. For a moment, I take in what Howard Schultz, chairman and founder of Starbucks, calls "the experience." The experience is the same here as it is in the two other Starbucks outlets in my neighborhood—the same easy chairs, the same bright color-schemes, the same soft rock and jazz piped at the same soothing volume, the same expensive cappuccinos and espressos. The frappuccinos. The macchiatos. The mochas. The experience makes me feel relaxed and uneasy in shifting proportions.

Intriguingly, some doctors now believe that painkillers, when taken frequently, actually cause the problem they set out to solve; Dr. Timothy Steiner, of Charing Cross Hospital in London, believes that one in thirty people suffer chronic headaches as a result of painkiller overuse. "If painkillers reduce the sensitivity of pain pathways, there is likely to be, over time, a compensation for that," Steiner told me, "which results in those pathways becoming more sensitive, leading to the requirement for more analgesia."

Painkillers give you pain.

Carbs make you hungry.

Mobile phones make you feel disconnected.

So what do people do? They take more painkillers to get rid of the pain, they eat more carbs to stave off the hunger pangs, they clutch their mobile phones to make themselves feel less edgy and paranoid.

Bad medicine.

The scariest thing about painkillers is that they now exist in a no-man's-land between medicine and product. Which means that they don't need someone to prescribe them—they need someone to market them. Don Williams is the man responsible for designing the Nurofen packet on my table. He works in Notting Hill, west London. His office is just what you'd expect—minimal furnishings, blond-wood floors. In the upstairs lobby there is a shopping cart full of products designed by his company, Packaging Innovations Global: Double Velvet toilet paper, Head & Shoulders shampoo, Pot Noodle—and Nurofen. A former session guitarist from Middlesborough, Williams is tall and trim, with wonderfully tasteful clothes and a shaved head. "That's our philosophy," he said, looking at the cart. "That's what we believe in. Getting things in trolleys. At the end of the day, that's what we're paid for."

One of Williams' innovations was to place the target in the center of the pack, with a chevron radiating out to the sides. He also wanted more of the silver foil on the packs to be visible. Consumers, he told me, are visually literate—they see the pack design before they read the words. When he took over the pack design of Benson & Hedges cigarette packs, Williams made sure that every pack was gold, even the packs containing low-tar cigarettes, which had previously been silver. "We believe that brand identities should be recognized at a distance," he said, "even through half-closed eyes, or sub-optimal conditions, or in peripheral vision." In supermarkets, said Williams, "we want a blocking effect on the shelf. The chevron links all the packs together, so you get a wave effect."

As I left, he said, "I get more kicks out of seeing a pack in a trash can than on a shelf."

I pick up and fiddle with my phone and sip my coffee and cast my eyes around the Starbucks. I look at the easy chairs, the blond-wood tables, the cheerful mugs on shelves. Everybody I know professes to hate Starbucks, although most of them still come here and drink the coffee, which is not great, and sit in the easy chairs. I think Starbucks makes us uneasy because it tells us something important about the world we live in; it tells us that we need somewhere like Starbucks. When I interviewed him in 2000, Howard Schultz said, "The environment that we create has given people a respite for themselves, or a sense of gathering and community with people at a time in their lives when there's no human connection. The PC, the handheld wireless devices facilitate levels of communication that are singular, that are not based on communicating with a human."

We were in Seattle, attending the annual Starbucks Employees' conference. In the conference hall that morning, people had been buzzing with corporate pride and near-religious zeal. One manager of a Starbucks outlet said, "Howard will tell you that it's not just about coffee. It's about people." Another employee looked me in the eye, and said, with quiet intensity, "It's not only about enjoying the beverage, but also the service, the aroma, the comfortable chairs."

At the time, Starbucks was worth $7.2 billion, but had

tangible assets of only $1.2 billion—it was rich in extrinsics, or, as one executive put it, "what's parked between your ears." In other words, the value of Starbucks consisted mostly of the consumer's need. Starbucks, it might be said, was a billion dollars' worth of real estate and coffee products, and six billion dollars' worth of human need. Scott Bedbury, Starbucks' vice president of marketing at the time, has said that "Consumers don't truly believe there's a huge difference between products." A former head of marketing at Nike, Bedbury has also said, "With Starbucks, we see how coffee has woven itself into the fabric of people's lives, and that's our opportunity for emotional leverage."

We took our seats in the conference hall. A man arrived on stage and unveiled a number—46.38. Everybody cheered. Starbucks stock had just gone up, and, since most people in the room owned Starbucks stock, they were now a little bit richer than they had been a short while ago.

One after the other, Starbucks executives took the stage, and made speeches. The first guy told us that Starbucks was the "most preferred" restaurant in Tokyo, that Koreans loved it, that, for the first time in U.K. history, the consumption of coffee had exceeded that of tea.

"Take a moment to congratulate yourselves," said the executive.

Later, he quoted Winston Churchill ("Success is never final") and Tom Hanks. "I don't often quote Tom Hanks," he said, "but he did get it in *A League of Our Own* when he said, 'If winning were easy, then everybody would be doin' it. It's the hard that makes it great.' "

Another exectutive said, "Our stores really are theaters. The store manager is the director."

Schultz arrived on stage. Like the self-help guru Anthony Robbins, he has the air of Ted Danson from *Cheers*. He wore a black shirt, no tie, black suit. Halfway through his speech, he told us that, as he watched the conference proceedings, he shed tears, thinking of his dead father, who would have been proud. People in the audience began to cry. Schultz defined the Starbucks concept as "something that is true, that is authentic, that is relevant, that enriches people's lives. We've touched their heart. You've touched their heart with the things that you do."

He said, "We have changed the landscape of America! Not only have we changed it—we have enhanced it!"

He said, "People said there would never be a time when the Japanese walked down the street holding a cup of coffee! But now, you can't walk down the street without seeing it!"

He said, "What they can't copy, what they can't take away, is the heart and soul of what makes this company great. Don't allow this moment to be dismissed!"

He said, "I believe—and I hope this is not coming across in some soppy way—take the moment! Seize it!"

Later, in the penthouse of the Westin Hotel, with views all the way across Puget Sound, Schultz described the experience of being in a Starbucks outlet: "You hear the music, you smell the coffee, you see the people. The lighting and the design have been put in place to almost take you away."

I sip my coffee. I cast my eye around the Starbucks, at the easy chairs, the blond-wood tables, the cheerful mugs on shelves.

At last! Some progress with my headache. The painkillers I have taken are beginning to deactivate a chemical in my brain called prostaglandin H synthetase, the catalyst that turns a chemical called arachidonic acid into messengers of pain called prostaglandins.

My brain has bad news: I am in pain.

My solution: shoot the messenger!

And, finally, my phone lights up, and rings, and the man sitting in an easy chair a few feet away from me, whose phone has the same ringtone, snaps his head toward his own phone, as if waking from a dream, and turns away again, disappointed, and I pick up my phone and put it to my ear.

"Leroy," I say, and then, "When?" and then "Yes," and then, "Good."

On the way out, I toss my Nurofen packet into the trash, where it nestles brightly against the beiges and browns and coffee-stained whites of the java jackets, the napkins, the waxed paper cups that Japanese people are now more willing to hold as they walk down the street.

Don Williams would get a kick out of it, if he happened to be passing.

A Net Loss

You know you shouldn't do it, you know it's not good for you, you know that, even if snorting coke will make you happier than you are now for a brief period, it will make you more miserable than you are now for a longer period; you know that, with coke, the economics are not good, that you'll end up with a net loss.

You know that coke works by fooling the brain, by

telling the brain to release large amounts of feel-good chemicals, and you also know that, when these chemicals, dopamine and serotonin, are released, the brain neutralizes them with brutal efficiency, leaving you with lower levels than before, and a raging hunger for more coke.

And you know that, when you snort more coke, you will not feel as good as you did the first time, and, soon afterward, you will feel much, much worse, with disastrously low levels of serotonin and dopamine, and a raging hunger for yet more coke, and a bitter, twisted gleam in your eye.

One thing that irks me is that, if you have problems with alcohol or drugs, some people think that you're just slacking off for a while, having a great time. Just like some people look at a fat person stuffing pizza into his face, and think it's all about enjoyment. People think greed is all about enjoyment. But it's not. Greed, as any self-help guru will tell you, is a compensation for pain. Greed is about deprivation. I was talking to a compulsive eater the other day, the one who didn't want to be identified, and I asked him or her to tell me what he or she had eaten during a binge the night before, and he or she listed the items—the two small frozen pizzas blitzed in the microwave, the sandwiches with avocados and cheese, the single doughnut, the chocolate bar. All this after having dinner—a salad. And I asked him or her if any of these things had given him or her any pleasure, and for a moment he or she looked shocked. The very idea! No, this was pure masochism, pure self-harm, every mouthful a self-administered laceration.

You know you shouldn't do it, but you go ahead, you soldier on. The mind of a coke fiend, pre-binge, is like the babble of an unpopular government leading a nation into war—there are evasions, omissions, calculated abuses of intelligence, outright lies.

It will make you feel bad, but that doesn't matter, because you will feel good first.

It will cost you money, but that doesn't matter, because it will also save you money. How? We'll come to that point later.

When you walk into the bar to meet Leroy, you will have the briefest and most formulaic of conversations, and soon you will find yourself in a dank, smelly toilet, scraping some powder onto the toilet lid, snorting the powder up your nose through a rolled-up banknote, fretting about germs. But that doesn't matter, because cocaine is an appetite suppressant, and you will not eat any more food today.

And, before you leave the cubicle, you'll have a nasty moment of clarity. For a second, you will see yourself. And you won't look good. But that doesn't matter, because very soon, you will forget about all these things. You will forget about the suspicious crusting on the toilet lid, the mulch of wet tissue on the floor, the fuzz of lichen on the grouting between the tiles, the money you have spent, the Faustian pact you have set into motion.

None of these things matter, in any case, because the decision has already been made, was in fact made a long time ago, for reasons that are obscure, classified, confidential. You never had a chance to put it to the vote. Some kind of Rumsfeld or Cheney figure deep in your brain took your prime minister to a quiet location and held a gun to his head, and that was it.

I hail a taxi, meet Leroy, lock myself in a smelly cubicle, snort a line, and then I'm talking to some people I don't, or at least didn't, know, and what I'm saying is mostly the word, "Yeah." As the drug takes hold, as my brain is filled with ersatz pleasure, the word shortens to "Yeh." I am pure assent. Everything says "yes" to me. Everybody looks good. The man I am talking to looks good. The barmaid looks sensational. I don't exactly want to have sex with the barmaid. I just want to look at her. Exciting thoughts come to me. I should have rum and a mixer! Rum is known as "ron" in Spain! And the man is talking to me about ferries, ferries versus trains, or of course you can fly, and I'm saying that I agree with ferries, the best, or not quite best, but certainly a good way to travel, or possibly not, or even probably not, not with all the accidents you get with ferries, but then again, flying is more dangerous than ever before, with the flight paths so crowded, now that everybody wants to be somewhere else all the time.

And I snort two more lines in the toilet cubicle, just in case my friends arrive and ask to share my drugs and take my drugs away from me, and now my nose is running, and I look at myself in the mirror, and I have absolutely no negative emotions, no real emotions at all, and I'm not worried about what will happen later, about feeling depressed and paranoid after the coke wears off, or even about stuff like death, which I can now quite happily think about, the fact that I'll die and probably be cremated and there will be a funeral and some of the people attending, my future children I suppose, have not been born yet, and neither is it too scary to think about all the bad things in my past life, my broken childhood, being shuffled about and locked up in nasty, violent boarding schools, the fact that my family always seemed to be moving outward, everybody moving away from each other, almost from the beginning, certainly not something I normally want to think about. Well. What doesn't kill you makes you stronger. I dab my nose and look at myself in the mirror, and this toilet, I decide, is not so bad after all. It has *character*.

A few minutes later, or maybe more than a few minutes later, it's hard to tell, I'm sitting at a table with a couple of my friends, they've got drugs of their own, are settling in for a binge, and I'm still feeling fine, maybe not as exhilarated as I was, back there in the toilet, but still fine, and one of my friends is saying something about a lap-dancing club, something about knowing the owner, and the girls would give him a private show, on account of the fact that he knew the owner, and this particular girl . . .

"The tits!"

"The tits?"

"They were . . ."

"Yeh."

"You know."

"Yeh."

"Just . . ."

And the other guy is saying that he was walking through some nightclub or bar and he saw a woman, short skirt, legs open, nothing on underneath, he swears this is the truth, actually thinks she was flashing him . . .

"What was it like?"

"Perfect."

"Perfect?"

"Absolute perfection. She knew it as well."

Patrolling her channel, the barmaid looks fine, no longer sensational but fine, and my train of thought drifts around, trying to focus on stories about lap-dancing bars and strip clubs. I remember being invited to some kind of escort bar, this was years ago, possibly decades, I was with some people from the city, people who were, compared to me, very rich indeed, and when I'd run out of money, one guy just opened his wallet and offered me a chunk of money, which I pulled out and waved at him. He nodded. It was about £200. Anyway, by the end of the evening it was gone, spent on three bottles of champagne, which I drank with a girl who would let me put my hand up her skirt, and touch her through her underwear, but no more. People who wanted to do more had to pay more money, a lot more money.

My mind alights on a time when I went to this place with a friend of mine, he'd had an operation and the operation had not, he felt, been a success, something to do with the nerves on one side of his face, and he'd retreated into himself. One day, I suggested we go to a strip club; vaguely, he assented. I remember walking down some narrow stairs, and paying a nominal sum, a tiny sum, and sitting down on a sofa in the dark in this nasty basement room, it might almost have been a garage or workshop, and I drank a warm glass of lager, followed by a glass of sparkling wine, and I thought that one of the last things I wanted to see, right at that moment, was a strange naked woman. I sat on the sofa, and when a woman did arrive, she was small and middle-aged, and she presented me with a bill for £245.

I said, "What?"

I said, "Look, I didn't think . . ."

I said, "Look, I'll just pay for the drinks and we'll go."

The woman, quite nasty I now saw, said, "You can't do

that. You've already undertaken a legal obligation to be hostessed."

"What?"

"If you want me to show you the law, where it's printed, then I'll go and get it right now." She had raised her voice. She shouted, "Winston! Come in here!"

A tall black man walked over to the table. The woman said to me, "Now, do you want me to ask Winston to go and get the legal documents?"

"No."

I said, "Look, why don't I just pay for the drinks?"

The woman put the bill in front of me. She said, "This is your bill. £30 each for drinks. £60 for the champagne. A £50 hostess fee. And £75 for the show."

We didn't have the money. We had to get the money from cash machines in the street, escorted through the streets by Winston, one at a time, while the other waited in the basement. Later, we sat on chairs in a small, bright room, and a tattooed woman with very pale skin took her clothes off and bent over in front of us, showing us her bottom, and afterward, we walked out into the rain and . . .

The coke, I can tell, is wearing off. Somebody once gave me a good description of this moment; it's as if you're enjoying yourself, surrounded by lovely scenery, and then somebody comes along and takes the scenery away, wheels it off, leaving you sitting in a horrible studio, looking at the dirty brickwork, the exposed pipes.

When you snort coke, you become the perfect consumer. Having more makes you want more; wanting more makes you want more. As a product, coke never works, because consuming it feels like an index of loss. As a product, coke works brilliantly, because consuming it feels like an index of loss. As you continue to snort, the coke you've had becomes your enemy, reminding you that the coke that's to come will never be enough.

And later, we're all at somebody's house, at some kind of impromptu party or gathering, a whole lot of stray people drinking and listening to music and rolling joints and snorting lines of coke from CD cases, there's a big pile of CDs stacked up by a radiator, and everybody is talking at once, telling each other bitter little stories about living in the city—about how they were nearly knocked down by cars, and pushed and shoved aside on public transport, and cursed by people who thought they had the wrong tickets, which maybe they did, but see, it wasn't their *fault,* and they tell stories about waiters who brought them the wrong food, and waiters who brought them what they ordered, but it was disgusting, really horrible, what a rip-off.

"I wish I was in Spain right now."

"I wish I was in France."

"What about a beach? A deserted beach, somewhere in the South Pacific? With, like, those birds, what are they called? And you can see the fish jumping in the sea."

I'm drinking a lot, drinking to cushion my fall. I make a calculation; if I eke out my drugs slowly, I might not feel too bad, might not crash. This is what always happens, a fact that my inner spin doctor had soft-pedaled. In the kitchen I find some kind of milky liqueur, which would make me sick, and a bottle of whiskey half-hidden behind a food blender, and I pour myself a big slug of the whiskey into an inappropriate glass, a glass decorated with some kind of soft drink motif that reminds me of childhood, and I try to drink most of the whiskey where nobody can see me, and, moving through the noisy room, I am the recipient of a familiar feeling, that there's nothing here for me, that I will get nothing more from the evening, that everything from now on will be damage control, and it occurs to me that I am alone here, as lonely as a Stone Age man, walking naked and hungry through the savanna with a sharpened stick.

I drink more and talk more about missed connections, people who look funny and just don't get it, people who are fat and eat too much, people who have serious drink and drug problems, or can't stop looking at porn on the internet, women who wear clothes too revealing for their overweight figures, celebrities who are putting weight on, celebrities who look suspiciously thin. Jennifer Aniston, we say, slimmed down and maintains a steady weight. Cameron Diaz can eat what she likes. Sophie Dahl is dropping, dropping. What's the matter with her? Jennifer Lopez employs a "food cop" to check her hotel room for possible trigger foods, which he removes before Lopez enters the room. Have you seen Kirstie Alley recently? Robbie Williams? Robbie Coltrane?

When I've Lost the Weight

Robbie Coltrane. When I interviewed Coltrane, I was trim, and he told me he'd recently lost 56 lbs.; he'd got his weight down to around 275 or 280. It was 1993, and he was still hugely fat, I couldn't tell he'd lost weight, and he said he wanted to lose more, he wanted to lose enough to start taking exercise again. As we sat and talked, I began to realize that there was something about this man that frightened me, although, at the time, I wasn't sure what it was.

The interview had not started well. Coltrane, who was promoting a series called *Coltrane in a Cadillac,* a show about driving across America, was being lionized like never before. We watched two episodes of the show, which was quite funny but not very. At one point, Coltrane, driving through a desert, put on a funny voice and said, "Whilst it might be some people's idea of ideal television to watch the rather enormous Mr. Coltrane driving an old banger across the salt flats, I found myself getting up to make a cup of tea after only ten minutes." Dear me, I thought. I sensed that part of him, out there in the middle of nowhere driving his 300-lb. bulk around in a 1951 Cadillac, thought that this view, however ironic, might be too close to the truth for comfort.

Coltrane presided over a press conference. When it was time for me to talk to him, I overheard him say to his publicist, "Well, that wasn't too bad. Nothing about the weight or the baby." (He had recently become a father.)

We sat down. I said, "Two things first of all, Robbie— the weight, and the baby."

He looked at me filthily. "Ha ha."

I asked him to tell me about his early life. When had he first wanted to be a performer?

"Oh, come on," he said. "That's all documented. That's all old stuff. Early seventies, I suppose. Mid-seventies, I suppose. Come on, this is old stuff. No, that's been in so many interviews. I did all that stuff about ten years ago."

He sat there, with his vast belly, his strangely perched head, his suit that fitted him like a burst condom, strange leopardette brothel creepers on his feet. Fat-guy shoes.

"Well, I mean, there's no point in going over old ground," he said. "People get sick of all that early origins stuff. I certainly do."

"But, say, your schooldays? Can't you . . ."

"Not really. It's all been done to death really."

I asked him about his shoes. Was he wearing them because of the series, because they were fifties shoes?

"You cheeky bugger."

"Well . . ."

"No," he said. "This is how I dress normally." Then he looked at me and said, "Well, I wouldn't walk around looking like a fucking student at your age. Cheeky bugger! I wouldn't! Who wants to be thought of as a student? God!"

I was wearing a denim jacket, jeans, sneakers, a T-shirt, an outfit I would not have considered if I was as fat as Coltrane. We sat there, looking at each other. He was losing weight. I was gaining. Soon, I would step into a nightmare of bingeing which would last almost a decade.

Why did Coltrane get so fat? He once said that, for several years in the 1980s—this is the era that his friends and colleagues referred to, gingerly, as "the hell-raising years"— he put on 14 lbs. a year. Another thing—why did such a talented actor do so much work? He was doing everything— terrible movies, stage plays, ads, comedy. He once said, "Brando always said that no moment in front of the lens is wasted—and that's absolutely true."

I said, "What made you do the Cadillac series?"

"Driving across America—it was just something I always wanted to do. I don't know why. It would have been easier and quicker without a film crew, obviously. But it occurred to me, I didn't really have the time to do it, and I wouldn't have done it on my own because of my commitments with work. I thought it would be a good idea to combine the two."

"But why couldn't you have just had a holiday?"

Coltrane said, "Because it would mean missing work."

"Do you feel that you always have to keep on the move? That you always have to be working?"

"Yeah, you do. You have to keep on doing things that interest you, really. And excite you. And bring out the best in you."

He lit up a cigarette. He told me he was on a strict diet, that he was going to quit smoking soon.

"I've lost 56 lbs.," he said.

"56 lbs? How?"

"Just by being on a horrendous diet. I don't eat any fat, don't eat any bread. I just eat the occasional baked potato. I do it all through Nutri-System. You pay the money, they give you the grub. And they say: if you eat no more than this, you will lose 7 lbs. a week. They send you the food; it's like aircraft food, or those Marks & Spencer meals you get, in the wee trays."

"What about exercise?"

"I'm still too overweight to do any serious exercise without damaging my heart. Once I've lost another 40 lbs. I'll go back and do some boxing training."

Coltrane had boxed at prep school in Scotland, just as he boxed a little at eighteen. But in his early teens, at his public school, Glenalmond, he was chubby, and unsporting. This is when, some of his schoolfriends told me, he became interested in being funny. When I asked him if he'd liked Glenalmond, he said, without hesitation, "No! I hated it!"

"He was the classic chubby young boy," one of his schoolfriends told me. "He was the fat boy who started telling jokes to protect himself."

After Glenalmond, he went to art school. And so began the unhealthy years, the years of eating and drinking and drugs, the years, as Coltrane himself put it, of "getting pissed and feeling people's arses."

"I wanted to be Rembrandt and I wanted to be Brando," he told me. "Neither has happened, so there you go."

He put on 14 lbs. a year. Why? Coltrane's friend John Sessions once said, "Robbie has a strong self-destruct streak . . . a deep, driving melancholy."

I asked Sessions about this. "I don't think he liked himself very much. That made him do it. He reconciled himself to the fact that he was going to get bigger and bigger and die. There was something in there."

Sessions also said, "I think he believed that, somehow, it was part and parcel of what sold him."

Coltrane lit another cigarette. I sat there, watching him, deeply uneasy, although at the time I wasn't sure why.

"If you smoke," he told me, sucking the smoke in with malicious enthusiasm, "you're doing yourself no good. But I will give up. I'll give up when I've lost the weight."

Collapse

And I drink more whiskey, and I find a bottle of vodka and drink some of that, I'm guzzling now, preparing a cushion for myself for when the drugs wear off. I'm flagging. I snort a line and I smoke a joint, the combined effect of which gives me a minor, barely perceptible rush, and I'm beginning to panic a little. The drink is running out. The drugs are running out. The party is beginning to break up. People are still here, people are talking to me, but I'm not listening.

I'm upstairs, in a bedroom, on my own, snorting the last of my drugs, preparing for one last assault, and now I know, of course, what it was that frightened me about Coltrane. He looked out of control. He looked like he couldn't help himself.

He didn't lose the weight, of course.

Why? Because dieting was not the answer.

I snort the drugs and scrunch up the little square wrapper and put it in my pocket, one melancholy moment in a series of melancholy moments, the whole experience a Groundhog day of wrong turns, and I take a last swig of vodka, and I remember the milky liqueur, which might and might not make me sick, and the thought of the liqueur, combined with the muted kick of the drugs, lifts my spirits, or possibly decelerates their fall, and I sit on the edge of a strange bed, not quite numb anymore, bad feelings and emotions beginning to break through, and I consider the condition of being out of control.

I've always had a morbid fascination with fat guys who lose control; I am drawn to them and disgusted by them in equal measure. Fatty Arbuckle, who hated himself, who pounded his liver with booze, who felt desperately unattractive, who tried to make people laugh, who wanted to be the center of attention all the time. John Belushi, who more or less invented the gross-out movie with his Bluto character in *Animal House*, who could not stop drinking and taking cocaine, and who once said, "I give so much pleasure to so many people. Why can I not get some pleasure for myself?"

Belushi and Arbuckle and Coltrane are similar cases; they were all driven by the need to work all the time, the need to entertain, and a desperate hunger for booze and food. This type of person does not want to sit still. Michael O'Donoghue, a writer who worked with Belushi, said, of his insatiable hunger, "He wants to grab the world and snort it."

Walking carefully down the stairs, I'm thinking about John Belushi, who would snort coke and drink alcohol for days on end, getting more and more terrified and paranoid. I'm thinking that, if I drink any more, I'll make myself ill; I'm also thinking, with a boozer's illogic, that, if I drink some more, my hangover will be less bad, because I will sleep better.

I remember talking to Michael VerMeulen about John Belushi. This was around the time I interviewed Coltrane. I was thin. Michael, by now editor of British *GQ*, was putting weight on. His appetites, for food, booze, and drugs, were getting out of control. Neither of us had yet written the article about fat guys; it was something both of us were planning, and also avoiding. I would get fat. He would get fatter. The process was already under way. It scared the hell out of both of us.

Michael said, "This is it. This is where he died."

We were in the Château Marmont hotel in Hollywood, the hotel where Belushi had died after taking a lot of cocaine and drinking a lot of alcohol. "I just asked for the Belushi room," said Michael. (Actually, we were not in the room where Belushi died, but another room—room 69—

where he'd stayed; the receptionist had applied a little artistic license.)

Michael said, "This is where he crashed out. The drugs and the booze just wiped him out."

"Apparently," I said, "when they found him he was a ghastly purple color. The blood had pooled on one side of his body."

"He put himself through a lot of abuse."

"He sort of . . . didn't like himself. He made people laugh, and he was a huge star. But he couldn't get the same respect as a leading man."

"Imagine that last night of his life. He would have collapsed about here. When he died, his head would have been . . . here."

I was in Los Angeles researching a story on Don Simpson, another man with a terrible appetite for food and booze and drugs, another fat boy who couldn't keep still. Simpson, a big fan of cocaine, produced films, along with his partner Jerry Bruckheimer, such as *Flashdance, Beverly Hills Cop, Top Gun,* and *Days of Thunder*—films that would later be dubbed "high concept." Simpson's movies always featured young people from the wrong side of the tracks, people who couldn't keep still. The films, like Simpson's life, were full of loud music and sexual innuendo, and endless conspicuous consumption, according to Simpson's biographer, Charles Fleming. Simpson himself owned forty pairs of cowboy boots; he once bought thirty-one Armani suits on the same day. He favored black Levi's jeans, but would only wear each pair once. "The color drops off just that much," he told an interviewer. "I like black to be what I call technical black. I can afford it. One time only, and they're out."

Fleming tells us about Simpson's heavy booze and drug consumption. One friend of Simpson's told Fleming, "He'd be like, 'Two lines? I'm doing *ten* lines, motherfucker.'" The same friend said, "If you took a shot of tequila, he'd guzzle half a bottle."

I'm thinking about this, about Simpson's gluttony, about what one Simpson acquaintance called his "inner fatboy," and about Belushi's inner fatboy, how his most famous moment was the scene in *Animal House* when he filled his mouth with food, puffing out his cheeks, and pressed on his cheeks so that the food spurted out, and said, "I'm a zit!" This is what I'm thinking about as I walk down the stairs and into the kitchen, wondering if I should have one last drink.

It doesn't take much. As soon as I take a swig of the milky liqueur, I don't feel good, not good at all, and after two or three swigs, I'm back in the sitting room, rocking on my feet. I can feel the nasty retribution of the blood leaving my head, saliva filling my throat, and at first I think I might not pass out, and then I think I might not be sick, and, finally, I think there is a chance that I will not do both of these things at exactly the same time, which is similar to the feeling I imagine Don Simpson might have had on January 18, 1996, when, after bingeing for years on coke and food and booze, his heart finally gave out, and which might also be similar to the sensations I imagine John Belushi had, when, after bingeing on coke and booze, he had a seizure and died in the early hours of March 5, 1982. And how the Chicago comedian Chris Farley, by then grossly overweight, who "dreamed of being John Belushi . . . I wanted to follow him" must have felt when, on December 18, 1997, he did indeed follow him. And the feeling I imagine Michael Ver-Meulen had when, on August 30, 1996, after a night on the tiles, a night bingeing on coke and booze, he, too, collapsed, passed out and died.

I've never vomited and passed out at exactly the same moment before. It's only in retrospect that you realize how dangerous it is. It would be salutary and rather neat if my thoughts, as I passed out, were "What makes me binge?" or "I need help," or "I'll get help." It would be interesting if, as oblivion beckons, you realize that oblivion is not what you want, not what you want at all. But actually, things happen much too fast for that. As you begin to lose control, as your stomach heaves, and as you begin to collapse, you just have time to wonder, briefly, what it will be like when your head smashes into the pile of CDs.

I never find out; I lose consciousness before I hit the ground.

A Forgettable Song

I wake up and I walk to the window and pull back the curtains and look out of the window for a while. I'm on the side of a hill and I can see right along the river valley, seven miles to the sea, and it's a clear, clear day so I can see beyond where the river hits the coast, right up the coast I can see, and then I get back into bed and lie there for a while, thinking nothing much, doing nothing much, just letting my mind go blank, which is something that, after seventy or eighty hours of therapy, I'm getting better at.

Diets are not the solution.

Of course diets are not the solution.

The problem is not the food.

The problem is far, far worse than just the food.

I'm looking around the bedroom, at the line of books along the wall, and the sink, and the crack in the ceiling where the water comes in when it rains. I'll go downstairs to make some coffee in a minute, and a few slices of toast. Sometimes, these days, I switch the radio on in the mornings and lie there, half-listening. But that's not what I do today. My girlfriend is still asleep. Sometimes she dozes longer than me.

I get out of bed and walk down the stairs and into the kitchen. I put the coffee on. I cut four slices of bread, two for me and two for her, making sure the slices are roughly even by turning the loaf around as I cut, which is something I never used to be able to do, but am fine about now. Before, I sliced downward in a straight line, pushing into the bread and sawing at it at the same time, and often ended up with wedge-shaped slices, which bothered me, but not enough to modify my technique.

As the coffee percolates I stare out of the window, at some trees, at the sky, at the planes angling up through the clouds from Gatwick airport, miles away when they appear, tiny dots at first and then perceptibly planes, and if I stand in the right place I can make the planes disappear in the exact corner of the window.

I drink the coffee outside the front of the house, sitting on a bench in the sun. I'll tell you something: I haven't stopped drinking. I just don't drink very much anymore. But I won't forgo the pleasure of what James Frey describes as "a nice glass of wine," or "a beer on a hot afternoon."

And I'm not on any particular diet. I eat bread and pasta and rice, and meat and fish and vegetables. There's a trifle in the fridge, and I want some of it, possibly even for breakfast. But I'm not so hungry all the time these days; I'm learning not to be so hungry.

I say, "I am learning."

I don't say, "I have learned."

I haven't stopped believing that carbs make you hungry. I still think that the Glycemic Index is important. It's easing itself into the culture. People are starting to say, "Forget Atkins—it's all about GI now." But, really, these are just two ways of spinning the same idea. Anyway, I don't think you should eat refined carbs if you can help it, unless you do a lot of exercise. But it's much easier to practice moderation if you're not hungry in the head. When you're hungry in the head—when you're spiritually needy—it's hard to resist your cravings. When you're happier, you can eat carbs and feel hungry and just ride it out. Go easy on the carbs, then, but don't flip out about it.

Drugs? Well, I don't want drugs so much anymore. I'm less interested in oblivion. I think alcohol and drugs, and food and sex for that matter, are no longer so dangerous when it's not oblivion you seek.

I've had four periods of problem drinking in my life—one when I was a teenager, for two years, one in my late twenties, for two years, one in my thirties, for about six years, and the recent one, which lasted a few months.

In my whole adult life, I've only been dry for twenty weeks.

So what was happening the rest of the time, when I was neither dry nor bingeing? Well, I drank a couple of times a week, mostly one or two drinks, sometimes a few more. I was drunk once in a while, but not often. I'd go into a bar and wonder what I wanted and sometimes decide on a coffee or a glass of water. During these times I didn't think about alcohol very much, but I remember going swimming or playing tennis and afterward having maybe two beers and absolutely enjoying them, totally savoring them. And that's a better relationship to have with beer, I think, than abstaining from it and being frightened of it.

Drugs? Well, maybe at a wedding, or on New Year's Eve, or if you see a group of old friends you haven't seen in a year or two.

I went to see Dr. Robert Lefever, who runs the Promis Centre, a place for recovering addicts, as the terminology has it, and Dr. Lefever, he's a former alcoholic, gambler, and overeater himself, said that he once asked his wife how she can leave half a glassful of wine. She told him she could leave it because she didn't want it anymore. Lefever then said that he hadn't asked her why she'd left the half-glassful of wine, but how.

He said, "She looks at me blankly because she doesn't understand the question. If I left half a glassful of wine it would sing to me—so strongly that I would have to go back to it to finish it off."

Well, there have been times when I haven't been able to leave half a glassful of wine, either. But I can now. It doesn't sing to me anymore.

Or rather, maybe it sings a bit, but it's a forgettable song, not one of those songs you get on the brain.

Vomit

When I woke up that morning, all those months ago, with my head in a pile of CDs, I felt better than I thought I would. First of all, I was breathing. Aside from that, I was caked in vomit. I had vomit in my nostrils and hair, vomit on my shirt, vomit stiffening the front of my jacket, which I had not, of course, taken off. The curtains were still open. The sun was bright. When I opened my eye, I felt savagely exposed, like a man on a battlefield under a flare. I could see the sun broken down into individual rays, which rippled off the broken pyramid of CD cases like heat haze. There are many bad things one might pass out into while vomiting, and some are better than a pile of CDs. They are sharp, they are shiny, they cut into your face.

I opened my other eye. I had pain *in* my eyes, pain *behind* my eyes, a pulsing tide of sickening discomfort clutching the inside of my head. The alcohol I had drunk had dehydrated the inside of my skull. Consequently, the dura, the cellophane-like membrane that encases my brain, was no longer fully supported. Cells inside my brain were being traumatized, and had responded by releasing chemicals ordering nerve endings in my head to tell my brain the bad news. My brain, in turn, was trying to get my attention, and succeeding. I was in pain. It felt as if something inside my head was being gently pulled away from my skull, which it was.

Quite apart from that, the cocaine I had snorted and the cannabis I had smoked, having raised my levels of serotonin and dopamine to unrealistically high levels, had created the knock-on effect of making my brain mop up these feel-good chemicals like a sponge.

The radiator was on. My head was pressed against the radiator. My eyes and mouth were encrusted with vomit. The radiator was encrusted with vomit. My head was heating up at an alarming rate. My cheek was pressed into the carpet. The carpet was tough and bobbled, hard knots of sea grass abrading my skin.

And when I moved my head, I felt as if a rotating implement had pared my brain from my skull. My throat, once again, was lubricated with juices. I considered my position. The grand ambitions I had entertained moments before—to wipe down the CDs and the radiator, to sponge the worst of the vomit off my clothes, to somehow pick the carpet clean with a knife or some other implement, to air the place— came and went. For a too-brief moment, my lesser ambition, of sneaking out unnoticed, so that I could retch in the street, unconstrained by the awkwardness of being in someone else's house, seemed a definite possibility.

And when the door opened, and the hostess of the impromptu party, the lady of the house, walked through the door, and said something, and walked straight back out, and slammed the door, I thought, "I need help."

And: "I don't need help."

And: "I need help."

And: "I'll get help."

"I'm Hopeful"

Susie Orbach, trim and girlish although she's well into middle age, opened the door to her office, which is a very neat, well-kept basement in north London, and welcomed me in, and we walked into her office and sat down, and we talked about why people become compulsive eaters. We agreed that people were intimidated by impossibly thin role-models in magazines and on television, by the cult of thin; we agreed that the cult of thin, in the end, made people fat. We agreed that girls were dieting at a younger age than ever before. She said she thought that "very very early on, babies' appetites are being thwarted."

We talked about the fashion for women to lose weight very quickly after giving birth, and how women often stop breastfeeding too early. We talked about Elizabeth Hurley, how Hurley lost her "baby body" soon after giving birth to her son Damian. We agreed that body fascism, which used to intimidate women, and hardly used to intimidate men at all, is now beginning to intimidate men. We discussed the theories of Susan Faludi, who believes that men are undergoing a terrible crisis of identity.

And then we talked about the rise of men's magazines, and how they were really vectors for advertising male grooming products, which means that, to be successful, they need to make men feel insecure, so they will want to buy the grooming products.

"It's a very very lucrative business," said Orbach.

We discussed the power of the cult of thin. The cult of thin is about wanting what you can't have, striving for impossible perfection, slipping into narcissism, judging yourself by your own dismorphia, and eventually becoming isolated, compulsive. I said that skinniness was such a ubiquitous and positive image in our world that it seemed almost hardwired in the brain.

Orbach said, "No, absolutely not. I completely disagree.

I think it's totally socially constructed. And the social construction is so powerful that it *feels* hardwired. Look—you go around the world. Look at Fiji. In 1995, you've got commercial telly going in. In 1998 they've got 12 percent of teenagers being bulimic. Now that is staggering. It's a very clear result. You've got economic penetration, and visual penetration."

I said I'd read an article in the *Daily Mail* which described two *Vogue* models as "ugly" and "skinny"; I said I thought this use of language demonstrated that the cult of thin was absolutely in the ascendancy.

I said, "I mean, a state of body has to be extremely powerful in today's PC world when you can call it ugly. You can't say fat people are ugly. You can't even say they're a bit dumpy. Surely the cult of thin has won."

"Watch this space."

"Do you think a change is possible?"

"Well it is. I'm around teenage girls, and they're sticking their bellies out, and wearing these crop tops, and they're not at all skinny. So there is a zeitgeist change about to happen."

Orbach said she thought the change might be brought about by fashion designers and high-end stores and magazines; things could be different if these people would only change their ways, make clothes in bigger sizes, use bigger models.

"I'm hopeful," she said.

I told her I'd had trouble with overeating, overconsumption in general. I said I needed help. She said she would not give me therapy.

But she could recommend somebody who would.

In Disguise

I'm sitting on the bench, drinking my coffee, and thinking that diets don't work because diets are about being fat and wanting to be thin. Diets, in other words, are about being one type of thing, and wanting to look like another type of thing.

And if your main motivation is to look thin, you will almost certainly fail, now or sometime soon. Mostly, fat people are fat because they're troubled, and if they lose weight, they become troubled thin people, and then they just start overeating again, and become fat people who are even more troubled than they were before.

I've laid out all sorts of statistics, but here's the most important one—95 percent of the people who lose weight find themselves back where they started, or somewhere even worse.

That's the problem with the whole of the diet industry. The diet industry says to millions of troubled people, "You don't have to look into the reasons why you're troubled."

The diet industry says, "Just follow these simple steps, and you can avoid any of the difficult stuff."

The diet industry says, "You have problems, and you don't want to talk about them, and, guess what—you don't have to."

If it's successful, a diet merely makes you temporarily *look* like a person who doesn't have your problems. You might lose weight, but the problems, which made you overeat in the first place, are still there. So you'll overeat again. Or, like me, you'll do something else—you'll use alcohol or drugs or whatever, and then you'll probably start to overeat again anyway.

So diets don't work. Diets are like facelifts, which aspire to making you resemble a different type of person, but which can never turn you into a different person.

To diet is to believe in the supremacy of the image; dieters are like people who believe they are more real in photographs than in person.

At best, diets, like facelifts, enable you to walk around in disguise.

No Trouble

I met a woman who wanted to walk around in disguise. To me, Anne's face looked fine. Certainly, there were some crow's-feet around the eyes and some lines between the nose and the mouth. Her brow was slightly wrinkled. She also had something of a double chin. But Anne was fifty-three. Her facial expressions, made from the movements of the lines, wrinkles, and muscles of her face, had an air of integrity. They were the outward manifestations of the thoughts of a woman in her early fifties.

To me, Anne's facial lines were part of why her face looked fine. But I was not Anne. Anne did not want to look like a woman in her fifties. She wanted to look like something which, to her, was significantly different—a woman in her forties. She wanted, superficially, to pass for someone who was born, not in the era of Glenn Miller, but around the time when Elvis was beginning to make an impression. She wanted to have the appearance of a younger version of herself. Looking less old, she believed, would improve her life.

Anne was due to have a facelift, and some liposuction, the next day. The operation would last nearly four hours. She invited me to watch it.

"It should take five or ten years away," Anne explained. She told me what would happen to her. It frightened me. Just the idea of it frightened me. She would be anaesthetized. The skin around her ear would be cut with a scalpel. Not pricked, or jabbed, but sliced. Next, her cheek would be separated from the flesh of her face. Her facial muscles would be rearranged. Her skin would be stretched. Excess skin would be cut off. Then she would be stitched up. The whole process, of course, would be repeated on the other side. Then her eyelids would be cut open with a laser beam. Fat would be removed from the eyelids.

Looking younger, Anne said, would improve her "confidence." She was already relishing the thought of looking in the mirror and seeing the difference.

She said, "You may think, Small problem, silly woman. But it's about what you feel like inside."

Anne's husband, Derek, who was fifty, said, "I'm passionately in favor. If it doesn't do any harm, then it's got to be good for everybody." He himself had had fat sucked from under his chin.

We discussed the reasons for Anne's facelift. Finally, she said, "Men mature, whereas women age. Men look quite good when they look older."

I said, "Why is that?"

"I don't know. I don't know why. But it's true. For instance, gray hair looks nice on a man. Not on a woman. It's very, very hard to say why, but it's a fact."

I drank the champagne Anne poured for me. Having entered the final twenty-four hours before the operation, Anne was not allowed to drink.

"Are you worried?"

She said, "Oh, yes, I'm anxious. I'd be abnormal if I wasn't."

Anne's facelift was to be performed in a small private clinic in Highgate in north London. As I approached the clinic the next day, feeling hollow and nauseated, I realized that I had mixed feelings about cosmetic surgery. I couldn't shake off a feeling of discomfort. But why is it wrong? If it is ageist, so is jogging. So is yoga. If it is a superficial change masquerading as a more significant one, so is wearing a suit. Did I believe that beauty was divinely ordained, or that there should be only so much of it around? My misgivings were elusive, but persistent.

The clinic was a former Edwardian house in a residential street. Anne was watching television in an upstairs room. She was quiet. She looked nervous. I was terrified. She had opted not to have a "pre-med," an injection to quell her nerves. The television rumbled away. We did not say much to each other.

To attend the operation, I had to wear "scrubs"—a blue, square-necked T-shirt, blue cotton pajama-like trousers, a blue elasticized paper cap, and white slip-on sandals with, for some reason, a little heel.

The administration of the anaesthetic was a shock for which I had not prepared myself. Anne was wheeled into the room on a trolley. She was lying on her back. Dr. Chang, the anaesthetist, who had himself had cosmetic surgery on his eyelids and his ears, stuck a needle into Anne's hand. The needle was joined to an open socket. Chang was whistling. Anne said, "I'm very calm, actually. Yes. Just a slight apprehension in the last few minutes, but nothing dreadful."

Chang said, "Anne, have a nice sleep." Then he took five syringes and, with practiced ease, pumped their contents, one after the other, into the socket in Anne's hand. There was a muscle relaxant, the anaesthetic itself (which is white and soya-based), a painkiller, a steroid to ease swelling, and an anti-sickness drug. (Later, Chang would tell me there is still some medical mystery about how the anaesthetic works.)

For a tiny moment, Anne concentrated on her hand. Then, horribly, all expression on her face collapsed. It was like watching the moment of death. The eyes rolled in their sockets and the head, suddenly heavy, slumped down on the pillow. I had an overwhelming sensation of disgust. (It's gone wrong! They've killed her!) While Anne's face was being injected with adrenaline, to reduce blood flow, I slipped out of the room, and, breathing deeply, took a seat in a room next door where a surgeon was eating a turkey sandwich. "I'm having lunch between faces," he told me.

A trolley was wheeled in. A nurse said, to a patient, "Come on, Julia. Julia! Time for you to wake up. Keep waking up! That's better. Listen! Stay awake for me." The patient's face was heavily bandaged. She was gently moaning.

Superficially calm, I walked into the operating theater. It struck me that my misgivings about cosmetic surgery might simply be a fear of blood and unnecessary violence. Also, the more people who do it, the more chance there is that, one day, it will be my turn to feel the pressure. Anne had talked of the influence of older film stars who looked good because they'd had facelifts. Julie Christie, Joan Rivers, Burt Reynolds: their nips and tucks have crept into the culture.

Anne was on her back, on a trolley. She looked like a corpse. She looked like a dead old bloke. She had tubes coming out of her mouth; a machine was breathing for her. Mr. Prakash, the surgeon, was standing by the side of the trolley, in scrubs. Two thick magnifying lenses were protruding from his glasses like frog's eyes.

The first thing Mr. Prakash did was to make a hole under Anne's chin, and insert a cannula, which looked like a thick needle. This was for liposuction, or, as cosmetic surgeons prefer to say, "liposculpture." The cannula was attached to a clear plastic tube. Mr. Prakash jabbed the cannula under the skin of Anne's neck. After a moment or two, a bubbly pink substance, like strawberry milkshake, was sucked back through the plastic tube. This was the fat. This was the double chin.

When Mr. Prakash took the cannula out of Anne's neck, it slurped, as if it were a straw sucking the last drops of the milkshake from a glass. He had, he told me, performed this operation seventy times. He replaced the cannula, and jabbed away, with a great deal more vigor than I would have expected.

There was more fat on the left side of her face than the right. The fat bubbled back through the tube. Mr. Prakash smoothed his gloved hand over the flesh, as if molding putty.

He said, "See how the bulkiness has gone?"

It was when Mr. Prakash picked up a tiny scalpel that I started to feel sick. The blood left my head. My legs felt hollow at the sight of a man, with a blade, preparing to insert it into the face of another human being. I found a chair and sat, head in hands, swallowing saliva. I needed a few moments.

One of the reasons often cited for getting cosmetic surgery is that it is a simple, painless process. You go into the operating theater unbeautiful, and, hours later, emerge, beautiful. All you have done is paid; somebody else has done the work. (I've heard people take the same tone with fake suntans: you don't have to work for them, so, in some way, you have taken an unfair advantage.) Looking at Anne, though, whose gray, open-mouthed, open-eyed face resembled that of an old man hovering between life and death, I dismissed this idea. In the end, she might look younger, or better; she might have fewer wrinkles and a taut neck. But, on some level—physical, mental, spiritual—she looked like she was paying for it.

Mr. Prakash told me that, to combat my nausea, I could try bending over Anne's face and concentrating on small details. It worked. Mr. Prakash sliced into Anne's flesh. He went around her ear with his scalpel. The wound did not spurt with blood. There was a slight welling. The adrenaline injections had done their job. Mr. Prakash said to the nurse standing on the other side of the trolley, "Have you seen the breast girl?" He was referring to his next patient.

Mr. Prakash said, "Pull the ear, please!"

Dr. Chang said, "Now comes the interesting bit." And, with a pair of tweezers, Mr. Prakash began to peel Anne's skin away from her cheek. Or was it that he was peeling her face away from her head? He started behind the ear and moved around to the front of the ear. Underneath, the flesh was pink and slightly runny, like raw veal. As he pulled the skin away, he cut the membrane joining it to the layer of muscle underneath. You can see why some people who have had facelifts lose sensation in their faces for a while. Their nerves have been cut.

Every now and again, there was a sizzle, and a smell of cooking. Mr. Prakash was cauterizing those blood vessels which were still seeping. When Mr. Prakash had cut the side of Anne's face, as it seemed, free of the muscles underneath, all the way down to the corner of her mouth, a clamp was inserted, tenting the cheek.

Now, there was a cavernous space, inside which were stalactites of fat, and glands, which resembled sweetbreads, and the flesh itself, stringy and bright red and gently oozing. With tweezers, Mr. Prakash inserted a cloth to mop up the blood. Then he placed the cloth on a tray.

Into the hole in Anne's face, Mr. Prakash inserted a needle-and-thread contraption. He put a stitch in each of the facial muscles and pulled them upward, holding on to the thread, his gloved hands dextrous, twirling. It took ages. The stitches, he said, would dissolve in 120 days.

"Ear, please." While the nurse held Anne's ear, Mr. Prakash gently pulled on her skin. And the skin, stretched, fit over the bottom half of the ear, as if it were a rubber mask. Mr. Prakash cut the excess away with a pair of scissors. He went around the ear, cutting little triangles of fleshy skin. He placed the skin on the tray. One bit had hair on a triangle of scalp. Again, the blood left my head.

Ninety minutes passed. Mr. Prakash repeated the procedure on the other side of the patient's face. When Anne was stitched up, he slid metal eyeball guards underneath her eyelids, which he would slice open with a laser gun. Anne looked like an android. We put on goggles, to protect our own eyes from stray laser beams.

Using the laser contraption, which looked like a dentist's drill, Mr. Prakash cut across each eyelid. As soon as the beam touched, the flesh seemed to spring apart. Then, with a pair of tweezers, he pulled out the fat. It came out in worms, and looked like bloody snot. Finally, he ran the laser along some of Anne's facial lines. His smock was smeared with blood. Next door, through a glass panel, I could see a man lying on a trolley. He was writhing and bucking. Minutes later, a young woman walked toward the operating theater with a trolley by her side. "I'm walking in," she said. It was the breast girl.

"My next victim." Mr. Prakash grinned.

Five months later, I knocked on the door of Anne's large Victorian house in the Sussex countryside. The door opened. The woman on the other side of the door, while recognizably the woman I met before the operation, looked changed. She looked . . . tighter. There was something different around the eyes. She smiled. Her smile was not exactly the same smile. She led me into her kitchen, where we both sat at the table.

I said, "Well!" She poured me a glass of wine. One of her eyelids looked slightly tighter than the other. She no longer had a double chin. She had a single chin, like a younger woman. She had a more defined bone structure. Her face conveyed her thoughts in a flatter, less complicated way, in a way that resembled the expressions of a younger woman, although her skin, as she pointed out, was not the skin of a younger woman. Her skin was fifty-three.

She looked younger, but not, I imagine, precisely like her younger self.

She was, she said, "very happy" with the operation. She had, she'd been told, "lost a good eight years." In a way, it was true. Having been a young-looking fifty-three, she could now pass for forty-five. "When I'm sixty-three," she says, "I'll probably look mid-fifties, or perhaps fifty-seven." Friends she had not told about the operation had been re-marking on how well she looked.

"My confidence," she said, "is boosted 100 percent." Her husband was "over the moon." There were pictures of him on the kitchen door before liposculpture and, younger looking, after. Anne's children, who had thought she was "mad" to have the operation, were pleased. Now she was no longer negatively conscious of her neck. "I hated looking down," she said. "To look down was awful."

After the operation, Anne felt "tight," as if she was "permanently blowing up a balloon." Later, there was discomfort, swelling, and bruising. The bruising takes weeks to go down. "I told my children I'd look horrible," she said, "but you can't prepare people."

Looking at Anne, I could see that her facelift both had and hadn't worked. She had dispensed with her double chin, which she hated, and various wrinkles. But it was not per-fect. She had the air of a woman who had had her wrinkles removed, rather than one who was too young to have wrin-kles. Looking at Anne, with her new smile and firmer chin line, made me understand a bit better my misgivings about cosmetic surgery. It is one more example, in the modern world, of the superficial being offered as a substitute for the profound, of image being traded for meaning. The terrible, secret worry I had been carrying around about cosmetic surgery, I began to realize, is that it might actually work.

"The thing that went wrong with my eyelid," Anne said, "was that it bled so much. It's very rare for this to happen. But that's why it's healed like this." She put her finger up to the eyelid. She said, "But that won't be any problem. Mr. Prakash can put that right. No trouble." She moved her finger across her eyelid, as if it were a surgical tool.

We sipped at our wine. Anne was getting the feeling back in her cheeks. The nerves were joining up again. You could see that the cheeks, tighter now, were almost back to a natural look. The scars around the ears were minimal. She nearly felt right again. Some people don't for a year. Some never do.

Extrinsics

No, I'm thinking as I drink the last of my coffee, facelifts are not the answer. At best, facelifts disguise you as a more attractive person, in the same way that credit cards disguise you as a rich person, mobile phones as a connected person, cocaine as a happy person, painkillers as a person without a hangover, diets as an untroubled person who never got fat, never stuffed their face. But, with all these things, the economics are not good. You end up with a net loss. Overwhelmingly, people who diet end up still feeling fat, and eventually getting fat. People who have facelifts still feel wrinkly; many book themselves in for repeat surgery. Credit-card debt is increasing exponentially; more debtors commit suicide every year. Cocaine makes you depressed. Painkillers give you headaches.

Treat the symptoms, not the cause. That's what we're always being told. What can you do if you're feeling sad? Take Prozac. Get a new kitchen. Have a wardrobe makeover, an operation, a new set of teeth. Have a Botox injection in your lunch break. Have a cushion inserted into the sole of your foot, so you can wear higher heels. Get a tattoo or a piercing. Play the lottery. Fly to a secluded beach. Become famous.

In an essay entitled "The Dark Side of the American Dream," sociologists Tim Kasser and Richard Ryan wrote about people who pursue what they call "extrinsic goals"—money, fame, and beauty—believing these things make them happy. But they don't, of course. They experience "lower quality of life" than people who are less materialistic. But they are not just miserable—they spread misery, too; they have "shorter, more conflictual, and more competitive relationships with others." People with extrinsic goals, writes the Australian economist Clive Hamilton, "tend to be more depressed than others, and they tend to suffer from higher levels of psychological disturbance." Romantically, they are more jealous. As teenagers, they commit more vandalism. And when they achieve their goals, Hamilton says, they are "no happier."

And when one person gets a facelift, others will want one, too. This exponentially increasing pursuit of the superficial, Hamilton believes, is the West's most significant problem. Every Western government, he says, is obsessed with economic growth. But how does the economy achieve growth in a time of abundance, when everybody has what they need?

By making them want what they don't have, of course.

By making them dissatisfied with what they've already got. By making them feel abject, hungry, isolated. And by making them overspend and overeat, by lending them money at high rates of interest, and pumping their bodies full of insulin, and then telling them the problem, the real problem, is fat, sugar, and salt.

That's what I'm thinking, sitting here on the bench with the last of my coffee. Extrinsic goals are not the solution.

But what, then, is the solution? Therapy?

Really, I Was Fine

I was late for my first session. Twenty minutes late.

"Sorry about this," I said. "You see, when you gave me your address, you gave the number as 130. Which is right, of course. But, see, I took it down as 30."

"Don't worry."

"I took it down wrong."

"That's fine."

"So I get to number 30, and nobody's around. No answer. And then this woman arrives, walks up the garden path, and says, can I help you? And I say, well, I hope so. And she says what do you mean, and I say, well, I think you're my therapist. And she looked really scared at this point. It was getting dark. So I said, actually, I might have the wrong number."

"I see."

"And that's when I worked it out. I thought, you know, this is a long street. And the only other number it could have been was 130."

"Right."

"So here I am."

I've read that, during therapy, you're not supposed to notice your surroundings, but I took everything in. I was sitting down on a small, neat armchair, not a couch, and my therapist, Naomi, was sitting on an identical chair. Sort of like the chairs you would get in a hotel lobby, chairs to be quite comfortable in, but not totally relaxed. The room was minimally furnished. White walls. Neat carpet. Journals on a shelf.

I was not sure what would happen next. I wanted to find out what my problems were. That was all. I was not unduly alarmed. I reminded Naomi about my "issues," which we'd briefly discussed on the phone. The eating. The drinking.

"So—eating and drinking. Anything else?"

I thought for a moment. I felt a sense of vertigo, as if standing on the edge of a crevasse.

"Well, obviously, procrastination."

"Procrastination?"

"Yes. I'm always . . . putting things off."

"That's interesting. Tell me about that."

"I always seem to leave things to the last moment. I'm always late. I don't like being late. In fact, I hate being late. But I can't bring myself to be on time. Something, a sort of malign force, always takes me over."

She asked me if I could think of any instances, and I told her stories—of nearly missing trains, nearly missing planes, actually missing trains and planes. I told her that, if I was ever early for something, I felt uneasy, gripped by anxiety.

"And has this caused you problems?"

"Oh, yes. Everybody hates it."

"Can you tell me about a specific time?"

"I was once on holiday, in Italy, with a girlfriend and her family. One day we went somewhere on this train. And we all got on the train. It was a tiny station. We were sitting there. The train was leaving in about five minutes. And I looked across the platform, and there was this lovely sort of coffee place, a tiny little coffee bar. And all I could think of was that I really wanted a coffee. I mean . . ."

"Go on."

"I mean, I *really wanted* a coffee. And I said, does anybody want a coffee? And my girlfriend just hissed at me. She said, you can't be serious. I said, look, we have, like, six minutes. How long do you think it will take me? And she gave me this look, just this mean look, as if to say, if you do this I will hate you. And I sat there for a while, and just when she thought I was definitely not going to do it, I got out of the train, walked across the tracks, got my coffee, and made it back, about a full minute before the whistle."

"And what happened?"

"She wouldn't speak to me."

"And how did you feel?"

"Well, great. For a moment. And the coffee was not bad, actually."

"But this wasn't about the coffee."

"Right."

"So what was it about?"

"I don't know. With me it's probably all about boarding school."

"What's the connection?"

"Well . . ."

And so began the procrastination phase of my therapy,

the hours when I talked about certain things, in order to avoid talking about other things. Of course, this is not necessarily a bad approach. As Freud pointed out, therapy is not something that should be brought to a swift conclusion. On the contrary, therapy should be long, drawn-out, painful—and, of course, expensive. "Cruel though it may sound," Freud wrote in *Lines of Advance in Psychoanalytic Therapy*, "we must see to it that the patient's suffering, to a degree that is in some way or other effective, does not come to an end prematurely."

"Were you happy at boarding school?"

"I was fine."

"Fine?"

"I just felt very . . . restricted."

Boarding school, although I hadn't liked it, was something I felt relatively comfortable talking about; if my troubled psyche was a crevasse, the subject of boarding school seemed like a visible ledge. I lowered myself down onto the ledge. At boarding school, I explained, I felt "trapped." I hated the rules. I hated the fact that you had to wear a strict uniform. I hated the fact that, for a day every week, you had to dress up, not just in uniform, but in *army* uniform, that you had to polish your boots and belt, actually polish your belt with boot polish, making it shine, as if it was itself a pair of boots. And why, in any case, do boots need to be polished? Boots that need to be polished, I said, made me sick. They made me think of old women scrubbing the pavement outside their terraced houses.

"So, you know, I think I'm always trying to escape, trying to kick against that stuff. Hence the procrastination."

"That's interesting."

"Once, I remember, I was walking along a corridor, and this master just grabbed me, and slammed me against the wall and just . . . sort of strangled me with my tie, because it wasn't done up properly. That's the kind of place it was, my school."

"And where were your parents while this was happening?"

"Oh. They were . . . they moved around a lot."

"Yes?"

"My father was an academic. He worked at all sorts of different universities. He went to conferences all the time. Where were my parents? They were abroad."

"We're going to have to stop in a couple of minutes. We can talk about this more next time. But how did you feel about your parents being abroad?"

"Oh, fine."

"OK then."

"No, really. I was fine about it. Because . . ."

"I'm sorry about this, but we've run out of time."

Only Nuts

When I walked out, thinking about my parents, about where my family had been when I was a kid, I went into a bar and drank a glass of red wine, trying to drink it slowly, but drinking it in two gulps, and quickly ordering another, and drinking that one in about four gulps, and I sat at the bar for a while, feeling woozy and reading a tabloid story about a survey claiming that six out of every ten women were unhappy with their bodies. One woman interviewed said she'd had liposuction, and was "delighted with the results." But she was still not completely satisfied with herself. "The shape of my nose has started to bother me," she said.

I walked out of the bar and tried to imagine doing something other than snorting some cocaine and getting hammered, absolutely hammered, and I wandered around for a while, went home, watched TV, tried to calm down. I was fine, I told myself. There was *nothing wrong*. I went to the deli across the road, and bought a packet of macadamia nuts. Standing there, in the street, I ripped the packet open, swallowed some nuts, went home, and put the rest of the nuts in the cupboard. I closed the cupboard door. I tried to breathe deeply. I was fine. It was only nuts. I opened the cupboard door. I looked at the nuts, thought about them.

Did I want the nuts?

No, I did not.

I closed the cupboard door. It was only nuts. I was fine.

That's how I felt the rest of the week. Fine. Well, that's not quite true. I lay on my bed and read books, more or less compulsively, about addiction and therapy. I sat at my laptop, scribbling notes on pieces of paper, on the dog-eared documents that formed a mound on my desk—restaurant bills, bar bills, electricity and phone bills, reminders, final demands, summonses. The words I kept writing were "compulsive" and "eating" and "food" and "alcohol" and "childhood" and "mother" and "father" and "procrastination" and "hypochondria."

I'd had trouble with hypochondria, on and off, for years. The next time I saw Naomi, I brought the subject up.

"I think I'm better now, though. It still flares up. But it's more or less totally under control, I'd say. Just occasionally, I have to, you know, keep it in check."

"Does it happen at any particular time?"

"Well, yes. That's interesting. Uh, I'd say it happens in two quite different situations. One is when I'm anxious about something."

"What sort of thing?"

"When I'm under pressure. You know. Deadlines. Work. But it's not as bad now. I mean, it's just little things, and I get them under control pretty quickly."

"How do you mean?"

"Well, it's nothing like it was. These days, it's just, say, if I switch on the radio, like I did the other day, and the first thing I heard, the first word, was 'cancer.' And then the word just keeps jumping out at me. I'll see it everywhere. In stations. On posters. Sometimes you open a magazine, and there's a picture of someone, and just a simple caption, 'I have cancer.' You just see the stark words. And that begins to haunt me."

"I see."

"But I must be getting better. Because there was a time when I wouldn't have been able to say the words, 'I have cancer.'"

"Uh-huh."

"Which I don't."

"Right."

"I mean, I don't have cancer."

"You said there were two different situations when you felt your hypochondria coming on."

"Right, yes."

"One is when you're anxious. And the other one?"

"Oddly, when I'm not anxious."

I went on in this vein for a while. I told Naomi about my hypochondria—its details, its quirks. I told her about how, usually, I focused my anxiety on one disease, and how, when my hypochondria was at its worst, I had hung around the medical sections of bookshops, reading about diseases I was not frightened of.

"Why?"

"Well, to see if I could displace the main disease with another disease."

Naomi said, "It's interesting that you keep talking about being trapped."

"Yes?"

"And yet you keep telling me how you impose these traps on yourself."

Little Pieces

Over the next few weeks, a pattern began to emerge. I would arrive, late, take my coat off, sit on the not-quite comfortable chair, and proclaim myself to be "fine, absolutely fine." Then I would tell Naomi something trivial—something I had noticed about the weather, or the traffic. Naomi would smile politely. Mostly, therapists don't comment on anything at all. For months, the only solitary fact I gleaned from Naomi was that she preferred to travel to hot places in the off-season, when the weather was not too hot—she liked Greece in September, for instance.

I kept talking about the same few things—my tendency to binge, my fears, my lateness, the fact that I tended to hold on to clutter, rather than throwing it away. For a while, it seemed that I knew exactly what my problem was, and yet, simultaneously, that I knew nothing. I'd thought about it a million times, and made sense of it, and later, when I thought about it again, it made no sense at all.

One day, quite early on, Naomi said, "Tell me about your childhood."

"Well, you know. We moved around."

I described the moves. As I went through the place names, I became very uncomfortable—filled, not with sadness or misery, but guilt. I kept expecting Naomi to challenge me, or at least to change the subject. When I had finished listing the places, I felt terrible.

"And did your difficulties with eating have anything to do with that, do you think?"

"Well, I always think they did. I was fine until I was eight, when we moved to Canada for a year, and then I got fat. I was exposed to a lot of fast food. Before that I'd had a pretty controlled diet. In Canada it was burgers, fries, lots of ice cream, popcorn, and all that stuff. And I just fell for it. I remember this particular ice cream, sort of very soft white ice cream between chocolatey wafers, which I had at school every break time, it was a sort of reward—"

"Rewarding yourself?"

"Yes. I hated that school. It was a Catholic school, very religious, very strict."

"Were your parents unhappy?"

"My mother, I think, hated being there. My father had wanted to go."

"So there was tension between your parents?"

"No. Not . . . Well, I don't know. If there was, they played it down."

I paused. This was making me uncomfortable. I didn't

mind talking about myself, about my own problems, my own unhappiness, my bingeing, drug taking, procrastination, untidiness—but my parents! How could my parents be unhappy? They were my parents. They were fine.

"Do you remember anything about being told the family was going to move?"

"Well, I must have been seven. I remember coming home from school, and saying something like, I'm going to be in Mrs. Phillips' class next term, and my mother saying, no you're not, because we're going to Canada."

"Right."

"And I said, how long for? And my mum said, for a year. And this sounded weird, but not too bad. And I said, so does that mean I'll be in Mrs. Phillips' class the year after, or will I go straight into the next class? And my mum said that, well, no, I wouldn't . . ."

"Yes?"

"And . . . I didn't understand. That was when she told me that, after we came back from Canada, we wouldn't be coming back home. We'd be going somewhere else."

"And how did you feel about that?"

"It was the way the information came out in little pieces. That was the killer."

And . . . here it was! I sat there for a moment, wanting to explore this emotion, not wanting to explore this emotion. Here was something I'd been repressing! At last—a beginning. Of course, you shouldn't expect too much from therapy— as Freud said, the best you could expect was an experience, over time, of "transforming your hysterical misery into common unhappiness."

I had hoped to find two things. The first was: what is my

real problem? The second: if I find out what my real problem is, how will this help?

And this thing I'd just seen, or rather felt, this thing I'd been repressing, was, I felt, related to my real problem.

I said, "That was the killer. The way the information came out in little pieces."

I Hadn't Even Noticed It

Sometimes I talked about my dreams. I kept having two recurring dreams. In one, I would wake up in a cell, on the day of my execution. Then I would wake up in my bed, and still think I was in the cell. In the other, I would have a visit from an old teacher, often my Latin teacher. He would produce documents, incontrovertibly proving that I had to go back to school. In the dream, there was always a period of wrangling about uniform issues. In one version I would have to wear shorts.

One day I said to Naomi, "At the age of nine I had this sort of breakdown. This was after we came back from Canada."

"Breakdown?"

"Well, I've never called it that. I would never call it that in front of my parents. But I was completely out of control. I stopped being able to write. I started eating my pens and pencils, and drinking ink. I used to put ink cartridges in my mouth and chew them. I mean, something weird, really weird, was happening."

This was interesting. It was definitely true that something very peculiar had happened to me. It started with a compulsion to press too hard with the nib of my fountain pen, rendering my handwriting scratchy and illegible. I broke one nib after another. I could not understand how other boys could have a pen and not be overwhelmed by the urge to destroy it. Soon, nearly everything I touched would break. At the time I wore glasses, and my glasses kept falling off and smashing. I began to chew, and then to eat, the contents of my pencil case. But this was the first time, the very first time, I had described this period in my life with any accuracy. It amazed me. Over the years, these events had been diminished, watered down, forgotten.

"And how was this resolved?"

"One day, after it had been going on for a while, we were in a Latin class, and the Latin teacher, who was the headmaster of the school, asked me to go to the staff room to get some chalk. So I did. And later, some of the other kids surrounded me, and started saying, 'Crying, were you? Crying? Well, I'm going to make you cry!' "

"What was that about?"

"Well, years later, I became friends with one of these kids who beat me up, and he told me that when I went to get the chalk, the headmaster had said something like, 'I had a call from this boy's mother last night. And she says he comes home crying every day. Now, why would this be?' And this kid said, 'That really got us going. I mean, we knew you were pretty weird. But crying? Crying to your mummy? That made us want to hammer you.' "

"So you were very vulnerable at this point."

"Right. Absolutely. But things did get better."

"Because there was more stability at home?"

"Oh, no. Not at all. There was *less* stability. Less and less."

"So how did things get better?"

"I began to adopt a sort of gallows humor. The next thing was, about a year after I started getting beaten up, in fact around the time people stopped beating me up, my mother gave me another piece of news. We were going to Germany! We were all going to Germany for the Easter holidays. But get this. My parents and my brother were going to stay in Germany. I had to go to boarding school."

"How did you feel?"

"Well, come on. I mean, part of me must have felt really frightened. And, you know, who would do this to a kid who's just recovered from a breakdown?"

"How do you feel now?"

"Well, you know, if I allow myself to feel anything, it comes out like pure rage. I am furious. I'm feeling furious now."

"Is that a difficult feeling to live with?"

"God, yes. I never allow myself to feel it. Well, I try not to. Not for any length of time."

"Who are you angry with?"

"My parents. The world in general."

"Think about it a bit more."

I did. After a while, I had another insight. I was furious with my mother. I'd known this all along. Or rather, I'd known it, but not known it. How could I be furious with my mother? I loved my mother. My anger, it seemed, was not about what had happened, but about what happened when I tried to talk about it.

"When I try to talk about it, when I've tried to tell her how I felt, she tells me it wasn't so bad."

"Tell me about that."

"I feel like I want to talk to her about the whole thing, but I can't. Over the years I've tried."

"Yes?"

"But every time, I blow it. It just comes out all wrong. Whenever I've tried to explain how I felt, it was as if this incredibly strong force was working against me. I get flustered. It's as if I'm in court, and I've forgotten my notes, and the judge, my mother, is losing patience."

"Go on."

"My position is always that I've never really told her how I feel, how full of rage I am, and her position is that I'm always talking about it."

"And what about your father?"

"What's funny is that I don't feel any anger toward him whatever. I saw less and less of him. After Germany, he came back to England for a while, and then he moved to Holland. And then came another bit of news, the thing I'd dreaded and half expected, really. When I was fourteen, my parents decided to move back to Canada. I would have to go to boarding school again. I hadn't realized it, but our time of living together as a family had come and gone, and I hadn't even noticed it."

Just Facts

Naomi said, "You said you were trying to defend yourself from certain feelings."

"I think I probably do it all the time."

"What sort of feelings?"

"I can't be sure, because I stop myself from feeling them. But it's about being abandoned."

"Tell me about that."

So I told her horror stories about being at boarding school. I said, "I really didn't want to be there."

And, "I wanted to be with my family, at home."

And, "But my family had moved."

And, "I didn't really know where my home was."

In therapy, I became self-pitying, but, I fancied, admirably stoical. I told bitter stories full of humiliation and pathos. These were stories that could not fail to bring tears to the eyes of any listener—any listener, that is, other than me or my therapist. I told stories about cruelty, violence, and my grit and determination in the face of this cruelty and violence. I had learned the art of not being bullied. I stabbed somebody with a screwdriver. I watched one boy being tortured, night after night, in the dormitory. His tormentor, a handsome, curly-haired boy, ordered the poor soul to explain, in painful detail, the litany of perverted things he wanted to do to his sister.

"Do you like your sister?"

"Yes."

"Do you want to fuck your sister?"

"No."

"Liar!"

"No!"

"I know you're lying. And you know what the punishment is if you lie. I get two people to hold you down, and I get another to twist your foot. Until I can hear a crack. So you have to be quiet, so I can hear the crack, otherwise goodness knows what might happen to your foot."

"Oh," said Naomi.

"So the guy is tortured for not telling us pornographic

stuff about his sister. So he tells us pornographic stuff about his sister. Then he's tortured for being a pervert."

"I see."

There were more stories, endless stories. I drank. I took drugs. I fought. I underwent ritualistic torture. I overate and vomited, sometimes in front of others. I became an accomplished overeater and vomiter. I replaced being fat with being disgusting.

"How do you feel about this?"

"Fine."

"Fine?"

"Well, it's hard for me to have feelings about it."

"How do you mean?"

"Well, to me, it's just facts." Talking to Naomi, I felt fine about the facts. When I was a kid, I was unsettled, displaced. Nasty things happened. These were the facts. What was worse, much worse, was the feelings beyond the facts. They were about my parents.

Of course, I hoped, I really hoped, that my parents didn't know how bad I felt. And yet, I couldn't stand the idea that my parents didn't know how bad I felt.

That Sublime Experience

Shelley Bovey's book *The Forbidden Body,* written when the author was forty, is all about the pain of being fat, the psychological agony. It gives the impression that being fat is a life sentence, that the best a fat person can hope for is to be fat in a kinder world, a world of fat-acceptance. It tells you that, when you're fat, your biggest problem is other people.

Other people hate you because you're different.

Other people hate you because you remind them what they would be like if they lost control.

Other people hate you because you're wearing your misery on your body, like an anti-fashion statement.

Bovey's solution: get these other people to change. "Fat women are not masochists—they hurt," she wrote. "If they could 'do something about it,' wouldn't they? Wouldn't we?"

But when, at last, I met Shelley Bovey, in her countrified cottage overlooking the market town of Glastonbury, she was not the 260-lb. fat-acceptance warrior she used to be; she'd lost weight. Now fifty-six, she was closing in on her "ideal" weight—somewhere between 160 and 170. Just as thin people were unkind to her when she was fat, the world of fat-acceptance has been unkind to her now she's lost weight.

Of the fat-acceptance movement, Bovey wrote, "I actually know from within the movement that most people who are overweight are really unhappy." Members of the movement felt "abandoned," "insulted," and "betrayed." One woman wrote on a website, "If she honestly felt that people who were fat were that unhappy, I have to question why she bothered to support size acceptance in the first place."

I said to Bovey, "So there's a way out? You didn't think so in *The Forbidden Body*."

"I didn't think so at the time. I'd been on so many diets. I was forty-ish when I wrote that. And I thought if I hadn't managed to crack it in thirty-odd years, what's going to be different?"

"And what was different?"

"Well . . . I went on being unhappy. And I got to the age

of fifty, approaching fifty. I saw fifty as quite a turning point. This is the last segment of my life. I've suffered for forty years, and I'm still suffering. A lot of assumptions were made about me being somehow in charge of myself, having risen above it all, but inside I was actually, if anything, more unhappy, and I had put on more weight. I was 273 lbs. And it was only me who knew how I was feeling inside. And so I thought, 'I can't diet, I know it doesn't work.' And I took about two years thinking about this. And what emerged was this often-quoted statistic, that 95 percent of diets don't work. And I thought, what is it about the 5 percent? And I couldn't find the answer. But I knew that it existed."

"What was the answer?"

"It was very simple. Working out very roughly what my intake was, and cutting it by a tiny amount, so I was taking just that little bit less energy in. And it worked. And I didn't suffer because it was such a tiny amount. It took about two years, and I've maintained it. I have to work at it. That's the other thing. There's no finishing."

Still, she hasn't yet lost her fat personality. "I know that when I was overweight as a child, and as a teenager particularly, that I wasn't thought of as being as good as everyone else. And so I did a lot to compensate. I was too much of a nice person. Too much of a clown. Making people laugh. Getting into trouble. All those things, instead of just allowing the person that I might have been to develop. I've never been able to lose that thing of being nice to people in case they don't like me. That's stayed, and I guess always will."

We talked all afternoon—about the pain of being fat, about how difficult it is to stop being fat, about the sinister, brain-sucking power of the thin world, making us anxious, making us hungry.

And then I asked her the million-dollar question. Why did she get fat in the first place?

"Since I've lost weight," she said, "I've gone back and thought more deeply about all of that and I realized that I was brought up in a pub by parents who didn't know what they were taking on, and who worked constantly, rushed off their feet, had no help, and had no time for me. And I really, really felt it. I really suffered. They weren't ever available. They were physically there, but that's almost worse, because they weren't available, and I can remember before I put on weight, at about eight or nine, I can remember being at primary school and feeling this *immense* hunger. And I don't know if that was physical hunger. I would guess probably not. But I can remember feeling intense hunger and intense cold, all the time. And I think those things were psychological. And they were so intense—gnawing, bitter feelings. And it must have been around the age of ten that I started to voice these feelings of loneliness to my mother, who did feel, I know, very guilty."

Bovey went on, "And we had a little village bakery that made their own doughnuts. And she'd buy them for me. And I can remember—I can remember the comfort. It didn't do the trick. But I can remember that feeling. I can remember the brown paper bag, with the greasy marks from the doughnuts inside, and that—aah, that . . . *sublime* experience of eating them."

OK, OK

So, is therapy the solution? Can therapy stop you bingeing? It's too early to tell, of course. I've only done seventy or eighty hours of it. But I'm beginning to see how the mechanism in my brain that caused me to binge might work.

I began putting the facts together, arranging them, looking at what they might mean. I was always late. I was always lounging around for ages and ages, and then rushing to get things done at the last moment. I preferred the limbo stage of any project or relationship. I hated being lonely. I had a string of mostly difficult relationships. My girlfriends were often compulsive in some way. Some were depressed. Some were drinkers, smokers, takers of drugs. One was a compulsive shopper. All the women I stayed with for any length of time had had bad childhoods, mostly worse than mine. And, when I talked about my childhood, I kept hearing the same thing, over and over: "Oh, not this again."

I remembered how one woman had said, "When you tell me about your bad childhood, how do you think that makes me feel? It's like a man with a broken leg coming up to somebody in a wheelchair and saying, 'I feel terrible. I've got a sore leg.' Now, how do you think that person in the wheelchair would feel?"

"OK, OK."

And I realized that this "OK, OK" was the "OK, OK" I'd been saying to my parents, particularly my mother, throughout my childhood. I was saying it still! It was the "OK, OK" of not being angry, of not allowing myself to feel anything, because if I felt something, it would be too much; my rage would be boundless. It was the "OK, OK" of pretending everything was fine, that everything was just facts. It was the "OK, OK" of procrastination, of hypochondria, of bingeing, of all the things that kept me busy, that took my mind off how I really felt, but how I desperately didn't want to feel. It was the "OK, OK" of boozing, and snorting coke, and eating endless slices of toast, just as it had been the "OK, OK" of pouring a jar of coffee creamer into my mouth, or bingeing on my grandmother's apple pie, and, a quarter of a century later, on the same grandmother's morphine supply. I would sneak into her room, the room she lived in at my parents' house after her accident, after she'd been knocked down by a car and had metal pins put in her legs, and I'd see the small bottle, and look away. And then, click.

I kept remembering things people said to me, and realizing they were the same things, over and over.

"How do you think that person in the wheelchair would feel?"

And: "Don't say that in front of your father."

And: "Don't say that in front of your mother."

And: "It would crush your father."

And: "I don't want you causing a fuss."

And: "You're exaggerating again."

And: "I think you're overdramatizing."

And: "It can't have been that bad."

And: "Can't you move on?"

"OK, OK."

It's the same "OK, OK" that made me chase oblivion all my life, the "OK, OK" of having one drink, and then another, and finding yourself in a different world, the "OK, OK" of sleeping with strangers, mostly strangers who smoked and drank, or had a weakness for drugs, or had been anorexic or bulimic, or suffered from a shopping compulsion.

I once lived with a girl who had a shopping compulsion—a shopaholic. A lot of people laugh at shopaholism, and I suppose that's an appropriate response. But actually, the belief that material goods, beyond a certain point, will make you feel better about yourself, is the modern disease. It's what all those doomy sociologists are talking about. It's what Juliet Schor, in her book *The Overspent American,* means when she says that 27 percent of Americans making more than $100,000 a year feel unable to buy "everything they really need." It's what Kasser and Ryan were talking about when they said that money-minded individuals feel less happy than people who were not money-minded, and that, importantly, money doesn't make them happier. It's what Barry Schwartz meant when he coined the phrase "the paradox of choice," and set out to demonstrate that, if you go to the supermarket, and see 85 varieties of crackers, 80 different types of painkiller, 61 varieties of suntan oil and sunblock, 150 types of lipstick, 90 kinds of nail polish, and 116 types of skin cream, and you see these things every day, day in day out, for years, eventually you might go nuts.

I used to watch my shopaholic girlfriend as she shopped. Her favorite things to buy, and also the things that disturbed her the most, were clothes and shoes. At home, she had around a hundred pairs of shoes, seventy dresses, an entire chest of drawers full of underwear. The more stuff she bought, the less she thought she had. She would often say, "I can't go out. I don't have the right shoes."

"What about these?"

"The heel is too low."

"The heel is not too low—it's fine."

"Look, I should know. They're my shoes."

"Well, what about these?"

"*Much* too high. With this dress, they make me look like a slut."

"But they're only a tiny bit higher than these."

"Don't you know anything? Look at the shape of the *toe,* dummy!"

In the store, the sequence of events was the same. She would agonize over different purchases. She would rack her brains. She would try the clothes on. And then she'd make a decision to buy something. This would always be a great moment. But only a moment. From then on, it was all downhill, an opera of regret. This was the logic of the market, played out to its absurd endgame; the thing you value is the thing you do not possess. The thing you possess is worthless. You are full, yet empty. You are sated, but hungry.

We would wait in line to pay for the item. The waiting was torture. Payment itself was an aria of discomfort; carrying the item out of the store in a bag a burden to be borne. And then the bitterness, the recriminations.

"Why didn't you tell me not to buy it?"

"I thought you wanted it."

"Don't you know *anything* about me?"

One day, we were passing a store she'd recently bought a coat in.

"I'm just popping in here for a moment."

"What do you want to look at?"

"The coats."

"But you just bought a coat in there."

"I know."

"But you don't need another coat."

"I'm not going to buy one."

We went into the store. She was walking faster than me. When I caught up with her, she was looking at her coat—or rather, not her coat, but a coat identical to hers.

"How do you think it looks?"

"Fine."

"No, you don't."

"It's fine."

"I can see it in your eyes. You don't like it."

Here she was, harming herself and returning to the scene of self-harm, like a killer who revisits the bodies of his victims. Later, she said she hated the coat, and never wore it.

Dr. Robert Lefever, of the Promis Centre, told me he thought that 10 or 15 percent of the population were susceptible to compulsive behavior, and that, since they were attracted to each other, the genes keep replicating. But he also says that if you have an addictive tendency, you'll always have an addictive tendency, and that if you don't, you don't, both of which I don't believe.

What I learned from seventy or eighty hours of therapy is that I'm frightened of certain emotions, and that I do compulsive stuff in order to stop myself from feeling these emotions. In fact, I've got so good at doing the compulsive stuff that mostly I don't even feel the emotions. The emotions, by the way, are responses to the rage and loneliness I felt as a kid.

But I'll tell you this. If you're a compulsive eater, or

drinker, or whatever, you've probably been running away from emotions for most of your life. And these are emotions you felt *as a kid,* when you were at your most vulnerable and powerless. As an adult, you're not so vulnerable, not so powerless. My advice: sit still, and allow the emotions to wash over you; they're probably less scary than you've always believed them to be. It took me a while to realize it, but sometimes I feel furious, absolutely furious, with my mother. And I really want to tell her how furious I am, but the idea makes me shrivel with guilt; my fury, I believe, would be a kind of violation. As for my father—he wasn't around much when I was growing up, and it's still difficult for me to summon up any strong feelings about this.

I don't want to rape my mother and kill my father. I just want to rage at my mother and, at worst, not worry about my father—an Oedipus-complex lite. It doesn't seem like much, does it? And maybe it isn't. But the chemistry of the brain, as the psychopharmacologist William Potter memorably said, is "like a weather system." A butterfly flapping its wings in childhood, as it were, might be the cause of terrible storms in the years to come. To me, these seem like relevant thoughts. It's possible, of course, that these are merely the thoughts I'm having in order to avoid other, more painful ones.

It's All About Your Parents

So is therapy the solution? I don't know. At the moment it's all about my parents. What a surprise. Sometimes I think therapists ought to have a sign on the door saying

"It's All About Your Parents." Still, I've only been doing it for seventy or eighty hours. And I'm not absolutely sure, but I think I know what I'll be talking about after another seventy or eighty hours. I think I'll be talking about my parents.

Moreish

My girlfriend has come out to the bench, and given me a backpack and two bottles of mineral water. We're going on a walk today, a long hike. Ten miles along the tops of the hills, the South Downs, and then five miles to the coast, and then ten miles along the coast; she reckons we can do the whole twenty-five miles in a day. That's our objective. I'm a lot better at walking, now that I walk all the time. I'm no longer a sloucher or a schlepper. I no longer totter along as if I'm walking on high heels. These days, I walk like a guy in Gore-Tex boots.

She's gone back inside to do the toast. I want the toast, possibly a couple of slices with lots of butter. But I'm not in a toast frenzy. I think I'll be needing the trifle, too, for the sake of energy. But I'm not in a trifle frenzy, either. I feel hungry, but I don't feel empty. And soon I'll feel full, but I won't feel too bloated. Food is beginning to look different. It looks bigger, for one thing. It looks like food, and not something to take my mind off how I'm feeling. At the moment, I'm not feeling too bad.

I take a swig of the mineral water. It tastes fine. It tastes of nothing. I've heard it said that, if the modern problem is overconsumption, then mineral water is part of the solution.

This is my "favorite" brand, Fiji water. It's supposed to taste soft and pure, and I sort of think it does. They say it's so pure because it comes from a spring a thousand miles away from the nearest city, which is Auckland, New Zealand. The spring is on the island of Viti Levu, the most populated of the Fijian islands; it is where, as Susie Orbach says, there has been a sudden influx of Westernization such as eating disorders and television. If you drive through the island, you can see it—the logos, the aerials, the teenagers in their new Nike T-shirts.

They want our affluence. We want their purity.

They want to be full. We want to be empty.

When I asked the owner of Fiji water, David Gilmour, what he thought it tasted like, he said, "Soft and moreish."

The First Line of Attack

I'd booked an interview with Neville Rigby, the director of policy and public affairs at the International Obesity Task Force. The address of the Task Force's office is North Gower Street, and I vaguely knew the area, north of the Marylebone Road in central London, where there has been a lot of activity lately—a clutch of gleaming glass towers, a bit of modern sculpture, a square fitted with a restaurant, a Starbucks, a Pret A Manger.

I walked through the square, and then through some back streets, and then some council housing. I couldn't find the street, let alone the office. When I did, I thought I'd made a mistake. It was a dingy office building from the 1960s. The IOTF was on the second floor. There was a note tacked to the door: "INTERCOM DOES NOT WORK. WAIT FOR SOMEBODY TO COME DOWN AND LET YOU IN."

I pressed the buzzer. A woman arrived and led me up the stairs. There were two people in the offices of the International Obesity Task Force. One was Rigby. The other was the woman, a trainee.

Later, another woman popped in. We drank tea and chatted about the problem of obesity, and about what the Task Force was doing to stop its spread.

I thought: this is the international scientific community's answer to the problem of obesity. In contrast, McDonald's opens premises this size every few days.

Rigby had an air of cautious optimism. There are many reasons, he said, for the growth of obesity. Many, many reasons. Families don't sit down for meals so much anymore. People, therefore, are snacking more. Snacks are fattening. In the Western world, he said, we are being driven into an ethic of overwork. People demand convenience, so they shop in supermarkets, where the food tends to be more fattening.

There was lots more. "Pressures are coming at us from all directions," said Rigby. "The simplest example I can think of is that when I first started driving a car, I couldn't go into a gas station and buy any food. It wasn't allowed by law. The gasoline companies persuaded the government to change the regulations to allow food to be sold in gas stations."

Rigby continued listing the things which were making us fatter. Vending machines are now more sophisticated. Electronic devices tell the vending company when they need refilling. Calories are everywhere.

The big problem, said Rigby, was the food industry. "Most of us," he said, "get information about food from the people who are selling it to us. They would like to control the message. They would like to shape the message to fit their marketing needs."

Rigby said, "They come up with this recital of 'there is no such thing as a good food or a bad food.' This is fundamental science, they say. Where is it fundamental science? Show me a textbook where it says so. And it *isn't*. There are no studies which definitively explain that there is no such thing as a good food or a bad food. It's an industry mantra. But if you have your largest proportion of your nutritionists and your dieticians and so on getting their income, in some way or another, from the food industry, then they tend to have views which reflect those who are paying them."

In the Starr Report, said Rigby, there is a passage describing Bill Clinton, in flagrante with Monica Lewinsky, breaking off his activities to answer the phone. "The caller was a sugar baron from Florida," said Rigby. "He actually stopped what he was doing to take the sugar baron's call. The call was about a particular tax on sugar. And the tax never materialized! The tax evaporated! The very people who were involved in that had donated huge amounts of money to his political campaigns!"

There was more, much more. The companies who make soft drinks are investing in "neuromarketing," advertising that makes use of medical research identifying areas of the brain involved in hunger, desire, and compulsion. More money is being pumped into the selling of doughnuts. Confectionery is up. Exercise is down.

But, said Rigby, there is some hope. The IOTF are lobbying the industry around the clock. A "slow food" movement is thriving in Italy. And, at last, the government has begun to listen, at least in the area of salt. A campaign to halt salt is imminent. Salt, said Rigby, is "the first line of attack."

I walked down the stairs and into the dingy street, remembering to click the latch on my way out.

Passing Out

We walk up the hill, and along the top of the hill, and down into a valley, and up another hill. The endorphins begin to take effect about halfway up the second hill. After about five miles, we sit down under a tree and eat a bar of chocolate each. After ten miles we take a detour into a village and buy some kind of pie, which is all we can find, and which is disgusting. It doesn't matter, because I've had a bowl of trifle—sponge cake with cream, custard, jelly, and glacé cherries—and a few slices of toast. I don't think there's any real answer to the obesity crisis. Getting fat—it's in the system. In a way, it *is* the system. I heard an item on the radio the other day, in which an obesity expert was asked, "If the government could do one thing to stop the obesity crisis, what would it be?"

The man paused, and said, "That's the trouble. There is no one thing you can do. You have to do . . . everything."

As a society, we're getting fatter and lazier and more anxious and depressed. Why? Because the alternative is unthinkable. The alternative is to change everything. The alternative is to stop investing in extrinsic values. And that's not going to happen, is it?

When she put on weight to play the part of Bridget Jones in *Bridget Jones: The Edge of Reason*, Renée Zellweger said she felt "really great. I got such positive responses from the fellows in my life while I looked like Bridget Jones. I had a lot of friends who said I should think about keeping some of the weight on. I have to say I agreed, because there were certain things about it I liked very much. But of course, I'm a girl, and I thought, 'Ugh, no.' Like anybody, I want to look my best."

We reach the river and walk along the river to the sea, a few more miles, and it's getting painful, and we cross the river and walk along the coast, on the tops of cliffs, and press on, through the pain.

In general, I'm not optimistic. I went to see this fat friend of mine again, the one who does not want to be identified, even by gender. We went for dinner, and he or she said, "You haven't asked me about my eating."

"Well, maybe you don't want to talk about it."

"Ask me a question."

"How much do you weigh?"

"I don't want to talk about *that*."

"Why?"

"I'm not talking about it."

"I'm not asking you to tell me how much you weigh. I'm asking you why you don't want to tell me."

"And I don't want to tell you that either."

"Why? What would happen if I knew how much you weighed?"

"I just don't want to tell you."

"I think that's interesting."

"I don't want to go there."

"But if you want to lose weight, you've got to make a start. You should talk to someone."

"Has it worked for you?"

"I think it's helping."

"Well, it wouldn't work for me. I know what my problem is."

"You know what it is, but you don't want to talk about it?"

"No."

"You know what this thing is, but it's too powerful?"

"Something like that."

"It's bigger than you."

"Yes."

"Or maybe you want it to be bigger than you. Maybe you're afraid of what would happen if you took it on, and won."

"Don't give me that *cheap shit*! I can't stand that *cheap shit*! All those stupid, meaningless catchphrases! I can't be summed up like that!"

"OK, OK."

"I'm not in denial! I'm not being defensive!"

"OK, OK."

And I thought: the fat society is just like the fat individual. I know. I've been fat.

After twenty miles, I start to feel twinges. I am creaky. My ankles are sore. My calves are sore. My knees hurt when I walk down hills. After twenty-three miles, I feel better; after twenty-four, worse.

When we reach the town, we're hobbling. Nobody is around. Dusk is falling. We check into a hotel, and walk out again, looking for somewhere to eat, and we find a pizza restaurant, and I order spaghetti with a meat sauce, and some garlic bread, and a bottle of wine, and the exercise has galvanized us, and the sugar in the wine and the carbohy-drate in the bread and pasta give me a wonderful blood-sugar spike, and now I like food and we laugh, and we talk about how odd it was that I went to her wedding all those years ago, that I wanted to look good at her wedding, and now she's divorced. I stop eating when I'm full, and we walk back to the hotel, and sit on the bed, gripped by fatigue, and we pass out without taking our clothes off, not even our shoes, and when I wake up the next morning I think of the exact moment of passing out, possibly the happiest moment of my life.

ABOUT THE AUTHOR

William Leith is a leading journalist whose columns often cover diet, sex, and relationships. He writes regularly for the *Guardian* and the *Daily Telegraph,* and he has worked at many other respected British newspapers, including the *Independent on Sunday,* the *Mail on Sunday,* and the *Observer.* He lives in Sussex, England.